COTTON

AS A

WORLD POWER

COTTON

AS A

WORLD POWER

A STUDY IN THE ECONOMIC INTERPRETATION OF HISTORY

JAMES A. B. SCHERER, PH.D., LL.D.

GYAN

Published by

Gyan Publishing House
5, Ansari Road
Daryaganj, New Delhi-110002
Phone: 011-47034999, 9811692060
E-mail: books@gyanbooks.com

Distribution Network
gyanbooks.com
India, USA, Canada, UK, Australia, France

ISBN : 978-81-212-9542-0 (PB)
First Published, 1916

2nd Impression 2023

Printed at: Gyan Press, Delhi.

COTTON AS A WORLD POWER
Author: JAMES A. B. SCHERER

COTTON
AS A
WORLD POWER

A STUDY IN THE ECONOMIC INTERPRETATION OF HISTORY

BY

JAMES A. B. SCHERER, Ph.D., LL.D.

PRESIDENT OF THROOP COLLEGE OF TECHNOLOGY

Author of "The Japanese Crisis," etc.

TO

GEORGE B. CROMER

ACKNOWLEDGMENT

The core of this book was used as a lecture at Oxford and Cambridge Universities in the spring of 1914 with the caption, "Economic Causes in the American Civil War." The preparation of that lecture involved much fresh scrutiny of the subject, and I wish to thank the authorities of the Bodleian Library and the British Museum for assistance. To my English friends Mr. Norman Angell and Sir William Mather I extend especial thanks for invaluable aid. On this side of the water I owe much to many friends and correspondents, including Major Harry Hammond, the late Mr. D. A. Tompkins, and Dr. Walter Hines Page, now the American Ambassador to England. I owe most, however, to my Pasadena friend, George Ellery Hale, without whose encouragement I should hardly have brought this book to completion.

I desire to thank my colleagues, Professors Barrett, Judy, and Simons, as well as Mr. James Ford Rhodes, Professor John Bates Clark, and Mr. R. L. Ashley, for valuable suggestions made while the book was passing through the press.

Alphabetical lists of the leading authorities will be found at the close of the volume.

JAMES A. B. SCHERER.

THROOP COLLEGE OF TECHNOLOGY,
PASADENA, CALIFORNIA.

CONTENTS

BOOK I

FROM INDIA TO ENGLAND

BOOK II

THE TRANSFORMATION OF ENGLAND

CONTENTS

BOOK III

COTTON IN AMERICAN HISTORY: SECTIONAL EVOLUTION

BOOK IV

COTTON IN AMERICAN HISTORY: THE GREAT CONTROVERSIES

CONTENTS

BOOK V

COTTON IN AMERICAN HISTORY: THE CIVIL WAR

BOOK VI

THE OLD SOUTH AND THE NEW

CONTENTS

BOOK VII

COTTON AND WORLD TRADE

BOOK I

FROM INDIA TO ENGLAND

COTTON AS A WORLD POWER

CHAPTER 1

THE NEW GOLDEN FLEECE

It was in the Bodleian Library, while rummaging among the quaint and musty index papers of the Upper Reading Room, that I heard one capped and gowned librarian muttering to another, as with an air of offended dignity:

"Writing on cotton! Why on earth should he want to write on such a subject as that?"

Yet it was another Oxford don, Professor James E. Thorold Rogers, who proved by his brilliant lectures on "The Economic Interpretation of History" that plants and fibers have interwoven with the development of civilization no less than fine-spun theories of government, while others, such as Gibbins and Arnold Toynbee, attributed to cotton and wool the controlling influence in that remarkable transformation of England which began in the eighteenth century.

While reading Frank Norris's fascinating California novel, "The Octopus," in South Carolina, fifteen years ago, the thought occurred to the writer: if "the epic of the wheat," as Norris has properly phrased it, holds so much of interest and suggestiveness, might not the tracing of the great cotton influence prove to be quite as alluring, like the quest of a new Golden Fleece? For I knew enough of American history, and was sufficiently familiar with the mysterious nomadic career of this "vegetable wool" from the Orient, to suspect in such a connection an unworked quarry of wealth. I have therefore at odd moments engaged myself, as administrative duties permitted, in mining a few random fragments of ore, and smelting them as best I knew how.

It is amazing the way the veins ramified—enticing one on to become, as it were, a nosing adventurous Jason, prying in all sorts of places. "The gods send threads for a web begun." Through pleasant highways of half forgot prose and along quaint hedgerows of verse the quest of this fleece has meandered; through mazes of myth as well as the straight paths of fact, through intimacies of obscure biography as well as large spaces of history, and along the avenues of trade.—All at once burst the tempest of war; and, lo! cotton was puffed into air like so much thistledown, sensitive as it is to the currents of civilization, and therefore blown into shreds like civilization itself by the shock of this world-wide storm.

The Great War brought home to the public mind as nothing else could have done the knowledge that this vegetable fleece is really golden, and that its golden values are so interwoven with the solidarity of mankind as to depend to a peculiar degree for their stability on the maintenance of an unbroken network of international trade. Who knew, before the Great War, that the world's cotton crop, of which three-quarters, or thereabouts, is produced in the United States of America, exceeds in value the whole world's output of the precious metals by fifty per cent?[1] Who realized that the United States, in

[1] Value of eleven years' cotton crop (1901-11) £1,607,000,000
Value of gold for same period 807,000,000
Value of silver " " " 213,000,000 } 1,020,000,000
—The *Financier*, Jan. 7, 1913.

addition to its large manufacture of cotton goods, exports raw cotton annually in a sum exceeding in value its next three greatest export groups put together? [2] Who among us had stopped to think that this enormous production is almost entirely confined to a little group of Southeastern States, or paused to wonder what would happen to them if this stupendous source of revenue should become suddenly clogged? How many intelligent Americans have been aware that this single Southern commodity has maintained an annual balance of trade in favor of the United States on the pages of the world's ledgers, by attracting a stream of European gold westward each autumn and setting in motion the current of liquidation necessary to sustain national credit? As Mr. Theodore Price points out, cotton is peculiar in that it is the only crop of importance all of which is sold by those who produce it. Only seventeen per cent of the corn crop, for instance, leaves the farms; the rest is consumed or fed to stock by those who produce it. Cotton, therefore, generates an enormous commerce and provides a medium of exchange that almost entirely takes the place of gold in the settlement of interstate and international balances.[3] The late William B. Dana, for many years editor of the *Com-*

[2] "The value of cotton exported during the fiscal year 1912 amounted to $565,849,271, or 26.1 per cent of the total value of all articles of domestic merchandise exported during the year. It exceeded the amounts for iron and steel manufactures, meat and dairy products, and bread stuffs combined, these three groups ranking next in importance among articles exported. These large exports, combined with the more than five million bales consumed in domestic manufacture, strikingly indicate the importance of cotton in the economic affairs of the nation."—*Report of the U. S. Department of Commerce*, July, 1913. For other financial facts and figures, see Chapters 67–68, 70–71.

[3] See Appendix A.

mercial and Financial Chronicle, once said that cotton, being practically imperishable and always convertible, possessed more of the attributes of a legal tender than anything produced by human labor except gold.[4] It is the world's Golden Fleece; the nations are bound together in its globe-engirdling web; so that when a modern economist concerns himself with the interdependence of nations he naturally looks to cotton for his most effective illustration, as witness the following:

"A manufacturer in Manchester strikes a bargain with a merchant in Louisiana in order to keep a bargain with a dyer in Germany, and three or a much larger number of parties enter into virtual, or perhaps actual, contract, and form a mutually dependent economic community (numbering, it may be, with the workpeople in the group of industries involved, some millions of individuals)—an economic entity so far as one can exist which does not include all organized society."[5]

And yet it is only within recent times that cotton has entered the Occident from its ancient home in the Orient, and affected the welfare and wealth of western men. A century and a quarter ago its influence had but just made its way from India through Europe as far as England, and meant as yet nothing whatever to North America. Its startling growth here is graphically exhibited in the following table,[6] showing the chief raiment supplies of Europe and

[4] Cited in the *Outlook*, New York, September 9, 1914. In this article Mr. Price undertakes to demonstrate that cotton in normal years takes the place of gold in the settlement of America's huge annual indebtedness to Europe, as shown in Appendix A.

[5] The Foundations of International Polity, by Norman Angell: London, 1914; p. xxiv.

[6] Major Harry Hammond in the *News and Courier* Centennial Number: Charleston, 1903; p. 33, The Century in Agriculture.

America ten years before Eli Whitney invented the gin (1793), and a century later:

	1783	*1883*
Flax	18.4%	6.22%
Wool	77.2%	20.65%
Cotton	4.4%	73.13%

To trace the skeins of this fleecy white fiber through mazes of fable and fact, from its cradle in India, where Alexander discovered it, to modern England by tortuous slow stages through Egypt, Rome, and Spain; to tell the story of its revolutionary influence in Great Britain and to suggest its wholly unappreciated effect on the history of the United States; to show the personalities and depict the times of some of the men whom it influenced and who in turn lent their vigor to increase its strength; and, finally, to indicate the peculiar importance of cotton in contemporary world trade, and its relation to the Great War, is the object of the following pages.

CHAPTER 2

THE VEGETABLE LAMB

ALEXANDER THE GREAT, who has perhaps influenced civilization more than any other personality except Christ, acquainted Europe with India; and not the least wonderful of the oriental curios described by his generals[1] on their home-coming was that singular plant from which the natives plucked a "vegetable wool" which they spun into admirable clothing. Nearchus, for example, reported that there were in India shrubs bearing tufts or bunches of wool, and that from this wool the natives made garments of surpassing whiteness,—"a shirt, or tunic, reaching to the middle of the leg, a sheet folded about the shoulders, and a turban rolled around the head;"[2] from which terse description it may clearly be seen that the costume of the conservative Hindus remains unchanged to this day.

Alexander's soldiers, Nearchus further reported, were quick to use this "vegetable wool" for bedding, and as pads for their saddles. It is highly probable, indeed, that they brought back with them assorted specimens of Indian cotton cloth: "Calicut cloth," or *calico*, with *muslin* from Mosul, and various other piece-goods.

Ages elapsed, however, before the cotton plant came to be cultivated in Europe, and during that

[1] Aristobulus and Nearchus are freely cited in Strabo's Geographia, xv.

[2] Fabius Arrianus, Historia Indica, xvi.

period a myth slowly interwove itself with the strands of this "vegetable wool," one of the strangest myths of which history holds record, unraveled only a few years ago by the patience of a British antiquarian.

Theophrastus (about 372–287 B.C.) unwittingly sowed seed for this myth in his Botany, as will shortly be shown. In an admirable description of the cotton plant he said:

"The trees from which the Indians make their clothes have leaves like those of the black mulberry, but the entire plant resembles the dog-rose. They are set out in furrows on the plains, at a distance resembling a vineyard. —These wool-bearing shrubs have leaves like the grape-vine, but smaller. They bear no fruit, indeed, but the pod containing the wool resembles a spring apple (μῆλον), while this pod is still unripe and unopened. When ripe, it bursts open. The wool is then gathered from it and woven into cloth of divers qualities; some inferior, and some of considerable value."[3]

The close resemblance between cotton fiber and lamb's wool must have led many Europeans to mistake one for the other; or, rather, to regard cotton as a strange new species of wool. But rumor, truthful in one essential detail, persisted that this Oriental importation was a vegetable product, growing in Indo-Scythia on shrubs and trees; especially since Herodotus[4] himself, the father of history, had described cotton as "wool from the trees"; writing elsewhere of "trees bearing, as their fruit, fleeces which surpass those of sheep in beauty and excellence."

[3] De Historia Plantarum, iv, 4, 9.

[4] Historia, iii, 47, 106, vii, 65.

Thus arose the fable of a vegetable lamb, or zoöphyte, an animal growing on a tree! The name of this fabulous creature finally became fixed as the Scythian lamb, through confusion of Scythia with Indo-Scythia; and subsequently also as the Tartary lamb, both because "Tartary" was loosely used to denote Scythia, and also because nomadic Tartar merchants brought with them in their caravans, together with the fleece of Tartary sheep and goats, "the fine white wool that grew on trees" in India.

Many years after he had written his Botany, and when Greek had become a dead language in Europe, Theophrastus, by his ambiguous use of the word melon, as above quoted, was thought to give final and, as it were, scientific confirmation to the story of the vegetable lamb. Melon, in Greek, may mean either tree-fruit or sheep, and of course there are spring sheep, or lambs, as well as spring apples. Had not Theophrastus, therefore, botanized of a lamb that grew upon shrubs in India? It was but a step, then, to modify the language of Herodotus so as to make him seem to describe "plants bearing fruit *within which there is a lamb* having fleece of surpassing beauty and excellence"; and the myth was wholly made!

In more modern times, when travelers in Tartary searched for this famous zoöphyte, naturally they did not find it. They did find, however, a shaggy toy made of the rhizome of a fern so as roughly to resemble a lamb, and this for a long time was supposed to be the prototype and justification of the enormous and confounding fable of the "Borametz," or "Barometz," these words being obscure derivatives from the Tartar word for "ram," and "Baranets" being Russian for the fern-plant *Lycopodium Selago*. It was not until 1887 that Mr. Henry Lee, acting on an ingenious guess of Erman's, conclusively identified the "Vegetable Lamb of Tartary" with the cotton boll which Alexander had discovered in India.[5]

[5] Henry Lee, The Vegetable Lamb of Tartary: London, 1887.

CHAPTER 3

COTTON MYTHOLOGY

IMAGINATIVE writers have dallied delightfully with the Vegetable Lamb in several languages. Among his collection of literary tributes to this supposed "miracle of Nature," Mr. Henry Lee translates a Latin poem written by the eminent French botanist, De la Croix, so recently as 1791.

The traveler who plows the Caspian wave
For Asia bound, where foaming breakers lave
Borysthenes' wild shores, no sooner lands
Than gazing in astonishment he stands;
For in his path he sees a monstrous birth,—
The Barometz arises from the earth:
Upon a stalk is fixed a living brute,
A rooted plant bears quadruped for fruit;
It has a fleece, nor does it want for eyes,
And from its brows two woolly horns arise.
The rude and simple country people say
It is an animal that sleeps by day
And wakes at night, though rooted to the ground,
To feed on grass within its reach around.
The flavor of Ambrosia its flesh
Pervades; and the red nectar, rich and fresh,
Which vineyards of fair Burgundy produce
Is less delicious than its ruddy juice.
If Nature had but on it feet bestowed,
Or with a voice to bleat the lamb endowed,
To cry for help against the threat'ning fangs
Of hungry wolves; as on its stalk it hangs,
Seated on horseback it might seem to ride,
Whit'ning with thousands more the mountain side.

Dr. Erasmus Darwin,[1] poetizing in 1789 with intent "to inlist Imagination under the banner of Science," went so far as to endow the fabled lamb with golden hair, a rosy tongue, melting eyes, and a voice:

Cradled in snow, and fann'd by Arctic air
Shines, gentle Barometz! thy golden hair;
Rooted in earth each cloven hoof descends,
And round and round her flexile neck she bends;
Crops the gray coral moss, and hoary thyme,
Or laps with rosy tongue the melting rime;
Eyes with mute tenderness her distant dam,
Or seems to bleat, a *Vegetable Lamb.*

The extréme antiquity of this marvelous plant was certified by the Sieur du Bartas, who in 1578 described its discovery by Adam in the Garden of Eden:[2]

Musing, anon through crooked walks he wanders,
Round winding rings, and intricate meanders,
False-guiding paths, doubtful, beguiling, strays,
And right-wrong errors of an endless maze;
Nor simply hedgéd with a single border
Of rosemary cut out with curious order
In Satyrs, Centaurs, Whales, and half-men-horses,
And thousand other counterfeited corses;
But with true beasts, fast in the ground still sticking
Feeding on grass, and th' airy moisture licking,
Such as those Borametz in Scythia bred
Of slender seeds, and with green fodder fed;
Although their bodies, noses, mouths, and eyes,
Of new-yeaned lambs have full the form and guise,
And should be very lambs, save that for foot
Within the ground they fix a living root

[1] The Botanic Garden, Part I: The Economy of Vegetation: London, 1791; Part II: The Loves of the Plants: London, 1790.
[2] Translation by Joshua Sylvester as given by Henry Lee, as cited.

Which at their navel grows, and dies that day
That they have browsed the neighboring grass away.

Oh! wondrous nature of God only good,
The beast hath root, the plant hath flesh and blood.
The nimble plant can turn it to and fro,
The nummèd beast can neither stir nor goe;
The plant is leafless, branchless, void of fruit,
The beast is lustless, sexless, fireless, mute:
The plant with plant his hungry paunch doth feed,
Th' admired beast is sowen a slender seed.

Passing now from poetry to sober prose narrative, we derive the following account of Borametz from the famous Dutch traveler, Jean de Struys:

"On the west side of the Volga is a great dry and waste heath, called the Step. On this heath is a strange kind of fruit found, called 'Baromez' or 'Barnitsch,' from the word 'Boran,' which is 'a Lamb' in the Russian tongue, because of its form and appearance much resembling a sheep, having head, feet and tail. Its skin is covered with a down very white and as soft as silk.—It grows upon a low stalk, about two and a half feet high, some higher, and is supported just at the navel. The head hangs down, as if it pastured or fed on the grass, and when the grass decays it perishes: but this I ever looked upon as ridiculous; although when I suggested that the languishing of the plant might be caused by some temporary want of moisture, the people asseverated to me with many oaths that they have often, out of curiosity, made experiment of that by cutting away the grass, upon which it instantly fades away. Certain it is that there is nothing which is more coveted by wolves than this, and the inward parts of it are more congeneric with the anatomy of a lamb than mandrakes are with men. However, what I might further say of this fruit, and what I believe of the wonderful operations of a secret sympathy in Nature, I shall rather keep to myself than aver, or impose upon the reader with many other things which I am sensible would appear incredible to those who had not seen them."[3]

Jean de Struys published this restrained account at Amsterdam in 1681. In the same year Claude Duret included in his "History of Plants" a chapter on "The Borametz of Scythia," which affords interesting new characteristics:

"It was in form like a lamb, and from its navel grew a stem or root by which this zoöphyte or plant-animal was fixed, attached, like a gourd, to the soil below the surface of the ground, and, according to the length of its stem or root, it devoured all the herbage which it was able to reach within the circle of its tether. The hunters who went in search of this creature were unable to capture or remove it until they had succeeded in cutting the stem by well-aimed arrows or darts, when the animal immediately fell prostrate to the earth and died. Its bones being placed with certain ceremonies and incantations in the mouth of one desiring to foretell the future, he was instantly seized with a spirit of divination, and endowed with the gift of prophecy."[4]

About the time that the imaginary and highly imaginative "Sir John Maundevile" professed to have set out from St. Albans upon his memorable journey, Friar Odoric the Bohemian wrote an account of his own recent travels in which he mentions Borametz as follows:

"Another passing marvelous thing may be re-

[3] Quoted by Henry Lee, as cited.
[4] Quoted by Henry Lee, as cited.

lated, which however I saw not myself, but heard from trustworthy persons. For 'tis said that in a certain great kingdom called Cadeli there be mountains called the Caspean Mountains, on which are said to grow very large melons. And when these be ripe, they burst, and a little beast is found inside like a small lamb, so that they have both melons and meat! And though some, peradventure, may find that hard to believe, yet it may be quite true; just as it is true that there be in Ireland trees which produce birds."[5]

Boldest of all these historians, however, is Odoric's plunderer, who, writing as "Sir John Maundevile, Knight," professes to have set out from England in 1322, and, as he says in his "Voiage and Travaile," passed through "manye diverse Londes, where dwellen many dyverse Folkes, and of dyverse Maneres and Lawes, and of dyverse Schappes of Men" and eke of beasts, including Irish barnacles, but especially the Vegetable Lamb, which he duly and intimately encountered in the kingdom of the great Cham of Tartary.

"And there growethe a maner of Fruyt," writes this mischievous author, "as thoughe it weren Gowrdes: and whan thei ben rype, men kutten hem a to, and men fynden with inne a lytylle Best, in Flessche, in Bon and Blode, as though it were a lytylle Lomb, with outen Wolle. And men eten bothe the Frut and the Best: and that is a gret Marveylle. Of that Frute I have eten; alle thoughe it were wondirfulle: but that I knowe wel, that God is marveyllous in his Werkes."[6]

[5] Henry Yule, editor, Cathay and the Way Thither: London, 1866; p. 144.

[6] Voiage and Travaile of Sir John Maundevile, Kt. (Halliwell), reprinted from the edition of 1725: London, 1883; xxvi.

To such substantial corporeality had grown the myth of the Indian cotton boll, at the very time when a few Flemish weavers were settling at Manchester (in 1328), and, under the shrewd patronage of Edward III, were beginning the manufacture of those so-called "Manchester cottons" that were destined to become the foundation of England's immense cotton industry.

It is little wonder that this plant has laid hold on the imaginations of men throughout the world in various ages. Known to the people of India for two thousand years before Alexander's soldiers discovered it there, and plied by nimble Hindu fingers on primitive looms into fabrics so fair and delicate as to evoke the poetic description of "webs of the woven wind," cotton wended its triumphant way westward with the course of empire, itself a captain of civilization, clothing Mark Antony's soldiers in the heat of the fierce Egyptian summer, bringing fame to Barcelona in the manufacture of sail-cloth, enriching Venice and Milan with fustians and dimities, and producing as by magic the industrial transformation of England, until at last in the new western world it wove itself inextricably into the web of the national history, and now shuttles all the oceans with bands of intercourse and trade.

CHAPTER 4

EARLIEST HISTORY

THE cultivation and manufacture of cotton would seem to have evolved independently on three continents, Asia, Africa, and South America; but Asia is of leading concern to us, since it was from India that the plant found its way into Europe. Three of the principal countries of the East have from remote antiquity been characterized by their more distinctive raiments: China as the land of silk, Egypt of flax, and India of cotton. India, preëminently the mother land of this plant, is to-day outranked as a cotton producing country only by the United States, and carries on a modern manufacturing industry of large proportions, as will appear in the final section.

The first known mention of cotton is found in a Rig Veda hymn, composed fifteen centuries before Christ, which honors the "threads in the loom," indicating that manufacture was already well advanced.[1] The Sacred Institutes of Manu, dating from 800 B. C., contain such frequent references to cotton as to denote a very high esteem among the ancient Hindus.[2] In fact, they had come to hold this mystic plant in actual reverence, beautiful as it was in both blossom and fruit, responsive to culti-

[1] Hymn 105, vs. 8. Cited by J. F. Royle in The Culture and Commerce of Cotton in India: London, 1851.

[2] Manu, ii, 44, viii, 236, 397. Cited in Bulletin 33, U. S. Dept. Agriculture: Washington, 1896.

vation, and so indispensable, indeed, with its copious perennial supply of strong and silken "vegetable wool," being far better adapted to their peculiar climatic conditions than the downiest fleece supplied by shepherds from the plains.

As indicating the reverential awe in which the Hindus held their white fiber, it is noteworthy that thefts of cotton thread were, according to the Institutes of Manu, punishable by fines of treble the value of the stolen goods; moreover, it was required by the religious law that the sacrificial thread of the Brahmin should always be spun from this plant. The laws also mention weaving and sizing. Herodotus said that the Hindus made their clothes of "tree wool," which is the name the modern Germans give to cotton (Baum-wolle). We have seen that Alexander found it in general use when he invaded the Punjab, and that it was he who introduced it into Europe.

In Persia it had attained to extensive use long before Alexander's invasion. The purdah (Persian *parda*), for excluding the heat, is no doubt a very ancient invention. Aristobulus, one of Alexander's generals, speaks feelingly of the severe heat of Susa, the capital city, not sparing his gifts of forceful imaginative expression. "Lizards and serpents could not cross the streets at noon quickly enough to prevent their being burned to death mid-way by the heat," he declares; while "barley, spread out in the sun, was roasted, and hopped about" like popcorn! "The inhabitants laid earth to a depth of three and a half feet on the roofs of their houses to exclude the suffocating heat."[3]

This was in the fourth century before Christ.

[3] See ch. 2, note 1.

Two hundred years earlier, the less fervid author of the book of Esther, describing a royal feast in this same capital city, mentioned the "white, green, and blue hangings"[4] of the royal palace, wherein the King showed "the riches of his glorious kingdom and the honor of his excellent majesty many days."

Just as Nearchus, the associate of Aristobulus, described the Hindu costume which still prevails (see page 6), so it is highly probable that these canopies of Ahasuerus were exactly the same as those hangings of white and blue striped cotton so common throughout India to-day; and that in the time of Aristobulus, as now, blue and white striped purdahs, stuffed with cotton, were hung before windows and doors in the summer to keep out the fierce Persian heat of which he complained with such vehemence.

That cotton was early known in Assyria is witnessed by an inscription on a cylinder in the British Museum, descriptive of the great gardens which Sennacherib (705–681 B. C.) laid out along the river above and below Nineveh: "The trees that bore wool they clipped, and they carded it for garments."

[4] Esther i, 6.

CHAPTER 5

HINDU SKILL

THOUSANDS of years before the invention of cotton machinery in Europe, Hindu gins were separating fiber from seed, Hindu wheels were spinning the lint into yarn, and frail Hindu looms weaving these yarns into textiles.

The churka, or roller gin, was a rudimentary teak-wood machine consisting of uprights supporting two cylinders, one above the other, this upper roller having a handle at the end. A woman turned this windlass, and the cotton fiber, fed between the rollers, passed on through, while the seeds, too large for passage, clattered against the base-board to the floor.

The separated lint was then bowed, or teased, for the removal of rubbish and kinks. The bow was an interesting contrivance of elastic wood, made still more vibrant by the tension of taut cords. A workman, placing his bow in contact with a mass of lint, would strike the resounding strings with a wooden hammer, so that powerful vibrations forced open the knots of the cotton, shook free the small rubbish of the fields, and produced a mass of downy fleece.

It is difficult for a modern man, used as he is to ingenious mechanical contrivances, to understand how such rude devices could be made to render any useful service whatsoever; but the fact remains that deft fingers wrought with the bow and the almost incredibly simple East Indian loom so as to produce delicate fabrics that have never been surpassed.

After the cotton had been bowed, Indian women spun it either upon a one-thread wheel, or on the ruder distaff. A Manchester manufacturer declared, only a quarter of a century ago, that the well managed use of the finger and thumb of the Indian spinner, patiently and carefully applied in the formation of the thread, and the moisture at the same time communicated to it, are found to have the effect of incorporating the fibers of the cotton more perfectly than can be accomplished by our most improved machines.[1] Mill, in his "History of British India,"[2] endeavored to explain this manifest manual superiority by remarking that the weak and delicate frame of the Hindu is accompanied with an acuteness of external sense, particularly of touch, which is altogether unrivaled; and the flexibility of his fingers is equally remarkable. "The hand of the Hindu, therefore, constitutes an organ adapted to the finest operations of the loom, in a degree which is almost or altogether peculiar to himself."

The introduction of modern implements has caused the decay of manual art in the India industry, and nowadays only the coarsest garments are produced by the rustic hand-looms.

The ancient Hindu weaver was the most wonderful workman of all. Cotton, having been ginned and bowed and then spun into delicate yarn, was passed on to this magical master-craftsman, plying his trade under the friendly shade of a tree. A handful of reeds, with balances suspended from

[1] Isaac Watts in Enc. Brit., 9th edition, vi, 487.

[2] ii, 8—cited by E. Baines, Jr., in History of the Cotton Manufacture in Great Britain: London, 1835; p. 75.

overhanging branches, made up his frail apparatus, the workman sitting in a pit beneath it, his great toes treadling with looped threads, his hands wielding the wide shuttle-batten, the warp being stretched out along the ground. Orme, an early traveler, reports that when not near the high road or a principal town, it was difficult to find a village in which every man, woman, and child was not employed in making up a piece of cloth;[3] and Mr. Lowes Dickinson, in a recent book of travel, still finds "the village weaver at his work, sitting on the ground with his feet in a pit working the pedals of his loom; while outside in the garden, a youth was running up and down setting up, thread by thread, the long strands of the warp."[4]

"Webs of the woven wind" these fabrics were anciently called because of their delicate beauty. Two Arabian travelers, writing of the Hindus in the Middle Ages, say that they made garments of such extraordinary perfection that nowhere else were the like to be seen; being woven to that degree of fineness "that they may be drawn through a moderate-size ring."[5] Marco Polo mentions the coast of Coromandel as producing "the finest and most beautiful cottons."[5] Tavernier, writing about 1660, describes some of the "calicuts" he saw as "so fine you can hardly feel them in your hand, and the thread, when spun, is scarce discernible." Of one muslin the texture was so delicate that "when a man puts it on, his skin shall appear as plainly through it, as if he was quite naked; but the merchants are not permitted to transport it, for the governor

[3] Historical Fragments of the Mogul Empire, p. 409; cited by Baines.

[4] Appearances: New York, 1914; p. 27.

[5] Cited by Baines, pp. 56–58.

is obliged to send it all to the Great Mogul's seraglio."[5] With the aid of a bamboo spindle not much larger than a darning needle, and rotated upon a piece of hollow shell to keep from breaking the thread, a single pound of lint could be spun by Indian craftsmen to a length of two hundred and fifty-three miles; while the delicate woven fabric was of both plain and ornamental variety, some white, and some beautifully colored. The Rev. William Ward, writing at Serampore early in the nineteenth century, describes a muslin manufactured there as so exceedingly fine that when "laid on the grass, and the dew has fallen upon it, it is no longer discernible."[5]

[5] Cited by Baines, pp. 56–58.

CHAPTER 6

ALEXANDER'S TRADE ROUTES

The genius of Alexander first made way for the wonderful cotton weaving of India to come into Europe, by means of new highways completed under his generals, both overland and through paths of the sea. We know that India carried on an export trade in cotton so early as the reign of Amasis, 569–525 B. C.; but the Persians, averse to water, content with their own mighty empire, and contemptuous of foreign intermixture, had not extended their commerce with India beyond their own borders. When Alexander turned back from the Hyphasis and sailed with his fleet down the Indus, his bold intention held fast to a demonstration of his belief that the opulent commerce of India could be transported through the Persian Gulf toward the interior of Asia Minor, as well as by the Arabian Sea to his noble namesake city, and so spread out to the world. After returning to Susa, he surveyed in person the courses of the Euphrates and Tigris, ordering the removal of cataracts and dams and of all those obstructions near the mouths of the rivers that had been used by the Persians for prevention of interior commerce.

Susa and other inland cities were thus directly connected with the sea. From Susa to Sardis, in the extreme west, there ran a great highway, fifteen hundred miles long, into whose paths were drawn all the diverse life of the busy ancient world.

"Carians and Cilicians, Phrygians and Cappadocians, staid Lydians, sociable Greeks, crafty Armenians, rude traders from the Euxine shores, nabobs of Babylon, Medes and Persians, galloping couriers mounted on their Bokhara ponies or fine Arab steeds, envoys with train and state, peasants driving their donkeys laden with skins of oil or wine or sacks of grain, stately caravans bearing the wares and fabrics of the South to exchange for the metals, slaves, and grain of the North, travelers and traders seeking to know and exploit the world—all were there, and all were safe under the protection of an empire the roadway of which pierced the strata of many tribes and many cultures, and helped set the world a-mixing.—The organization and regulation of Alexander's empire was later made possible through the roads, and they were the conductors by which East and West were joined and the first cosmopolitanism brought into being."[1]

More important even than such channels of intercourse was the water-way, opened by Alexander's successors, in conformity with his brilliant designs, through the Indus and the Arabian Gulf to Alexandria. Ptolemy Philadelphus, with the intention of binding Indian commerce the more firmly to Alexandria, undertook to dig a canal between Suez and the eastern branch of the Nile. Although this task was never finished, Ptolemy did build the port of Berenice, into which Indian commerce could come without incurring the ancient danger of navigating the northern end of the Arabian Gulf; and the Indo-Egyptian traffic thus established was prosperously maintained for ten centuries. Goods landed at

[1] B. I. Wheeler, Alexander the Great: New York, 1900; pp. 196–197.

Berenice were packed camel-back three hundred miles across the desert to Coptos, and thence floated down the Nile to Alexandria, from which they were trans-shipped to the various countries served by the Mediterranean Sea. Even in the time of Julius Cæsar and Mark Antony, Alexandria, as Ferrero[2] has said, was the Paris of the ancient world. "What was there at Rome to compare with Alexandria?" he asks,—Rome, in spite of its imperial power, abandoned to a fearful disorder by the disregard of factions, encumbered with ruin, its streets narrow and wretched, provided as yet with but a single *forum,* narrow and plain, the sole impressive monument of which was the theater of Pompey; Rome, where the life was yet crude, and objects of luxury so rare that they had to be brought from the distant Orient? At Alexandria, instead, the Paris of the ancient world, were to be found all the best and most beautiful things of the earth. There was a sumptuosity of public edifices that the ancients never tire of extolling—the quay seven *stadia* long, the light-house famous all over the Mediterranean, the marvelous Zoölogical Garden, the Museum, the Gymnasium, innumerable temples, the unending palace of the Ptolemies. There was an abundance, unheard of for those times, of objects of luxury—rugs, glass, stuffs, papyruses, jewels, artistic pottery—because they made all those things at Alexandria. There was an abundance, greater than elsewhere, of silk, of perfumes, of gems, of all the things imported from the extreme East, because through Alexandria passed one of the most frequented routes of Indo-Chinese commerce. Arrian, writing in the

[2] Characters and Events of Roman History: New York, 1909; p. 55.

year 131 A. D., says that at that time "Indian cottons of large width, fine cottons, muslins, plain and figured, and cotton for stuffing couches and beds," were brought by water from India and launched by way of Egypt toward the countries of the West.[3]

In view of the proximity of Egypt to Persia and India, and of the great importance of the cotton crop in Egypt to-day, it is a striking and unexplained fact that Egyptian cotton as we know it has developed from a garden plant of the Peruvian type into a field crop only within the last two hundred years, the earliest record of it going back no further than the end of the sixteenth century. This is all the more strange in view of the fact that the history of the Nile Valley, which has been laid bare to the period of five thousand years before Christ, contains abundant remains of other textile fabrics, of the very earliest periods; but fragments of cotton are not found at all, and even the literary trace of it ends with about two hundred years before Christ, such "antiquity" being quite negligible in the history of Egypt. There is a reference to it on the famous Rosetta stone, Herodotus describes a gift of a fine cotton corselet sent by Amasis to the Lacedæmonians,[4] Pliny records the growth of the plant in Upper Egypt, and there are hints of it in the time of the Ptolemies; but here the scant record ends. Professor Balls does indeed infer, from the existence of several wild cottons in the Sudan, that some lucky excavation, or perhaps a casual glance through a microscope, may suddenly extend the known history of cotton in Egypt by two or three thousand

[3] Periplus Maris Erythræi, cited by Henry Lee.
[4] Herodotus, iii, 47.

years;[5] but as yet it is regarded as a modern upstart in comparison with the linen mummy-wrappings that establish the Egyptian antiquity of flax.

[5] W. Lawrence Balls, The Cotton Plant in Egypt: London, 1912; p. 2. See also Chapter 73.

CHAPTER 7

EGYPTIAN MUMMIES AND THE MICROSCOPE

THE microscope, which disclosed in 1834 the surprising fact that Egyptian mummies never wore cotton, revealed at the same time the secret structure of the cotton fiber that gives it such peculiar excellence in weaving. Mr. James Thomson of Clitheroe presented to the Royal Society, in the year just named, a paper "On the Mummy Cloth of Egypt,"[1] in which he proved incontestably, from innumerable microscopic investigations of mummy-wrappings, that cotton was not thus used by the Egyptians; basing his conclusion on the interesting fact, discovered in the course of his investigations, that cotton invariably shows, under the microscope, a twisted or corkscrew structure, while the fibers of linen are straight. Never once, throughout experiments conducted from 1834 to the present, has a trace of the distinctive corkscrew structure of cotton been detected in the ancient fabrics of Egypt.

The filament of cotton, as Mr. Thomson pointed out in his paper, resembles a transparent glassy tube, flattened, and twisted around its own axis. This twisted form of the filament, which distinguishes cotton from all other fibers, characterizes the fully ripe pod; the filaments in the unripe pod being simple untwisted cylindrical tubes, which never afterwards twist if separated from the plant

[1] Given as Appendix by Baines, as cited.

in an unripe condition—but when the bolls ripen, the cylindrical filaments collapse in the middle, so that a cross-section roughly resembles the figure 8.

The characteristic twist of the cotton fiber is permanently retained throughout all the processes of ginning, spinning, weaving, bleaching, and dyeing, and even through the hardest wearing and washing, until the material is worn into rags. In fact, the violent process of reducing these rags to pulp for the manufacture of paper produces no change in the native twist of the fiber, so that the presence of any smallest vestige of cotton may be detected, with the aid of a microscope, in paper of supposedly all-linen manufacture.

Now, it is precisely this corkscrew character of the cotton fiber that affords its advantage in cloth making. "The reason why cotton can be spun into very fine, strong yarns is because the cotton fibers are of a very fine diameter and are flat, *twisted* ribbons in structure, which fact enables them to 'kink' together and interlock, thus forming a strong, compact thread."[2] Mercerized cotton is formed by stretching yarn on a frame and submerging it in a solution of caustic soda, which makes the fibers swell and to a greater or less extent lose their twisted structure. They thus become smoother, and take on a luster like silk.

The microscope also discloses the fact that wool, as it comes from the back of the sheep, is covered with scales, so that, when the wool fibers are worked and massed closely together, the scales open out and interlock with one another, the interlocking of these scales enabling the wool to be "felted."

[2] K. B. Lamb on "Textile Fibers and Their Characteristics," in *Scientific American:* New York, Jan. 8, 1916, p. 56.

CHAPTER 8

FROM ROME TO SPAIN [1]

If India was the land of cotton, while China was characterized by the production of silk as Egypt by the manufacture of linen, then Greece and Rome were preëminently the almost exclusive dominion of wool. It is true that the Greeks knew of fine muslins as a precious curiosity, naming these goods "Gangitiki" because of their source near the Ganges; and that by the beginning of the second century before Christ, Indian raiment had so far encroached on the aristocratic dominion of the peplum and the toga that a popular comedy of that period contains reference to muslins and calicoes; but the importation does not seem either then or later to have attained to any great commercial importance. Yet cotton became eventually the Roman cloth of luxury, at least. From India and Persia the Latin conquerors borrowed the custom of using cotton awnings as protection against the rays of the sun. Livy, for example, says that Lentulus Spinther in the year 63 B. C. introduced cotton awnings in the theater at the Apollinarian games; and that Cæsar afterwards covered the forum with them, as also the sacred way from his own house to the Capitoline hill—"which appeared more wonderful than the gladiatorial exhibition itself." Moreover, cot-

1 Chief authorities: Baines, as cited; Henry Lee; Bulletin No. 33, as cited.

ton sails were sometimes seen on Roman ships. But it is doubtful whether the Oriental weavings ever broke beyond the bound of luxuries at Rome, although in Egypt they became so abundant and inexpensive that Antony could afford to give his men the comparative comfort of light cotton clothes. But linen persisted in its domination of the Egyptian clothing market for a very long period, so that the cultivation of cotton was not undertaken there on any considerable scale until the beginning of the seventeenth century.[2]

This was a thousand years after its cultivation and manufacture had become an important item in the industries of Arabia and Syria, and had even fringed the northern coast of Africa. By the Saracens and Moors a knowledge of the plant and its uses was brought into Spain in the year 712 A. D., vast fields being whitened with its fleecy growth and looms set up in almost every hamlet, cultivation and manufacture alike increasing in importance until the expulsion of the Moors at the end of the fifteenth century. It was during this Spanish régime that cotton paper began to be made; not to be confused, however, with the paper from linen rags that writers so highly esteemed; and thus cotton began to take the literary scepter away from the ancient papyrus plant in Egypt.

During Mahometan rulership in Europe the Egyptian maritime commerce was closed, and transportation once more followed overland routes by means of the stately and picturesque caravan. Those famous "Damascus" cottons of early times were so-called merely because that city was a great distributing depot for India goods, the two great

[2] See Chapter 73.

annual caravans of merchants and pilgrims which started from there and from Cairo meeting by prearrangement at Mecca, where they exchanged commodities and then turned homeward again,—great fleets of the desert, touching at port after port on their interminable voyages, and thus sowing the cotton influence, whether in the form of the actual staple or in guise of fabulous legends of the Vegetable Lamb, through all the principalities of the East.

Caravans for strictly commercial purposes proceeded at fixed times on voyages of enormous extent, penetrating even to the farthest confines of China. Until only a few years ago China and Russia maintained a regular system of intercommunication by caravan, this system covering a distance of more than six thousand miles, and stretching for much of this distance through uninhabited desert, although the tedium of the journey was lightened now and again by touching at towns in the midst of their festival fairs, such as the famous annual fair at Nijni Novgorod.

As many as a thousand camels sometimes made up the medieval caravan, harnessed in strings of fifty or more, the leaders gay with colorful trappings and tassels, an unladen donkey preceding the party "for luck." Packed on the back of these swaying ships of the desert, or wafted by its own sails from the shore of one sea to another, or floating down the Indus and the Nile, cotton wended its journey westward through the centuries, until its strands at length girdled the globe.

Cotton sail-cloth became the distinguishing product of Barcelona after the advent of the Saracens and Moors, Spanish looms also becoming famous for fustians and other stout stuffs. Grenada, Cordova, and Seville were celebrated seats of the industry for several hundreds of years. But with the expulsion of the Saracens the European cotton manufacture fell into decay, not to flourish again until it participated in that great efflorescence of human achievement known as the Renaissance, which unfolded in Italy and spread over every country in Europe.

CHAPTER 9

COTTON AND THE RENAISSANCE

REYBAUD has deftly indicated the influence of the Renaissance upon raiment. During the Middle Ages, he says, scant attention was given to refinement in clothing. "Neither chivalry nor the Middle Ages had any taste for it; monks wore the cowl, the men of the sword wore armor; clean linen became almost a matter of over-refinement.—But the epoch of the Renaissance," he continues, "lends itself more to it; the awakening of the arts then introduces luxury, and with luxury the care of the person.—From this moment the sphere of activity extends, and unexpected riches are acquired for the needs and enjoyment of man."[1]

Cotton was very early responsive to the reawakened needs of mankind, being quickened into life again in Italy, chief source of the mighty Revival. First Venice, then Genoa, and then Venice again, sought control of East Indian trade; the Genoese uniting with the Greeks to recapture Constantinople, with its oriental commerce, after Venice had held it for half a century; the Venetians then turning successfully to the acquirement of the Indo-Egyptian trade-routes through a treaty with the Mahometans, so that Alexander's channels of intercourse were once more opened to the world.

From this moment cotton weaves itself continu-

[1] L. Reybaud, Le Coton; Son Régime, Ses Problèmes, Son Influence en Europe: Paris, 1863; p. 4.

ously through the history of Europe, in an ever-widening pattern. Venice becomes preëminent for the distribution of cotton supplies, especially sought after by the people of Northern Europe, who, within fifty years, established a great manufacture of their own in Saxony, Suabia, and Holland, but especially in Flanders. Venice was the cotton market of the world, the Liverpool of those days; Antwerp, the seat of manufacturing, corresponding to Manchester.[2]

But the impulse of the Italian Renaissance, not to be hemmed in even by continental confines, again set in motion that world movement which had been retarded for so many centuries since Alexander first pushed it westward from the Himalayas and the mouth of the Indus. Influenced by a desire for freer intercourse with the commercial store-houses of India, wherein by no means the least precious commodity was the world's cotton supply, Italy and Portugal sent forward in opposite directions two quests for the key to the Orient—Columbus the Genoese sailing westward in 1492, and Vasco da Gama from Lisbon eastward in 1497, both seeking India.

Gama was successful. Rounding the continent of Africa and touching near Zanzibar, he sailed across the Indian Ocean described by Arrian in connection with the early history of the cotton commerce, and landed at Calicut, the city of calicoes, ten months and two days out of Lisbon. Here he set up a marble pillar as a sign of conquest and in proof of discovery of India. After his return to Portugal another fleet was sent out under Cabral, who established a factory at Calicut.

[2] G. von Schulze-Gaevernitz, Der Grossbetrieb: Leipzig, 1892; p. 25.

Vasco da Gama, commanding a second expedition several years later, founded a factory at Mozambique, in the Portuguese possessions on the east coast of Africa,—these being probably the first examples of the penetration of western mechanical enterprise into the Orient. A whole chain of forts and factories was shortly established for the protection of the Portuguese trade, ships plying between all the ports from the Cape to Canton.

Venice, thrown into alarm, formed an alliance with the Turks, but the dauntless Portuguese maintained, at the cost of much blood and treasure, their mastery of the Indian Ocean, routing the Venetians completely in this contest for Oriental supremacy, and reshaping the channels of commerce by shipment from India around Africa to Lisbon. The immediate result was a plentiful supply throughout Europe of Indian products, including cotton goods, and a consequent reduction in price; but this situation, in turn, brought about a greatly increased demand for these plentiful and inexpensive goods from the Orient, so that the cotton trade received the greatest impetus that had thus far occurred in its history.

Vasco da Gama's voyage, as Draper says, was to the last degree important in its effect on the future development of Europe. The commercial arrangements of Europe were completely dislocated; Venice was deprived of her mercantile supremacy; the hatred of Genoa was gratified; prosperity left the Italian towns; Egypt, hitherto supposed to possess a preëminent advantage as offering the best avenue to India, suddenly lost her position; the commercial monopolies so long in the hands of the European Jews were broken down. The discovery of America and passage of the Cape were the first steps of that prodigious maritime development soon exhibited by Western Europe. And since commercial prosperity is forthwith followed by the production of men and concentration of wealth, and, moreover, implies an energetic intellectual condition, it appeared before long that the centers of population, of wealth, of intellect, were shifting westwardly. The front of Europe was suddenly changed; the British Islands, hitherto in a sequestered and eccentric position, were all at once put in the van of the new movement.[3] Englishmen took to the sea, and the great Age of Adventure, led by Cabot, Hawkins, and Drake, laid the foundations of a new international commerce. Shipbuilding became a famous British business. By means of newly developed trade-routes, both East and West were tapped for such wares as cotton, silks, tobacco, tea, coffee, cocoa, sugar, rum, spices, oranges, lemons, raisins, currants, rice and other strange products with which Englishmen had theretofore somehow dispensed. The carrying trade of the world became an international bone of contention. Spain and Portugal having been crippled in warfare, England next struck a blow at Holland in the famous Navigation Acts of 1650–1651, requiring that all imports for England or any crown colonies should be carried in English bottoms or in ships of the producing country. The ensuing wars resulted in British acquisition of the New Netherlands colonies, embracing the present States of New York and Pennsylvania, thus driving out the wedge that had divided New England from Virginia and Maryland. With the subsequent settlement of the Carolinas and Georgia, the thirteen American colonies were com-

[3] J. W. Draper, A History of the Intellectual Development of Europe: New York, 1863; pp. 449–450.

plete. New imports from the colonies and the Orient called for an increased body of exports, and thus provided a powerful stimulus to British manufacturing industry as a means in the development of this newly established international commerce.[4]

But this is to run ahead of our story.

[4] A. F. Pollard, The History of England; a Study in Political Evolution: London, n. d., ch's vi, vii. ("The Discovery of the New World began that economic revolution which changed every manufacturing town into a mere booth in the world's fair."—George Bernard Shaw in Fabian Essays: London, 1889; p. 174.)

CHAPTER 10

THE WEAVER KING

King Edward III (1327–1377) is called by Hallam "the father of English commerce." He taught his people, who monopolized the sheep culture of Europe at a time when Europeans wore woolen garments almost exclusively, to weave wool as well as to grow it; and thus augmented the national wealth by adding the profits of manufacture to the revenues derived from a monopoly of production. A hundred and fifty years before Vasco da Gama "discovered India," and just at the time when "Sir John Maundevile" professed to be forming a personal acquaintance with the Vegetable Lamb of Tartary, Edward was taking advantage of dissensions among the Flemish experts in wool weaving to invite them to settle in England.[1]

This he did with such marked sagacity that throughout his entire reign, and for the better part of a century, Flemish weavers continued to emigrate to England, and by the introduction of that "mystery" for which Flanders had become famous, improved so greatly the crude British business in weaving that wool became what cotton now is to the Southeastern States in America—the chief source of

[1] H. Hallam, View of the State of Europe During the Middle Ages: New York, 1896, vol. ii, p. 512.

revenue, and, indeed, the principal article of national export; so that wool was styled in ancient records "the flower and strength, the revenue and blood of England," as is still symbolized by the wool-sack whereon the Lord High Chancellor sits as he presides over the House of Lords.

Down to Edward's time England had been almost entirely dependent on the Netherlands for comfortable clothing; but the "father of English commerce" brought it to pass that instead of importing more than half of its cloth and practically all of its comfortable clothing, as England had done when he ascended the throne, by the close of his reign the realm was exporting British cloth of three times the volume of its imports.

Edward for his pains was nicknamed "the wool merchant" by his royal brother in France, but, nothing daunted, he utilized to the fullest extent his marriage with the daughter of a Flemish count to woo the weavers. The quaint Fuller, in his "Church History," gives a delightful account of the persuasive arguments used by the King's agents in Flanders to show how much "better off" the operatives would find themselves in England. In Flanders, he says, it was a case of early up and late in bed, and all day hard work and harder fare, and all to enrich their masters without any profit to themselves. But, oh! how happy should they be if they would but come over to England, bringing their mystery, which would provide them welcome in all places! Here they should feed on fat beef and mutton till nothing but their fulness should stint their stomachs. The richest yeomen in England would not disdain to marry their daughters unto them, and such the English beauties that most envious foreigners could not but commend them![2]

In 1328 the first important colony of persuaded Flemish weavers settled at Manchester, and three years later seventy families came over. These weavers produced the famous "Manchester cottons," which in reality were not made of cotton at all, but of wool. The fact remains, however, that the settlement of these Flemings in Manchester provided the means of developing that part of Lancashire to a high degree of expertness in the weaving industry, so that when time at last was ripe and "vegetable wool" began to be manufactured in England it was Lancashire that gave the country that primacy in cotton manufacture which England still maintains, and which constitutes to-day its greatest industry, although all the raw material must cross either the Red and Arabian Seas or the Atlantic Ocean.

The immediate result of Flemish immigration was, as Edward so shrewdly had planned, an enormous stimulus to the wool trade. Fuller says that before the Flemings came to Manchester the English knew no better what to do with their wool than the sheep that wore it, for their best clothes were no better than friezes; while Thorold Rogers proffers the chilling assertion that a man in an English winter might as well have dressed himself with a hurdle as with English woolen cloth;[3] but from this time on Britain grew able to compete even with Flanders itself, and by a unique policy of protection in the exportation of raw wool so fostered the weaving in-

[2] Cited by T. Ellison, in The Cotton Trade of Great Britain: London, 1886; pp. 4–5.

[3] J. E. Thorold Rogers, The Economic Interpretation of History: London, 1909; p. 286.

dustry at home as to develop heavy exports of the manufactured article,—Flanders, with Germany, Russia, Italy, and Spain ranging up at length among the buyers, and Spain at the last playing into her enemy's hand by destroying the Flemish weaving industry altogether, the weavers fleeing in large numbers to augment the earlier immigration into England.

Thus from the thirteenth to the sixteenth century "wool was king" in England quite to the same degree that cotton came to be king south of Mason and Dixon's line in America during the nineteenth century. From 1360 British resources were enormously enlarged by adding to a natural monopoly the increment accruing from skilful manufacture thereof, just as the Carolinas and other Southern States are now undertaking to do with their cotton crop.[4] In this way woolen manufacture had become, prior to the Renaissance period, the pet industry of England, and a lively struggle ensued when cotton began to come in by way of Gama's new route, and dispute the primacy.

NOTE. The practical monopoly which the English possessed of wool was less due to the climate and soil of England, than it was to the maintenance of order in the kingdom. For a long time, every one in England, from the King to the serf, was an agriculturist. After the landowners had been constrained to give up arable farming, they still remained sheep masters, produced wool and sold it. Now when, owing to the diffusing or distribution of property, every one is interested in maintaining the rights of property, there is very little temptation given to theft or violence, and every inclination to detect and punish it. Hence, Englishmen could keep sheep, the most defenseless of agricultural animals. Every one who knows anything about the state of western Europe from the thirteenth to the seventeenth century, knows that the husbandmen did not keep sheep, for they would have certainly been plundered of them by the nobles and their retainers if they had. The King's peace was the protection of the sheep master.—England then had a monopoly of

---

[4] See Chapter 69.

wool. The monopoly was so complete, and the demand for the produce so urgent, that the English Parliaments were able to grant an export duty on wool equal to more than the market value of the produce without diminishing its price. In other words, the export duty was paid by the foreign consumer, a financial success which every government has desired, and in which all, with this English exception, have failed.—Rogers, as cited, pp. 9–10.

CHAPTER 11

COTTON ENTERS ENGLAND

COTTON first makes its appearance in English history as a luminant, the first recorded importation, so early as the year 1298, being one of candle-wicks, at that time a most important commodity.[1] Other shipments wandered in from time to time, but the aspect of the East Indian trade was insignificant until the new routes had become fully established, and Lisbon's plenty began to overflow her own narrow borders. By the end of the sixteenth century the Low Countries were casting jealous eyes toward Portugal, so lucrative had the Oriental commerce become; and expanding England vied with Holland in the establishment of a great trading agency for the exploitation of East Indian markets. On the last day of the year 1600 the British East India Company received a royal charter. Having obtained permission from native princes to establish forts and factories, this East India Company was in 1624 invested with the plenary rights of government. Shortly thereafter the importation of cotton fabrics began in earnest, and the spider goddess of India enlisted straightway in a contest with the stout Minerva of British industry for the weaving supremacy of the world.[2]

The first arrival of Indian fabrics occurred in 1631. Ten years later one hears of Manchester

[1] Baines, as cited, p. 96. [2] See Appendix B.

weavers buying in London cotton wool imported from Cyprus and Smyrna, working the same into fustians, vermillions, and dimities, and then returning it to London, "where the same is vented and sold, and not seldom sent into forrain parts, who have means, at far easier termes, to provide themselves of the said first materials."[3]

Almost immediately the cry of the commercial patriot was uplifted in hoarse clamor for the protection of home industries. The war of the pamphleteer raged violently, all of the arguments being on the side of British wool, while the insidious cotton fiber silently spun its webs over England. "Instead of green sey," cried one voice of woolen lamentation, "is now used painted and Indian-stained and striped calico; and instead of a perpetuana or shalloon to lyne men's coats with, is used sometimes a glazened calico, which in the whole is not above 12*d* cheaper, and abundantly worse. And sometimes is used a Bangale, that is brought from India, both for lynings to coats, and for petticoats too; yet our English ware is better and cheaper than this, only it is thinner for the summer. To remedy this, it would be very necessary to lay a very high impost upon all such commodities as these are, and that no callicoes or other sort of linen be suffered to be glazened."[4]

Measurable legislative relief was granted, at least to the dead, by the passage of a parliamentary Act in 1666 providing that every dead person should be buried in a woolen shroud, in default of which the persons directing the funeral should forfeit the sum

[3] Lewes Roberts in The Treasure of Traffic, 1642, cited by Baines, p. 100.

[4] The Ancient Trades Decayed and Repaired Again: London, 1678; pp. 16–17; see Baines, as cited, p. 77.

of £5.[5] "If the people while alive were so perverse and unpatriotic as to prefer foreign to domestic fabrics for their vestments," says Ellison, "they should at all events not be allowed to carry their fripperies with them to the grave."[6]

In 1696 a pamphlet entitled *The Naked Truth* declared that muslins were "becoming the general wear in England"; and then the writer, intending to be contemptuous, pays a tribute rivaling that of Tavernier to the delicate shadow-like quality of the Indian weave. "Fashion is truly termed a witch," he says; "the dearer and scarcer any commodity, the more the mode; 30*s.* a yard for muslins, and only the shadow of a commodity when procured!"[7]

But fashion's slaves continued to bow down before the cotton boll, as Brahmin priests had done three thousand years before them; although "the effect of such frippery was that our gold and silver went abroad, and that much excellent English drapery lay in our warehouses till it was devoured by the moths.—And was it not a shame to see a gentleman whose ancestors had worn nothing but stuffs made by English workmen out of English fleeces,

[5] 30 Car. II, st. i. c. 3. Blackstone, in his discussion of personal liberty, gives an amusing defense of this law: "The statute of King Edward IV, which forbade the fine gentlemen of those times (under the degree of a lord) to wear pikes upon their shoes or boots of more than two inches in length, was a law that savored of oppression; because, however ridiculous the fashion then in use might appear, the restraining it by pecuniary penalties could serve no purpose of common utility. But the statute of King Charles II, which prescribes a thing seemingly as indifferent (a dress for the dead, who are all ordered to be burried in woolen), is a law consistent with public liberty; for it encourages the staple trade, on which in great measure depends the universal good of the nation." —Sir Wm. Blackstone, Commentaries on the Laws of England: London, 1809 (first edition, 1765).

[6] Ellison, as cited, p. 8.

[7] Cited by Baines, p. 78

flaunting in a calico shirt and a pair of silk stockings from Moorshedabad?"[8]

In 1700 an Act was passed by Parliament which forbade the introduction of "India silks and printed calicoes for domestic use, either as apparel or furniture, under a penalty of £200."[9] This, however, appeared to give little relief, for in 1708 we hear the genial author of "Robinson Crusoe" lifting up a mournful philippic against the growing rule of King Cotton.

"The general fansie of the people," says Daniel Defoe, "runs upon East India goods to that degree, that the chints and printed callicoes, which before were only made use of for carpets, quilts, etc., and to clothe children and ordinary people, become now the dress of our ladies; and such is the power of a mode as we saw our persons of quality dressed in Indian carpets, which but a few years before their chambermaids would have thought too ordinary for them: the chints was advanced from lying upon their floors to their backs, from the foot-cloth to the petticoat; and even the queen herself at this time was pleased to appear in China and Japan, I mean China silks and calico. Nor was this all, but it crept into our houses, our closets, and bedchambers; curtains, cushions, chairs, and at last beds themselves, were nothing but callicoes or Indian stuffs; and in short, almost everything that used to be made of wool or silk, relating either to the dress of the women or the furniture of our houses, was supplied by the Indian trade.—The several goods bought from India are made five parts in six under our price, and, being

[8] Macaulay's History of England: New York, 1873; vol. vi, pp. 165–166.

[9] Cited by Ellison, p. 11; Act 11 and 12, William III, cap. 10.

imported and sold at an extravagant advantage, are yet capable of underselling the cheapest thing we can set about."[10]

Meanwhile, there are whispers that the woolen weavers at Manchester are busily engaged in making shrewd imitations of the much denounced Indian imports! This marks the beginning of England's stubborn surrender. Parliament, however, made a final and desperate stand for the wool-sack. In 1720[11] it prohibited the use or wear in Great Britain, in any garment or apparel whatsoever, of any printed, painted, stained, or dyed calico, under the penalty of forfeiting to the informer the sum of £5—thus virtually establishing the universal office of clothes-warden, after the modern fashion of some of the American States in the protection of game by awarding a fine to informers. It was also enacted that persons using printed or dyed calico "in or about any bed, chair, cushion, window-curtain, or any other sort of household stuff or furniture," should be fined £20, and that dealers selling the stuff should be mulcted an equal amount.[12]

This was just twenty years before the beginning of the Industrial Revolution, which with great suddenness transformed rural England by introducing the modern era of machinery.

10 *Weekly Review:* London, Jan. 31, 1708.

11 Ellison, p. 12.

12 F. Wilkinson, The Story of the Cotton Plant: New York, 1906; p. 119.

BOOK II

THE TRANSFORMATION OF ENGLAND

CHAPTER 12

THE INDUSTRIAL REVOLUTION

WRITING of the Industrial Revolution in England, Professor Gibbins says: "The French Revolution took place about the same time, and as it was performed amid streams of blood and flame, it attracted the attention of historians, who have apparently yet to learn that bloodshed and battles are merely the incidents of history.—Nothing has done more to make England what she at present is than this sudden and silent Industrial Revolution, for it increased her wealth ten-fold, and gave her half a century's start in front of the nations of Europe." [1]

Cotton chiefly produced it—the struggle of cotton with wool. How complete the triumph in this battle, appears in the simple fact that cotton now takes the leading rank in British industries, whereas wool occupied the supreme position when the Industrial Revolution began. Cotton dispossessed wool; and yet every circumstantial advantage was arrayed on the side of the wool-sack, as has been shown. Townsend Warner sums the case aptly in Traill's "Social England," pointing out that the term "revolution" is amply justified by the three-fold test of trade expansion, a transformed economic system, and the transfer of industrial sites.

In the first place, then, this revolutionary era was

[1] H. de B. Gibbins, The Industrial History of England: London, 1904; pp. 156–157.

characterized by an enormous increase in trade. In 1740 there had been no true cotton manufacture at all; which is to say, that all of the so-called "cottons" were made with the aid of linen warp. Even the import of cotton for fustians, candle-wicks, and other purposes amounted to only 1,645,031 lbs.; whereas in 1815 cotton imports reached a volume of nearly one hundred millions.

Cotton, however, was by no means the only industry affected; other trades borrowed its stimulus. For example, in 1740 England made 17,350 tons of pig-iron; but in 1806 there were 258,206 tons, and in 1825, 581,367 tons. In 1740 England exported hardly any iron, but imported much; in 1815 it exported 91,000 tons: while conversely, between 1792 and 1812 the quantity imported dropped from 51,000 tons to 24,000 tons. The total merchandise exports rose from a value of £8,197,788 in 1740 to £58,624,550 in 1815, while the revenue increased from £3,997,000 to £71,900,005, and the population itself rose from 6,064,000 to more than ten millions.

A change in mere volume, however, hardly justifies the term "revolution." A change in nature, far more important than a mere change in volume, also occurred. All industry was domestic in 1740; spinning and weaving being cottage occupations entirely. While the husbandman managed the loom at odd hours, wife and children spent all of their spare time in spinning. Factories in the modern sense did not exist. Except for Kay's fly-shuttle, the loom stood unchanged as from primitive ages, while spinning was equally ancient in all its methods. But in 1815 the master and mill had arrived, while men had become "hands," working on a time schedule, assisted by women and children.

But industry had not only changed in nature as well as in volume, it had also changed its location. Weavers, no longer scattered through the rural districts at random, had been attracted to the vicinity of the spinning mills, so as to work up the yarn which the master spinners gave out. Then water-power came into use, mills clustering on the river banks, and gradually moving up-stream. One incidental result of this movement was the abandonment of the woolen manufacture in the low countries, and, in fact, wherever water-power was not available. By 1802 steam power began to supersede water, whereupon industry drew in from the streams and built up large manufacturing towns, wherever coal was cheap and labor fairly abundant.

The Industrial Revolution of England, as summarized so compactly by Warner,[2] serves to typify and typically illustrate those stupendous changes that were to be wrought throughout human society by the invention and large use of machinery; and the cotton plant of the Orient is historically responsible for an important share in this Revolution, which brought about unnumbered benefits, with numerous attendant evils in their train.

Perhaps the most startling feature of the English change was the rapidity with which it was accomplished. In little more than twenty years almost all the great cotton inventions were achieved, Watt's new engine had applied steam power to novel looms, and the modern factory system had usurped the seat of a scattered and unorganized rural industry.

England, with its accustomed phlegmatism, had been almost the last country in Europe to take up

[2] H. D. Traill, Social England: London, 1905; vol. v, pp. 600-604.

the manufacture of cotton; but England, slow to arouse herself, makes a mighty stir when once awake. Convinced finally that the seductive Indian goods had permanently enchanted the fancy of her people in spite of political eloquence and excise laws and penalties, she taught her weavers surreptitiously to imitate the forbidden fripperies, and then at length the spirit of indomitable enterprise awakened, so that England resolved to take this fleecy stuff from the Orient, and, by the sheer application of brain power, turn disaster into opulence through a manipulation more dextrous than that of the Hindus themselves.

CHAPTER 13

BRITISH GENIUS

JUST on the unguessed verge of the Industrial Revolution, Daniel Defoe,[1] the eloquent champion of wool, went on an inland journey which he fully reported, giving a vivid picture of domestic England before machinery had made its appearance. "The land was divided into small Enclosures from two Acres to six or seven each, seldom more, every three or four Pieces of Land had a House belonging to them;—hardly an House standing out of Speaking-distance from another.—We could see at every House a Tenter, and on almost every Tenter a piece of Cloth or Kersie or Shaloon. At every considerable House there was a Manufactory. Every clothier keeps one horse at least to carry his Manufactures to the Market; and every one generally keeps a Cow or two or more for his Family. By this means the small Pieces of enclosed Land about each house are occupied, for they scarce sow Corn enough to feed their Poultry.—The houses are full of lusty Fellows, some at the Dye-vat, some at the looms, others dressing the Cloths; the women and children carding or spinning; being all employed, from the youngest to the oldest."

Next to agriculture, the handiwork connected with cloth manufacture had come to be, since the time of

[1] Tour Through the Whole Island of Great Britain: London, 1727; iii, 144–146.

Edward III, the chief occupation of the English; but it was essentially a rural and domestic handiwork, as far as possible removed from the factory-town system of to-day. Pieces of goods, once made, were painfully collected in the huddled hamlets; slowly gathered from the hamlets into towns; and then from the inland towns to seaports, over the worst of roads, and by the most rudimentary conveyances. There was certainly acute need of manufacturing improvement, as well as of better transportation.

Professor Cheyney's terse sketch of the old processes of domestic manufacture may be still further condensed for the present purpose. The raw material, whether coming from the back of the sheep, the boll of the cotton plant, or the crushed stems of the flax, is in any case a mass of tangled fiber; so that it is first necessary to straighten the skeins of this fiber, by "combing" in the case of wool, and otherwise by "carding"; simple hand implements having been used from time immemorial, and a thin fluffy roll of fiber resulting, known as the slubbin, or rove. Spinning, the next task, consisted in attenuating the rove into yarn, which in the same process was twisted to secure greater strength; the implement being first the high hand-wheel, and then the low foot-wheel which left the hands free for more rapid manipulation of material. The thread thus produced was then set upon the loom, which required strong substance for the lengthwise threads of the warp; while the weft, or woof, which might be of weaker material, was wrapped on a shuttle and thrown horizontally by hand between the two diverging bands of the warp. The woven cloth, being then subjected to various processes such as finishing, fulling, shearing, and dyeing (unless this had already been done in the yarn), the finished product was ready for the market.[2]

After British weavers had begun to imitate the fabrics of India they encountered their chief difficulty in being unable to spin a cotton yarn of sufficient strength to serve as warp; the lengthwise threads being subjected to severe longitudinal strain as well as to the friction of the cross-flying shuttle. Linen warp, used, perforce, as a substitute, failed to deceive those keen-eyed ladies and dandies that were addicted to the fashionable craze for calicoes and other "fripperies" of Oriental origin.

This difficulty was hardly relieved by the first invention in the notable series, when John Kay, in 1738, made a fly-shuttle for his loom, and thus enhanced its efficiency; on the contrary, the troubles of the spinners were only intensified, since Kay's invention made the looms so voracious for yarn that it was difficult to keep them supplied even with weft. Weavers generally had their weft spun for them by the women of their families, as already remarked; whence the modern connotation of "spinster," a proficient unmarried female. But the time came, as Guest says, when those weavers whose families could not furnish the necessary supply of weft, had their spinning done by their neighbors, and were obliged to pay more for the spinning than the price allowed by their masters; and even with this disadvantage, very few could procure weft enough to keep themselves constantly employed. It was no uncommon thing for a weaver to walk three or four miles in a morning, and call on five or six spinners, before he could collect weft to serve him for the remainder of

[2] E. P. Cheyney, An Introduction to the Industrial and Social History of England: New York, 1905; pp. 205–206.

the day; and when he wished to weave a piece in a shorter time than usual, a new ribbon or gown was necessary to quicken the exertions of the spinner, or spinster.

This augmented demand for ordinary weft, due largely to Kay's contribution to the efficiency of the loom, was at length met by the ingenious spinning-jenny of Hargreaves, invented about 1764; while the need of stronger thread for warp was supplied by the patent taken out on the spinning-frame or "water-frame" by Arkwright in 1769, a year still further signalized by Watt's patent of the steam engine, which was to furnish the chief motive power of modern machinery; while the gifted Crompton presently joined the "jenny" of Hargreaves to Arkwright's invention, thus producing the efficient composite "mule"; and so the spinners' troubles were finally ended.

The loom, having now ample provender, was transformed by Cartwright in 1787 into a machine of great power, and hitched to the engine of Watt; while full provision was beneficently made for the transportation of this enormously increased manufacture by the bold canals of Brindley, connecting Manchester with Liverpool, and by improved roads; so that it only remained for Humphry Davy, through his invention of the miner's safety lamp (in 1815) to light the way to untold storehouses of coal for the driving of James Watt's steam-engines.

Such, in brief, was the closely knit series of inventions by which England, her genius aroused, seized the entangling threads of the cotton boll and out of them wove a new destiny. It remains now to examine that genius as exemplified in the lives of the inventors.

CHAPTER 14

KAY AND HARGREAVES [1]

"THE strength in the heart of her poor is the hope of Sweden" conveys a sentiment that England might borrow with which to emblazon the story of that wonderful group of men whose patience and skill, in a brief span of years, filled her waste places with plenty and her silent spaces with the incessant hum of industry through making of their meager island home the rich and busy "workshop of the world." Arkwright was a barber, Brindley could hardly write his name, Watt and Robert Kay began life as mechanical apprentices and Davy as an apothecary's clerk, while Hargreaves, Crompton, and John Kay were humble weavers. Only Cartwright, of all the illustrious group, commenced with the background of influence behind him, being a clergyman when he invented his loom; but even he, like most of the others, got much pain and trouble as reward. It is little wonder that Baines, after a study of this period, should reach the hard conclusion that inventors, when failing in their projects, get no pity; and when they succeed, persecution, envy, and jealousy are their reward.

John Kay (1704–1764?) became doorkeeper to "the golden age of cotton," as it is called, by increasing

[1] Chief authority: B. Woodcroft, Brief Biographies of the Inventors of Machines for the Manufacture of Textile Fabrics: London, 1863.

the efficiency of the loom, and thereby rendering new spinning devices imperative if England was to capture the cotton industry from India. A weaver at Bury, he was used to the common type of "Dutch engine loom" brought over by the first Flemish settlers. This was a cumbrous machine, requiring, in addition to the labor of the weaver himself, the services of men standing on either side of the loom to fling the heavy shuttle to and fro whenever wide goods were in process, so that Dyer in his quaint poem on "the Fleece" could appropriately compare the casting of the "strong-flung shuttle" with the wielding of the spear.[2] For more than five thousand years, North[3] says, by millions of skilled workmen, one generation following in the exact footsteps of another, had the clothing of the people been woven, with but little attempt to expedite or simplify the process. John Kay, by the application of his prolific genius, brought the ancient hand-loom essentially to the form in which we now use it, by extending the lathe, or container in which the shuttle moved, and attaching spring fixtures and cords to both ends, so that the weaver, while treadling, could with one hand drive home the weft, while with the other he now merely released the racing shuttle, spring hammers being substituted for muscle power; thus not only saving labor, but operating the machine with such celerity as to double its output. Woodcroft thinks that no division of labor between the two hands of one operative ever produced results equal to those which this invention secured; leading a fervid versifier to exclaim:

[2] See Appendix C.

[3] S. N. D. North, The Development of American Industries since Columbus: New York, 1891; *Popular Science Monthly*, xxxix.

"Success to the shuttle, respect be the doom
Of John Kay, as our trade's benefactor!
What impulse he gave to the use of the loom,
What a boon to the world's manufacture!"[4]

Kay's device, called the "fly"-shuttle on account of its swift movement,[5] was patented in 1733, and by the year 1760 had been adopted by the manufacturers of Lancashire. It was in the latter year that his son Robert further increased the efficiency of the Dutch engine loom by inventing the "drop box," which enabled the weaver to ply at his pleasure any of three separate shuttles, each containing a different colored weft, without disturbing the box that contained them.

But before Kay's fly-shuttle could command general use it had to overcome not only the bitter prejudice of artisans who condemned it as a supplanter of labor, but also the opposition of the "upper classes," who were straightway alarmed at the prospect of an increased tax rate for the support of supposititious workmen that would be thrown into the alms-houses by reason of lack of employment! Neither the ignorant laborer nor the elegant gentleman of leisure had sufficient sagacity to perceive that machinery, by at once improving and cheapening manufacture, causes an extended demand for its products and thereby provides employment for more hands than have been for the time superseded. The rioting of weavers at Leeds compelled John Kay to shut up his mill there; and when it was learned that he planned further

[4] "D. F. P." in An Exposition of Facts Relating to the Rise and Progress of the Woollen, Linen, and Cotton Manufactures of Great Britain, by Thos. Sutcliffe: Manchester, 1843.

[5] A "pick" is the passage of the shuttle across the loom. Before the invention of Kay's fly-shuttle, looms could not average 20 picks a minute; they now range from 135 to 230.

machinery for the improvement of spinning, a mob broke into his house, and, after destroying everything it contained, would have killed the inventor had he not been smuggled away in a wool-sheet. His troubles did not end here, however, for manufacturers violated his patents, and at length the man who had added untold wealth to his country was permitted to be driven into France as an exile and to die there, about the year 1764, in direst poverty.

Within the last generation Bury dedicated a monument to the memory of Kay, bearing the following appreciative inscription:[6]

PRESENTED TO HIS NATIVE TOWN
BY HENRY WHITEHEAD, ESQ.,
TO PERPETUATE THE NAME AND FAME OF JOHN KAY,
OF BURY
WHOSE INVENTION OF THE FLY SHUTTLE IN THE YEAR 1733
QUADRUPLED HUMAN POWER AND PLACED THIS COUNTRY IN THE FRONT RANK
OF THE MARKETS OF THE WORLD
FOR TEXTILE MANUFACTURES.

The loom having now been greatly improved, there ensued, as already noted, an emphasized demand for better and more copious spinning. The next three inventors accordingly busied themselves with satisfying this increased hunger of the looms by devising machinery for the production of yarn: Hargreaves providing more weft, Arkwright making possible the first genuine cotton warp, and Crompton uniting the essential features of their two machines, jenny and frame, in his comically nicknamed "mule"—one of the choicest titbits of etymological fun in all the dictionary larder.

[6] London *Times*, June 27, 1913; p. 46.

James Hargreaves (——1778), carpenter and weaver, literally stumbled upon his invention about the year 1764, when, entering his cottage near Blackburn, his back bent with heavy bundles of yarn that he had been laboriously collecting for his loom, either he or his wife accidentally overthrew the hand-wheel at which she was spinning; whereupon James perceived that the spindles, although thrown into an unwonted upright position, still continued revolving; and on the instant there flashed into his mind the picture of a spinning machine with upright spindles, which he translated straightway into an instrument so simple that children could and did operate it, thus dating the introduction of child labor into the cotton industry.

The chief characteristic of the new spinning-jenny, besides its rows of upright spindles, was a moving carriage; the operator's right hand turning a wheel which caused the spindles to revolve rapidly, while with his left he pulled a miniature carriage towards him, and thus drew out to tenuity the rovings attached to it, the spindles twisting this material into yarn, and then winding it. The first jenny, working eight rovings in a row, multiplied the power of the hand-wheel eight times; when the machine was patented, in 1770, the number of spindles had been doubled; soon there came to be twenty or thirty, and afterwards a hundred—thus, according to the argument of ignorance, throwing ninety-nine spinsters out of work.

Hargreaves kept his invention secret as long as possible, his ambition extending no further than the use of it in his own family, so as to increase the supply of weft for his own loom; but when rumor had at length wrought its mischief a mob broke into his house, as into John Kay's before him, and, after destroying the spinning-jenny, compelled him to flee for his life. Establishing himself finally at Nottingham, he formed a partnership with Thomas James in conducting what was probably the first spinning mill in all England. His patents were stolen, however, and he died a poor man (in 1778), directing in his will that a guinea be given to the vicar for preaching his funeral sermon, while Mr. James gave the widow £400 for her husband's share in the factory.

Before his death his machine had worked its way into both the cotton and linen industries to such an extent that twenty thousand hand-jennies of eight spindles each were operating in England; [7] but in the year after his death a mob of weavers scoured the country for miles around Blackburn, demolishing all the jennies they could find with more than twenty spindles, the smaller ones being by this time conceded to be useful; and also destroying every machine, of whatever kind, driven by water or horses.

A pretty legend has long attributed the word "jenny," by which the spinning machine is universally known, to a chivalrous desire on the part of James Hargreaves to perpetuate his wife's name; it is said to have been named after her. Unfortunately, however, a grandson of the inventor is known to have denied this; and the origin of the tale may be traced to Miss Maria Edgeworth's didactic

[7] "From the year 1770 to 1778 a complete change had gradually been effected in the spinning of yarns; that of wool had disappeared altogether, and that of linen was nearly gone; cotton, cotton, cotton, had become the universal material for employment; the hand-wheels were all thrown into lumber-rooms; the yarn was all spun on common jennies."—Wm. Radcliffe's Narrative, cited by P. Gaskell in Artisans and Machinery: London, 1836; p. 374.

story for the edification of children, entitled "Harry and Lucy," published in 1825; wherein Lucy, having been told by her father the story of the Hargreaves invention, exclaims: "A Spinning Jenny! Very right! I suppose his wife's name was Jenny."

The word is probably either a feminine variant for "jack," frequently applied to pieces of machinery, such as jack-screw, or else a variant of "gin,"—formerly spelt "ginne,"—a colloquial abbreviation of engine, as "bus" is for omnibus.

CHAPTER 15

ARKWRIGHT THE BARBER [1]

RICHARD ARKWRIGHT (1732–1792) is the only one of the great cotton inventors endowed with sufficient business sagacity to transmute his genius into tangible wealth. Beginning life as a barber, he became high sheriff of Derbyshire, and died as an opulent knight—having been rewarded by George III for his eloquence when as high sheriff he presented the King with an address of congratulation on escaping death at the hands of one Margaret Nicholson. The youngest of thirteen children in a humble family of Lancashire, he was early apprenticed as a barber, and followed this calling until thirty years old. But he was by no means an ordinary barber, for he made money by doing an itinerant business with wig-makers, and, further, by monopolizing a secret manufacture of hair-dye. He also tampered with perpetual motion, and, having married a shrew, separated from her in order to be rid of her noisy alliterative complaints that "he would starve his family by scheming when he should be shaving"—as also out of a natural resentment toward her for having smashed some of his precious models.

This ingenious Lancashire barber could not escape the cogs of the great industrial revolution in the midst of which he was moving, and about the year 1767 gave himself up completely to the development

[1] Chief authority: E. Howe, Memoirs: New York, 1857.

of spinning machines. Securing the aid of the clockmaker Robert Kay, inventor of the drop box, he set to work in a house belonging to the grammar school at Preston, and there produced the first effective "water frame" (so called because driven by water), which was based, whether consciously or innocently, on the uncompleted work of Wyatt and Paul, done thirty years earlier.

Lewis Paul had in 1738 invented, in coöperation with John Wyatt, a machine that was providing the now numerous spinning-jennies with a plentiful supply of good roving. The characteristic feature of Paul's carding machine consisted of rollers in contact, like those of the modern clothes-wringer, and this is also the chief characteristic of the machine patented by Arkwright in 1769. These rollers were laid out by Arkwright in four pairs, all the lower rollers being fluted, and the upper ones covered with leather. Since each successive pair of rollers revolved with increased rapidity, the roving was by the pressure of the first pair reduced to a thick cord, and then by the next pair, revolving much more rapidly, drawn out to be thinner and stronger, until, when the end of the process had been reached, a cotton yarn could be obtained sufficiently durable to be used as a warp. To this day, the Arkwright principle, even in our most elaborate spinning mills, is used for the production of warp, while the moving carriage of Hargreaves is utilized in the manufacture of weft.

Like Hargreaves, Arkwright moved to Nottingham, where he became the dominant partner in a knitting firm, which in the year 1773 manufactured from Arkwright warp the first piece of genuine British made calico—by horse-power. Arkwright afterwards set up an extensive water-power factory at Cromford, in Derbyshire, where his business talents served him so well that, notwithstanding his patents were thrown open by the courts, he laid up a great fortune, living in "patriarchal prosperity." Dr. Erasmus Darwin, whose poetic faculty exercised itself in extolling the Vegetable Lamb of Tartary without his ever guessing of its identity with the cotton boll, thus described, in the same poem,[2] the mill on the river Derwent:

Where Derwent rolls his dusky floods
Through vaulted mountains, and a night of woods,
The nymph, *Gossypia*,[3] treads the velvet sod,
And warms with rosy smiles the watery God;
His ponderous oars to slender spindles turns,
And pours o'er massy wheels his foamy urns;
With playful charms her hoary lover wins,
And wields his trident,—while the Monarch spins.—
First with nice eye emerging Naiads cull
From leathery pods the vegetable wool;
With wiry teeth *revolving cards* release
The tangled knots, and smooth the ravel'd fleece;
Next moves the *iron-hand* with fingers fine,
Combs the wide card, and forms the eternal line;
Slow, with soft lips, the *whirling Can* acquires
The tender skeins, and wraps in rising spires;
With quicken'd pace, *successive rollers* move,
And these retain, and those extend the *rove;*
Then fly the spoles, the rapid axles glow;—
And slowly circumvolves the laboring wheel below.

Arkwright, this barber who became knight, was a good deal of a man. When considerably more than fifty years old he undertook the study of English grammar, not only devoting an hour a day to it, with

[2] The Botanic Garden, as cited.
[3] The botanical name of the cotton plant is *Gossypium*.

another hour to the improvement of his writing and spelling, but taking this time from his sleeping allowance, which was scant, as he labored assiduously from five until nine o'clock daily. Yet at this time he was exceedingly rich for those days, having amassed a fortune of nearly half a million pounds sterling. A vivid glimpse of the "patriarchal prosperity" in which he had lived is gained from the following lively description of his funeral, from the pen of a contemporary traveler who happened to be passing through the town:

"As the ground I was on was much higher than the Tor, or any of the hills at Matlock, I was at once surprised and delighted with the grand and awful scene that expanded below me; all the rich profusion of wild nature thrown together in an assemblage of objects the most sublime. To heighten the view, the Tor, and rocks near it, were covered with people.—The roads were nearly impassable, from the crowds of people who had assembled to witness the procession. The ceremony was conducted with much pomp, and, as nearly as I can remember, was thus: a coach and four with the clergy; another with the pall-bearers; the hearse, covered with escutcheons, and surrounded by mutes, followed; then the horse of the deceased, led by a servant; the relations, and about fifteen or twenty carriages, closed the procession, which was nearly half a mile in length. The evening was gloomy, and the solemn stillness that reigned was only interrupted by the rumbling of the carriages, and the gentle murmurs of the river; and, as they passed, the echo of the Tor gently returned the sound."

Thus ended the dramatic career of the Englishman who may properly be called the father of the cotton manufacture. During his lifetime the imports of lint grew from a million and a half pounds to 34,907,497 lbs. (1792), and its manufactured exports from a value of less than £20,000 to almost £2,000,000, although the "golden age of cotton" was but just beginning.[4] This "golden" period, which covered the years from 1788 to 1803, saw the cotton trade treble itself, leading Erasmus Darwin to say: "It is probable that the clothing of this small seed will become the principal clothing of mankind."[5]

[4] See Appendix F 1. Radcliffe designated the "golden age" of cotton in his Narrative, as cited.

[5] The Botanic Garden, as cited.

CHAPTER 16

CROMPTON [1] AND CARTWRIGHT [2]

SAMUEL CROMPTON (1753–1827) had learned at an early age to spin on one of the Hargreaves machines, in the beautiful old house known as the Hall ith Wood, which is still standing near Bolton, a town famous from his time until the present for the manufacture of fine muslins and quiltings. Losing his father in infancy, he came under the care of a wise and industrious mother, who gave her son an excellent education. He was never able, however, to emulate the business ability of Arkwright. At the age of twenty-one he began his experiments, and succeeded after five years of the most diligent labor; the result being a combination of the Arkwright rollers with the moving carriage of Hargreaves, greatly improved, in a machine which eventually—during his own lifetime—carried upwards of 350 spindles. "He applied the principle of roller drawing in order to first attenuate the cotton, and he utilized the traveling carriage as a reserve power with which to improve the quality of the thread and draw it out finer." As Baines said in his paraphrase:

> The force of genius could no farther go—
> To make a third he joined the other two.

This "mule" was far more than a clever adaptation; it manifested original ability, in accomplishing

[1] Chief authority for Crompton: F. Wilkinson, as cited.
[2] Chief authority for Cartwright: E. Baines, Jr., as cited; B. Woodcroft, as cited.

for the first time by automatic mechanism the movement of the spinner's left arm and forefinger and thumb, which held and elongated the sliver, while the spinner was twisting it into yarn. North says that it produced a yarn of much greater fineness and evenness than it had been possible to make by any process previously in use. This invention was the prototype of the mule of which thousands are at work throughout the world to-day.[3]

Crompton was of a gentle and retiring disposition. Fond of music, he built an organ for his enjoyment, and also played the violin in the orchestra at the Bolton theater at a wage of one shilling sixpence the night, and served as honorary choirmaster of the Swedenborgian chapel. Shunning publicity, and moreover aware that rioters were smashing cotton machinery in the neighborhood of Blackburn, he took elaborate pains to conceal his invention above the ceiling of his work-room at the Hall ith Wood. But his yarn, when sold, attracted the attention of the Bolton masters by its unique excellence, and from that time life became a burden to him. "Hundreds of manufacturers visited Samuel to purchase, but many more came out of curiosity," writes Director Wilkinson of the Bolton Engineering School. One individual is said to have hidden himself five days in the cock-loft and, having bored a hole through the ceiling, feasted one eye at least by a sight of the marvelous mechanism which Crompton had invented. Being plagued for his secret, he at length gave it up in return for a promised subscription, which, when collected, amounted to the munificent sum of £67 6*s.* 6*d.*, while the recipient lived to see great fortunes realized from the muslin indus-

[3] S. N. D. North, as cited.

try as cultivated by his wonderful mule. So early as the year 1811 more than four and a half million spindles operated by mules were in use in various British factories. The Government voted Crompton a paltry grant of £5000, but he made little use of it, becoming dependent upon a friend, and dying at the age of seventy-four in poverty.

The effect of these several inventions of Hargreaves, Arkwright, and Crompton was to set the spinning business far in advance of the weaver, who now had his hands full. The man who helped the weavers catch up with the spinners, by completing the cycle of cotton machinery, was a poet and a genial Kentish parson.

Edmund Cartwright (1743–1823) himself describes his invention in an interesting letter which tells of a visit to Arkwright's spinning factory at Cromford. It will be noted that he had never seen a weaver at work when he achieved his revolutionary invention.

"Happening," he says, "to be at Matlock in the summer of 1784, I fell in company with some gentlemen of Manchester, when the conversation turned on Arkwright's spinning machinery. One of the company observed that as soon as Arkwright's patent expired, so many mills would be erected, and so much cotton spun, that hands would never be found to weave it. To this observation I replied, that Arkwright must then set his wits to work to invent a weaving-mill. This brought on a conversation upon the subject, in which the Manchester gentlemen unanimously agreed that the thing was impracticable; and in defense of their opinion they adduced arguments which I was certainly incompetent to answer, or even to comprehend, being totally ignorant of the subject, having never at the time seen a person weave. I controverted, however, the impracticability of the thing by remarking that there had lately been exhibited in London an automaton figure which played at chess. 'Now you will not assert, gentlemen,' said I, 'that it is more difficult to construct a machine that shall weave, than one that shall make all the variety of moves that are required in that complicated game.' Some time afterwards a particular circumstance recalling this conversation to my mind, it struck me that, as in plain weaving, according to the conception I then had of the business, there could be only three movements, which were to follow each other in succession, there could be little difficulty in producing and repeating them. Full of these ideas, I immediately employed a carpenter and smith to carry them into effect. As soon as the machine was finished, I got a weaver to put in the warp, which was of such materials as sail-cloth is usually made of. To my great delight, a piece of cloth, such as it was, was the produce. As I had never before turned my thoughts to mechanism, either in theory or practise, nor had seen a loom at work, nor knew anything of its construction, you will readily suppose that my first loom must have been a most rude piece of machinery. The warp was laid perpendicularly, the reed fell with a force of at least half a hundred weight, and the springs which threw the shuttle were strong enough to have thrown a Congreve rocket. In short, it required the strength of two powerful men to work the machine, at a slow rate, and only for a short time. Conceiving in my simplicity that I had accomplished all that was required, I then secured what I thought a most valuable property by a patent, 4th of April, 1785. This being done, I then condescended to see how other people wove; and you will guess my astonishment when I compared their easy modes of operation with mine. Availing myself, however, of what I then saw, I made a loom in its general principles nearly as they are now made. But it was not till the year 1787, that I completed my invention, when I took out my last weaving patent, August the 1st of that year."

Cartwright's machinery was at first worked by a bull, but he introduced the newly discovered steam power into his factory at Doncaster in 1789. In 1791 a Manchester firm contracted for four hundred looms, but the factory was burnt to the ground, probably by laborers who thought that the "iron men," as the machines were called, would take the bread out of their mouths. Sarcastic popular verses by John Grimshaw[4] of Groton began as follows:

Come all you cotton weavers, your looms you may pull down;
You must get employed in factories, in country or in town,
For our cotton masters have found out a wonderful new scheme,
These calico goods, now wove by hand, they're going to weave by steam.

Not until 1801,—the very year in which his patent expired,—did Cartwright's invention come into general favor. In 1813 there were 2400 in use; in 1820 there were 14,150; and in 1833, over 100,000. The elaborate machines of to-day have evolved gradually, one improvement following another, out of the

[4] Lancashire and Its Ballads, in London *Times*, June 27, 1913; p. 46.

clumsy devices invented in the eighteenth century by Kay and Cartwright.

To the end of his days Cartwright remained a gentle Oxonian poet, unspoiled by his inventions, which he regarded as a contribution to the welfare of his fellows. He devised a machine for combing wool, and experimented with steam engines. It is even recorded that he once constructed a model of a steam engine attached to a barge, which he explained about 1793 to Robert Fulton, then a student of painting under West; and that he predicted the day when both ships and land-carriages should be propelled by steam. Of an absent turn of mind, it is said that he would sometimes fail to recognize his own poems, and that on one occasion he expressed amazement on being shown the small model of an ingenious machine that he himself had devised! Among his unpatented projects may be mentioned the application of the tread-wheel to the working of cranes; an apparatus for beating or kneading dough, which was used in his own family; a reaping machine; a "dibbling machine" for planting wheat; and a carriage to be moved by human labor, that is to say, a precursor of the bicycle and automobile.[5] Parliament bestowed on him a grant of £10,000, which was barely sufficient to reimburse him for the loss of a handsome private fortune that he had thrown into the development of his loom and of his unsuccessful factory at Doncaster. Living to a ripe age, he became in his eightieth year the patriarch of contem-

[5] Rummaging in the Bodleian Library among the pamphlets of this period, the writer found an amusing evidence of inventive genius in the claim of one J. Dubois that he had devised a machine that could "Shave 60 Men a Minute"! In 1745 Dubois published *"A perspective view and section of an engine proposed to be built . . . which will shave 60 men a minute."*

poraneous British poets, numbering 407 individuals, as Woodcroft quaintly assures us. Crabbe left among his Letters a terse sketch of Cartwright's appearance and manners: "Few persons could tell a good story so well, no man make more of a trite one. I can just remember him, the portly, dignified old gentleman of the last generation, grave and polite, but full of humor and spirit."

CHAPTER 17

WATT AND DAVY [1]

By the startling development of the cotton trade the whole face of England had been altered. Towards the end of the century zeal for the new industry became so intense that, as Radcliffe reported, "Fabrics made from wool and linen vanished, while the old loom-shops being insufficient, every lumber-room, even old barns, cart-houses, and out-buildings of any description, were repaired, windows broke through the old blank walls, and all fitted up for loom-shops. This source of making room being at length exhausted, new weavers' cottages, with loom-shops, rose up in every direction; all immediately filled, and, when in full work, the weekly circulation of money, as the price of labor only, rose to five times the amount ever before experienced." [2]

But the growth proceeded further. Villages became towns, towns grew into cities, and factories started up on barren heath and desert waste. As Toynbee says, we are accustomed to think that, however the life of man may alter, the earth on which he moves must remain the same. But here the revolutions in man's life have stamped themselves upon the very face of nature. The great landmarks, such

[1] Chief authority: H. Brougham, Lives of Men of Letters and Science Who Flourished in the Time of George III: London, 1845; vol. i.

[2] Wm. Radcliffe, Origin of Power-Loom Weaving; cited by Baines, pp. 338–339.

as mountain ranges, river channels, inlets and estuaries, are for the most part unaltered; but nothing else remains the same. "For desolate moors and fens, for vast tracts of unenclosed pasturage and masses of woodland, we have now corn-fields and orchards, and crowded cities with their canopies of smoke."[3]

It was the general application of steam to the driving of machinery, and the consequent erection of gigantic factories grouped in towns and cities, that struck down the little master, half-manufacturer and half-farmer, while in his place there sprang up as by magic the great capitalist employer, dubbed "captain of industry" by Thomas Carlyle in 1843[4]—owner of hundreds of looms, employer of thousands of men, women, and children; buying and selling in every market on the globe.[5]

James Watt (1736–1819) took out his first patent on the steam-engine in 1769, the year in which Arkwright invented the spinning-frame. Leaving his home at Greenock when eighteen, he had served for a year as apprentice to an instrument maker in London; but in 1757 gained the opportunity of his life, as it proved, by securing appointment as maker of mathematical instruments to Glasgow University, where he came under the patronage of Adam Smith, who in 1776 published "The Wealth of Nations." Here, in the winter of 1763–64, the professor of physics asked Watt to repair a small model of Newcomen's engine, owned by the University; and out of his study of this incomplete and defective machine came his steam-engine.

[3] A. Toynbee, Lectures on the Industrial Revolution of the Eighteenth Century in England: London, 1908; p. 194.

[4] Past and Present, ch. iv.

[5] Toynbee, as cited, p. 205.

Into this invention Watt threw genuine scientific research. His predecessors in the Industrial Revolution were mechanicians of genius, but Watt was a scientific investigator. "Even the double and triple and quadruple expansion engines," declared Lord Kelvin, "by which the highest modern economy for power and steam engines has been obtained, are splendid mechanical developments of the principle of expansion, discovered and published by Watt, and used, though to a comparatively limited extent, in his own engines."[6] Lord Jeffrey's eloquent tribute to the perfection of Watt's machine is well known: "The trunk of an elephant, that can pick up a pin or rend an oak, is as nothing to it. It can engrave a seal, and crush masses of obdurate metal before it; draw out, without breaking, a thread as fine as gossamer, and lift a ship of war like a bauble in the air. It can embroider muslin and forge anchors, and impel loaded vessels against the fury of the winds and waves."[6]

The use of the new invention spread very rapidly. In 1781 Watt's partner, Matthew Boulton, wrote to him that "the people in London, Manchester are all *steam-mill* mad." In 1785 the new power was introduced into the cotton industry, an engine being built for Robinson's cotton mill in Nottinghamshire; in 1790, Arkwright adopted steam in his own factory. By the year 1800 it was established as the motive power of the day.

Its use was by no means confined to the cotton trade. Saw-mills in America, sugar-mills in the West Indies, paper-mills, flour-mills, engines for flint grinding in the potteries, were ordered in quick suc-

[6] Cited by Andrew Carnegie, James Watt: New York, 1905; pp. 227–229.

cession. The iron trade, among many others, was heavily stimulated, and the demand for wood fuel became so great that the forests were by way of becoming completely denuded, so that Parliament seriously considered the suppression of iron manufacture to save the woods. Just at this juncture it was proved possible to substitute coal for wood; and thereupon only one other invention was needed to make England "the workshop of the world."

Sir Humphry Davy (1778–1829) supplied this want by his invention of the safety lamp for miners in 1815. Coal diggers, constantly exposed to the dangers of fire-damp, had been subject to destruction, without a moment's warning, in the most frightful catastrophes. Davy's invention, by enabling the most dangerous mines to be worked with comparative safety, augmented to an extraordinary degree the available supplies of coal.

Walpole has admirably summed up the work of these great men who did so much to bring about the Industrial Revolution of England. A series of extraordinary inventions, as he says, had supplied Great Britain with a new manufacturing vigor. Hargreaves, Arkwright, Crompton, and Cartwright had developed, to a remarkable degree, the producing power of man; Watt had given a new significance to their inventions by superseding the feeble and unequal forces which had hitherto been used, with the most tractable and powerful of agents. And Davy, by his beneficent contrivance, had enabled coal to be won with less danger, and had relieved the miner's life from one of its most hideous perils. The ingenuity of these great men had been exercised with different objects; but the inventions of each of them had given fresh importance to the discoveries of the others. The spinning-jenny, the water-frame, and the mule would have been deprived of half their value if they had not been supplemented with the power-loom; the power-loom would, in many places, have been useless without the steam-engine; the steam-engine would have been idle, had it not been for coal; the coal would not have been won without danger, had it not been for Sir Humphry Davy.[7]

The close association of this group of inventors strikingly illustrates the fact, which Professor Taussig points out, that the genius who reaches the crowning achievement is not isolated; he is borne forward by the sweep of a large movement.[8] This is the history of most inventions. The pressure of industrial circumstances directs the intelligence of many minds towards the comprehension of some single central point of difficulty, the common knowledge of the age induces many to reach similar solutions: that solution which is slightly better adapted to the facts or "grasps the skirts of happy chance" comes out victorious. Hobson says that no one of the textile inventions that were greatest in their effect, the jenny, the water-frame, the mule, the power-loom, was in the main attributable to the effort or ability of a single man, after all. Each represented in its successful shape the addition of many successive increments of discovery; in most cases the successful invention was the slightly superior survivor of many similar attempts.[9] These considerations, however, need not prevent us from honoring the memory of

[7] S. Walpole, History of England since 1815: London, 1878; cited by B. Rand in Selections Illustrating Economic History since the Seven Years' War: London and New York, 1903; pp. 53–54.

[8] F. W. Taussig, Some Aspects of the Tariff Question: Cambridge, 1915; p. 277.

[9] J. A. Hobson, The Evolution of Modern Capitalism; a Study of Machine Production: London and Felling-on-Tyne, 1906; p. 79.

those persistent workers who, when triumphant in the culmination of a response to the needs of that society of which they formed a part, were so often robbed of the fruits of their labor and rewarded only with obloquy.

CHAPTER 18

BRINDLEY'S CANALS[1]

It only remains to name one other great English inventor, whose inborn and amazing genius as a transportation engineer linked factory towns and seaports by means of artificial water-ways so that the great cotton trade and the other industries of England might find an easy and economical channel to the markets of the world. While the locomotive and steamboat still lay dormant in the engine of Watt, Brindley's canals had harnessed rivers as servitors to "captains of industry." To him water in a river was a furious giant overturning everything, whereas, "if you lay the giant flat on his back, he loses all his force whatever his size may be."

Interrogated on another occasion before the House of Commons he showed so great contempt for unharnessed rivers that an amused member asked him for what purpose, then, he deemed rivers to have been created. "To feed canals," replied this self-taught engineer, whose name is well worth remembering at this time when the river-fed Panama Canal ties oceans together and bridges the space between worlds.

James Brindley (1716–1772), a self-made man if ever there was one, sprang from a millwright apprenticeship to be the foremost engineer of his time by the sheer force of his unaided genius. Although

[1] Chief authority: H. Howe, as cited.

to the end of his life he could hardly write his name, and is reported as being barely able to read "on any very pressing occasion," his mind was characterized by comprehensiveness and grandeur of conception, as well as a keenness of analytical penetration that laid open at a stroke the most intricate engineering difficulties. The Duke of Bridgewater, acquainted with Brindley's rare genius, and aware of his success with the novel Sankey Canal, challenged him to connect Manchester with Liverpool, across both the Irwell and the Mersey. Brindley leaped to this challenge, and defied all discouragement by spanning the rivers with aqueducts, on which might frequently be seen one vessel passing along, while another, with all masts and sails standing, held undisturbed to a transverse course beneath its keel.

While this undertaking was in progress, Brindley was engaged by Lord Gower to connect the Trent with the Mersey, thus uniting the East and West coasts. This meant not only many aqueducts, but five tunnels, one of which, through Harecastle Hill, had to be bored through the rock for a distance of 8,640 feet at a depth of two hundred feet below the surface. The amazement excited by the successful execution of this plan is well reflected in a contemporaneous "journalese" account, as follows:

"Gentlemen come to view our eighth wonder of the world, the subterranean navigation which is cutting by the great Mr. Brindley, who handles rocks as easily as you would plum-pies, and makes the four elements subservient to his will. He is as plain a looking man as one of the boors of the Peak, or one of his own carters; but when he speaks all ears listen, and every mind is filled with wonder at the things he pronounces to be practicable. He has cut a mile through bogs which he binds up, embanking them with stones, which he gets out of other parts of the navigation, besides about a quarter of a mile into the hill Yelden, on the side of which he has a pump, which is worked by water, and a stove, the fire of which sucks through a pipe the damps that would annoy the men who are cutting towards the center of the hill. The clay he cuts out serves for brick to arch the subterraneous part, which we heartily wish to see finished to Wilden Ferry, when we shall be able to send coals and pots to London, and to different parts of the globe."

Once begun, canal building went forward rapidly, but not more so than the construction of new and better roads. Sir Henry Wood estimates that between 1760 and 1774 no fewer than 452 Acts were passed for making and repairing highways;[2] and quotes a writer of 1767[3] as thus contrasting the conditions of the roads in his own time with their state in the time of Queen Anne: "There never was a more astonishing Revolution accomplished in the internal system of any country, than has been within the compass of a few years, in that of England. The carriage of Grain, Coals, Merchandise, etc., is in general conducted with little more than half the number of Horses with which it formerly was. Journies of Business are performed with more than double expedition. Improvements in Agriculture keep pace with those of Trade. Everything wears the Face of Despatch; every Article of our produce becomes more valuable; and the Hinge, upon which

[2] H. T. Wood, Industrial England in the Middle of the Eighteenth Century: London, 1910; p. 31.
[3] H. Homer, Enquiry into Public Roads.

all the movements turn, is the Reformation which has been made in our Publick Roads."

Between 1760 and 1790 the shipping cleared out of English ports rose from 471,000 tons to 1,379,000 tons, and no doubt the increase in the national movements of trade was quite as great in proportion. This rapid development of consuming power, made possible by better transportation facilities, greatly cheapened the cost of the highly popular cotton goods, and led to an enormously augmented demand for the raw material. During the twenty year period between 1751 and 1771 the annual import of raw cotton was doubled, while from 1780 to 1800 it actually increased almost ten-fold.[4] It is little wonder that grave fears were entertained as to an adequate source of supply. The chief sources for a long time had been Turkey and the West Indies; but manufacturers felt certain that a larger supply would be necessary, and in 1788 the East Indian Company was accordingly urged to spur the cultivation of cotton in India—a noteworthy change from the earlier years of the century, when cotton lay under the ban.[5]

Within a short time, however, assistance arrived from an entirely unexpected quarter, the Southern

[4] P. Gaskell, Artisans and Machinery: London, 1836; p. 336.

[5] By the year 1836, the changed relations of Great Britain and India were indicated by the following remarks of M. Dupin to the Parisian operatives: "The British navigator travels in quest of the cotton of India; brings it from a distance of 4,000 leagues; commits it to an operation of the machine of Arkwright, and of those that are attached to it; carries back their products to the east, making them again travel 4,000 leagues; and in spite of loss of time, in spite of the enormous expense incurred by this voyage of 8,000 leagues, the cotton manufactured by the machinery of England becomes less costly than the cotton of India spun and woven by the hand, near the field that produced it, and sold at the nearest market. So great is the power of the progress of machinery!"—Cited by Gaskell, pp. 320–321.

States of the American Union, where, owing to the invention of the Whitney gin, the production of lint made such wonderful progress that West Indian and Turkey cottons were not only superseded, but the desired augmented supply from India was rendered unnecessary.[6]

[6] For table showing the relation between textile invention and cotton manufacture in England, see Appendix F: 1a.

CHAPTER 19

GENERAL RESULTS

THE Industrial Revolution in England profoundly influenced the development of the arts and sciences in general, but naturally in a practical direction. While wool had been deposed from its lordly ascendency, the same machinery that built up the cotton manufacture advanced the facility with which wool could be woven, rendering it cheaper and better, the linen and silk industries both profiting in a similar manner. It has already appeared how intimately the iron and coal trades were associated with the new movement, which also gave impetus to the production of tin,—most ancient of British exports,—with lead, glass, pottery, copper and brass, paper, gunpowder, and various metals; while brewing, distilling, tanning, watch-making, and printing all leaped to unaccustomed activity.[1] Capital rapidly accumulated, so that England was financially prepared for the Napoleonic wars when they came, her exports amounting to more than £58,000,000 in 1815 as against £17,000,000 in 1793. This gave her an enormous advantage over the battlefield nations of the Continent,[2] an advantage which is still felt.

[1] H. T. Wood, as cited.

[2] "The spinning-jenny and the steam-engine were the true moving powers of our fleets and armies."—G. R. Porter, The Progress of the Nation in Its Various Social and Economic Relations from the Beginning of the Nineteenth Century: London (1838), 1912; p. 288.

With this large accumulation of capital came a strange increase of human assets, a striking growth in population. Previous to 1751 the largest decennial increase was three per cent. For each of the next three decades the increase was six per cent. Between 1781 and 1791 it rose to nine per cent; then to eleven per cent, and then to fourteen, while between 1811 and 1821 it reached eighteen per cent, the highest rate in the history of England. Gaskell[3] shows that between 1801 and 1831 the whole population increased "rather more than fifty per cent," while that of the manufacturing towns increased 140 per cent. According to his statistics, the population within thirty years (1801–1831) increased in three cities as follows:

Liverpool	138 per cent.
Manchester	151 per cent.
Glasgow	161 per cent.

So striking was this feature of the Industrial Revolution, even in its earlier stages, that Sir Robert Peel said in 1806: "In the cotton trade, machinery has given birth to a new population; it has promoted the comforts of the population to such a degree that early marriages have been resorted to, and a great increase of numbers has been occasioned by it, and I may say that they have given rise to an additional race of men."[4]

This is the Robert Peel who brought calico printing to the highest stage of efficiency that it reached in England until Bell invented the cylinder process in 1785. The art of printing by blocks had been invented by the Arabs, who thus accomplished a great

[3] As cited, pp. 197, 199.
[4] Parl. Report, p. 440; A. Toynbee, as cited, p. 67, note.

advance over the ancient Hindu method of painting by hand. Print work in England was curiously fostered by the act of 1700 prohibiting the importation of the beautiful India calicoes, in response to such complaints as that cited on page 45. Foreign prints being thus shut out by law, the growing taste for such gewgaws could only be satisfied by domestic production; so the infant trade of British printing expanded, with the adventitious aid of this law, until at length the Peels took it up on their great estate near Blackburn with such energy and intelligence that the history of their house may be said to constitute the history of the calico business in Lancashire for many years.

No doubt the eminent statesman, Sir Robert Peel, grandson of the Peel who first took up the cotton printing trade, was more or less influenced by the traditions of his family when, in 1846, he secured the repeal of the Corn Laws, thus lifting the cotton manufacturer to at least an equal footing with the agriculturist, or land-owner, by the adoption of a free trade policy. The British system of protection (unlike that of the United States) had protected the land-owner at the expense of the manufacturer; so that the repeal of this protective system reacted favorably on the English cotton trade, being a victory of cotton over "corn,"[5] a triumph of the newly arrived captains of industry and commerce over the hereditary "landed aristocracy."

In fact, the entire British commerce now entered an epoch of the most extraordinary development, leading Professor Pollard to declare that the commercial expansion of England, as well as its political emancipation, resulted from the Industrial Revo-

[5] See Appendix D.

lution. "Not till the Industrial Revolution had changed the face of England did the old political forces acknowledge their defeat and surrender their claim to govern the nation against its will;" while the development of trading footholds into great self-governing communities—"the unique and real achievement of the British Empire"—depended for accomplishment upon the effects of the changes known to us as the Industrial Revolution.[6]

Arnold Toynbee emphasizes the interesting fact that the opening and closing years of the Industrial Revolution in England were signalized by the appearance of two famous works, dealing, singularly enough, with wealth and poverty respectively—"The Wealth of Nations" by Adam Smith in 1776, and Malthus's "Essay on Population" in 1798.[7] The work of Malthus, with its far-reaching effects, we shall shortly consider.[8] For the present it may be found of interest, in this brief survey of the social changes with which the Industrial Revolution had something to do, to note the impression made on Toynbee's mind by the association of Adam Smith and James Watt at Glasgow,[9] together with an interesting development of the same idea by a leading American economist.

The production of wealth was what Adam Smith had primarily before his mind's eye; "the great object of the Political Economy of every country," he wrote, "is to increase the riches and power of that country." He was, moreover, an enemy to the political, industrial, and commercial restrictions

[6] A. F. Pollard, as cited; pp. 192, 149, 173, 190, 196.
[7] Toynbee, as cited, pp. 64–65.
[8] See Chapter 21.
[9] See page 79.

that enthralled the England of his time, restrictions which, as we have seen, the unsuspected but imminent Industrial Revolution was destined to throw off. Nothing could be more interesting, thinks Toynbee, than the story of James Watt, threatened in the practise of his trade by the guild of mechanics in Glasgow, but admitted by Professor Smith within the walls of the University, and allowed to set up his workshop,—wherein, by inventing the steam-engine, he was to make possible the realization of that industrial wealth and commercial freedom which Smith himself regarded as Utopian. The England described by Adam Smith, says Toynbee, differed more from the England of to-day than it did from the England of the Middle Ages. The cotton manufacture is mentioned only once in his book. The staple industries of the land were still wool, tanned leather, and hardware, silk and linen coming next in importance. Wool, flax, and silk were spun and woven in scattered villages by families who eked out their existence by agriculture. "Manufacturer" meant not the owner of power-looms and steam-engines and factories, buying and selling in the markets of the world, but the actual weaver at his loom, the actual spinner at her wheel. Seven years before the publication of "The Wealth of Nations," however, Arkwright had patented his water-frame and James Watt his steam-engine. A few years after its publication Cartwright invented the power-loom, Crompton the mule. It was by these discoveries that population was drawn out of cottages in remote valleys by secluded streams and driven together into factories and cities. Old restrictions became obsolete by sheer force of necessity, and the invention of the steam-engine literally called into being "the wealth of nations" of which Adam Smith had dreamed.[10]

Dr. John Bates Clark [11] applies the same idea to America. "How far," he asks,—"how far into the intimate recesses of social life and individual life have gone the influences that emanated from the invention of James Watt and from those of Hargreaves, Crompton, and the endless succession of men who followed after them? They have done much more than merely to multiply the physical results of labor. We have become different mentally and morally from what we should have been if the mechanical improvements had never taken place. As a matter of fact the steam-engine led to the multiplying of textile machinery, that to the factory system and that to a course of centralization which has gathered vast populations into producing centers. As the use of machinery in America has extended to almost every productive operation, it has carried this centralizing process to very great lengths and in the briefest time. It has led to a fierce competition in every department of business, and this struggle has sought to end itself by the building up of what we call 'trusts.' During the period of competition and well into the period of growing consolidation another type of contest has been waging—that between employers and employed in each of the different occupations. While the automatic machine, the modern genius of the lamp, has been turning out forms of utility in profusion, masters and workmen have been contending over the sharing of

[10] Toynbee, as cited, pp. 151–152.

[11] In the General Introduction to a Documentary History of American Industrial Society: Cleveland, 1910; vol. i, p. 38 ff.

them; and here again organization has played its part and the effects have been far reaching. We have our national unions of employees on the one hand, and of employers on the other.

"We look to England for the beginnings of the use of machinery, but we find in our own country the largest application of it and the greatest results it has as yet produced; and it has resulted from this that American class struggles offer especially fertile fields of study. If there be any probability in the legend that the steam-engine is traceable to the suggestion which James Watt got from watching his aunt's kettle and seeing the pressure of steam raising the lid of it and the escape of the steam letting it fall, then that mythical scene might well be the special symbol of American development. It is without doubt true that what James Watt accomplished, as a young man working in a room in the University of Glasgow under the patronage of Adam Smith, had everything to do with this development. The year 1776, which made the United States an independent nation, and which also saw the publication of Adam Smith's 'Wealth of Nations,' saw the steam-engine, which was destined to play so important a part in shaping the life of the country, assuming an efficient form. In a way the industrial life of America, if it was not brewing in the mythical tea kettle, was taking shape in the Glasgow workshop. Steam and its consequences have been all important.

"It would be too much to claim that the effect of machinery has reached other nations by way of the United States, although in the case of many specific appliances this has been true. In some departments we have been leaders and teachers. What is clear is that the effects which machinery has produced in the United States have resembled in kind and exceeded in number and degree those which it has produced elsewhere. The mechanical genius of the lamp has in this country gone into every part of the field of production.

"With this transformation there has come in America, in a conspicuous way, the centralizing of industries, the fierce competition, the combination of rival producers, and the struggle against monopoly, which are the features of present-day life. We have more trusts and stronger ones than have most countries, and we have strong trade unions and growing socialistic parties. We can see how all this is connected with that complete transformation of practical life which machinery has produced."

CHAPTER 20

"CAPTAINS OF INDUSTRY"

THE Industrial Revolution in England was attended with very grave evils. As Pollard says, most of our present social problems may be traced, directly or indirectly, to this source.[1] For it is true, as Karl Marx pointed out, that in changing the modes of production, mankind changes all its social relations: the hand-mill creates a society with the feudal lord, the steam-mill a society with the industrial capitalist[2]—Carlyle's original "captain of industry," whose only idea of hell was the idea of "not making money," and whose attitude toward philanthropy was expressed in the declaration of Lord Brougham that "charity is an interference with a healing process of Nature, which acts by increasing the rate of mortality, thereby raising wages!"[3]

This first generation of industrial chiefs, newly rich, uneducated, rough and brutal, were strangers to those family traditions and moral considerations

[1] As cited, p. 197.

[2] Misère de la Philosophie, pp. 99–100; translation of E. R. A. Seligman, in The Economic Interpretation of History: New York, 1912; p. 35.

[3] Schulze-Gaevernitz, Social Peace (Zum Socialen Frieden): London, 1900; p. 25. This statement of Brougham's is well matched by the dictum of Malthus: "Benevolence indeed as the great and constant source of action would require the most perfect knowledge of cause and effect, and therefore can only be the attribute of the Deity. In a being so short-sighted as man, it would lead to the grossest errors, and soon transform the fair and cultivated soil of civilized society into a dreary scene of want and confusion."—Essay on Population, ed. 1872, p. 492.

that impose some restraint on hereditary wealth. They were in the habit of talking, not of their men, but of the "hands" they employed; regarding them not as human beings, but as mere instruments for production of capital.[4] Operatives were not only herded like cattle in unsanitary surroundings,[5] but treated as veritable slaves;[6] labor was actually bought from the workhouses, it being sometimes stipulated by the parish authorities that one idiot must be taken with every score of sane children, so as to be rid of the imbeciles.[7]

Women as well as children were victimized. Lord Ashley's report to Parliament[8] showed that so recently as 1839 factory "hands" were classified as follows:

	Male	*Female*
Over 18 years of age.......	96,569	130,104
Under 18 years of age.....	80,695	112,192
	177,264	242,296

Dr. Gaskell says that the factory was not seldom the harem of the employer;[9] mothers of fifteen years of age not being exceptional, and a condition approaching "free love" existing among the opera-

[4] Schulze-Gaevernitz, Social Peace, as cited, pp. 18, 26, 30, 32; Gaskell, ch. iii.

[5] Gaskell wrote in 1836 that upwards of 20,000 individuals were living in cellars in Manchester alone.—p. 82. His work is the best source-book for this general topic; being accurately described by its sub-titles, "The Moral and Physical Condition of the Manufacturing Population Considered with Reference to Mechanical Substitutes for Human Labor." It is the chief source of the well-known work by Friedrich Engels, *Die Lage der Arbeitenden Klassen in England* (1843).

[6] "There can be no doubt that far greater misery prevailed than in the Southern States during the era of slavery."—Wm. Clarke in *Fabian Essays:* London, 1889; p. 75.

[7] Gibbins, as cited, p. 179.

[8] Social Peace, p. 35.

[9] Artisans and Machinery: London, 1836; ch. iii.

tives.[10] Children were often worked for sixteen hours of the twenty-four, the term of their labor being sometimes marked only by exhaustion after various forms of torture had been applied to "stimulate" them. To prevent their running away, suspects frequently had irons riveted on their ankles, with chains reaching up to their hips, and in this harness were compelled to work and sleep.[11]

It must not be forgot, on the other hand, that measures for the protection of factory operatives had their beginning with two British "captains of industry," Sir Robert Peel the elder and Robert Owen, founder of English Socialism. In addition to the management of his great calico factory near Blackburn, already mentioned, Sir Robert Peel was an active member of Parliament, wherein he used his great powers for the benefit of that "additional race of men" to whom, as he said, the great new industry had given birth.[12] He declared that on visiting his own factory, which employed about a thousand children, he was struck by their unhealthy appearance and stunted growth; and in a speech in the House of Commons in 1802 he said expressly that his main object in advocating Factory Laws was the improvement of the religious and moral condition of the children.[13]

In that year he secured the passage of the first of the Factory Acts, known as the Apprentice Bill, which limited the working day to twelve hours, except in the case of children residing near a mill, who were supposed to be under the supervision of their parents. The Act of 1819, which was also

[10] Social Peace, p. 38.
[11] Gibbins, as cited, p. 180.
[12] See page 90.
[13] Social Peace, as cited, p. 71.

introduced by him, merely adapted that of 1802 to altered conditions. Subsequent Acts accomplished but little by way of amelioration until Lord Shaftesbury, in 1833, secured the passage of a law prohibiting night work for children and providing for their attendance at school; while the famous Act of 1847 reduced the labor of young persons and women to ten hours.

In 1823 Robert Owen addressed a circular letter to his fellow capitalists in which he said: "Since the general introduction of inanimate mechanism into British manufactories, man, with few exceptions, has been treated as a secondary and inferior machine. Give but due reflection to the subject, and you will find that man, even as an instrument for the creation of wealth, may still be greatly improved."[14]

In his own business he put his principles to the test. The spinning mills at New Lanark, with their workmen's cottages and manifold educational and benevolent institutions, were celebrated far and wide. The socialistic community that he founded in 1823 at New Harmony, Indiana, lasted only two years, it is true; since he forgot that his success at New Lanark depended on special conditions, such as his own unusual power of inspiring love and respect, and the exceptional character of the working people he had educated.[15] With Owen originated the demand for universal compulsory education. He was far ahead of his times.

Although they were not legalized until 1871, Trades Unions originated during this period, in the effort of the working classes to protect themselves against oppression and injustice. The eighteenth century has been called "the century of strikes," so

[14] The same, p. 68.

[15] The same, p. 68.

common were these economic and social disturbances—culminating in the earlier years of the century following, when, with banners inscribed "Bread or Blood," oppressed factory hands marched plundering through the country until put down by the military forces, as at "Peterloo." The truth is that the Industrial Revolution wrought havoc among laborers for a protracted period, the lowest depth of superinduced pauperism being reached about the beginning of the Victorian age, although the national wealth was all the while increasing as never before. Professor Macgregor says: "The years from 1800 to 1825 were suited to almost any doctrine of despair. It was the age of everything done wrong."[16] Toynbee said, "I tremble to think what this country would have been but for the Factory Acts;" while Professor Gibbins adds that he dares not trust himself to set down calmly all that might be told about this awful page in the history of industrial England.[17] Carlyle was moved by it to Jovian wrath in his "Past and Present." Mrs. Gaskell specifically portrayed the distressed conditions in her "Mary Barton," while the contemporary poetry reflects the sad facts of the times, as do also some of the well known novels of Kingsley, Dickens, and Disraeli.[18] Townsend Warner wisely says, however,

16 D. H. Macgregor, The Evolution of Industry: London; pp. 14–15. Gaskell wrote in 1836: "Upwards of a million of human beings are literally starving, and the number is constantly on the increase."—as cited, p. v.

17 Gibbins, as cited, p. 80.

18 See especially the writing of Samuel Bamford, himself a Lancashire weaver, one of whose poems ends as follows:

God help the poor, who in lone valleys dwell,
Or by far hills, where whin and heather grow;
Theirs is a story sad indeed to tell;
Yet little cares the world, and less 'twould know
About the toil and want men undergo.

that periods of progress and change are often hard; temporary hardships should not be allowed to blind us to the real progress denoted by this great era of industry in England. Schulze-Gaevernitz, while recounting the terrible abuses of the period, discerns behind the outer forms of the social life a great and worthy inner movement,—"the vast revolution in thought which was to carry men from an individualistic political economy and a utilitarian philosophy to an organic view of society and of the place and duties of the individual." [19] Carlyle himself, in his great classic of denunciation, distinguishes carefully between transitory and permanent. Discharging the shafts of his wrath at greedy "captains of industry," he gives ardent praise to the inventive geniuses who made this captaincy possible; while the romance of the unvanquishable cotton plant wrests from him an irresistible eloquence:—

"Unstained by wasteful deformities," he writes, —"by wasted tears or heart's-blood of men, or any defacement of the Pit, noble fruitful Labor, growing ever nobler, will come forth,—the grand sole miracle of Man; whereby Man has risen from the low places of this Earth, very literally, into divine Heavens. Ploughers, Spinners, Builders; Prophets, Poets, Kings; Brindleys and Goethes, Odins and Arkwrights; all martyrs, and noble men, and gods are of one grand Host; immeasurable; marching ever

The wearying loom doth call them up at morn;
They work till worn-out nature sinks to sleep;
They taste, but are not fed. The snow drifts deep
Around the fireless cot, and blocks the door;
The night storm hurls a dirge across the moor;
And shall they perish thus—oppressed and lorn?
Shall toil and famine, hopeless, still be borne?
No! God will yet arise and help the poor!

[19] Social Peace, p. xx.

forward since the beginning of the World. Arachne started with forefinger and thumb, and had not even a distaff; yet thou seest Manchester, and Cotton Cloth, which will shelter naked backs, at twopence an ell.—So answers Nature: 'Waste desert-shrubs of the tropical swamps have become Cotton-trees; and here, under my furtherance, are verily woven shirts,—hanging unsold, undistributed, but capable to be distributed, capable to cover the bare backs of my children of men. Mountains, as old as the Creation, I have permitted to be bored through; bituminous fuel-stores, the wreck of forests that were green a million years ago,—I have opened them from my secret rock-chambers, and they are yours, ye English. Your huge fleets, steamships, do sail the sea; huge Indias do obey you; from huge *new* Englands and Antipodal Australias comes profit and traffic to this Old England of Mine!' So answers Nature.—What is immethodic, waste, thou shalt make methodic, regulated, arable; obedient and productive to thee. Wheresoever thou findest Disorder, there is thy eternal enemy; attack him swiftly, subdue him; make Order of him, the subject not of Chaos, but of Intelligence, Divinity and Thee! The thistle that grows in thy path, dig it out, that a blade of useful grass, a drop of nourishing milk, may grow there instead. The waste cotton-shrub, gather its waste white down, spin it, weave it; that in place of idle litter, there may be folded webs, and the naked skin of man be covered." [20]

[20] Carlyle, Past and Present (1843): London, 1889; pp. 251, 113, 142, 169–170. See also his essay on Chartism, in Critical and Miscellaneous Essays, vol. iv (1839, 1869).

CHAPTER 21

MALTHUS AND DARWIN

OTHER writers besides Carlyle and Mrs. Gaskell were perceptibly influenced by the manifold changes wrought in England by means of the Industrial Revolution. Not only such masters of eloquent persuasion as these, but also those scholars whose brains were skilled in cold analysis to confront new economic problems in order to suggest a logical mode of solution therefor were challenged by the social upheaval, and none with more notable results than Thomas Malthus,[1] who applied the keen scrutiny of a highly gifted scientific mind to the startling increase in English population already noted (see page 90).

By way of his father, who had been a friend and correspondent of Rousseau's, young Malthus found himself stimulated to a keen interest in social and political problems. He was little disposed, however, to accept off-hand the plausible political optimism of this brilliant Frenchman, with whose social theories, singularly enough, the biological doctrines of Rousseau's fellow countryman, Lamarck, formed a cheerful and suggestive parallel,—both pointing, as they did, toward the "Progress of Humanity" as the assured and cheerful goal of both biology and politics.

[1] An Essay on the Principle of Population: London (first ed., 1798).

Malthus, applying himself like the matter-of-fact country parson that he was, to the evidence of things that surrounded him, and especially to the misery of "the masses," reached with a sort of mathematical exactitude the conclusion that the enormous increase in population which Sir Robert Peel attributed to the cotton industry would, if maintained, soon exceed the whole means of subsistence, and result in national calamity. Embodying his argument in a famous "Essay on the Principle of Population as it Affects the Future Improvement of Society," Malthus seemed to evince a certain gratitude for those "positive checks" on the increase of population, such as unwholesome occupations, severe labor, extreme poverty, large towns, epidemics, wars, plagues, and famines, without which his mathematical formula might execute itself with annihilative force. Expressed technically, the idea of Malthus refers to the disproportionate increase of organisms as compared with their means of subsistence; it is the phenomenon of overcrowding, which, combined with that of "variation," necessitates an automatic "selection" leading to a "struggle for existence" and the consequent "survival of the fittest."[2]

These terms are sufficient in themselves to suggest the enormous influence which the ideas of Malthus have exerted throughout the whole world of thought by virtue of the lodgment of one of his principles, forty years after its promulgation, in the mind of Charles Darwin, then singularly ripe for it. In the earlier pages of his work on "Animals and Plants under Domestication," Darwin expressly acknowledges his indebtedness to Malthus in thinking out his car-

[2] J. T. Merz, A History of European Thought in the 19th Century: Edinburgh and London, 1912; vol. iii, p. 554.

dinal principle of natural selection. After the study of domestic productions had given him a just idea of the power of selection, he found, he tells us, "on reading Malthus 'On Population,' that natural selection was the inevitable result of the rapid increase of all organic beings." In his autobiography he adds that his reading of Malthus occurred in October, 1838, and that, being well prepared by the results of systematic inquiry to appreciate the struggle for existence, he was at once struck with the idea that the operation of that principle would tend toward the destruction of unfavorable variations and the preservation of favorable ones, resulting in the formation of new species.

Wallace, strange to say, underwent the same remarkable experience, quite independently of Darwin. He gives a circumstantial account of the event, saying that the exposition which Malthus had given of those "positive checks" on increase and of their mode of operation recurred to him, during a period of enforced leisure, with the force of a universal law, as it suddenly flashed upon him that "this self-acting process would necessarily *improve the race,* because in every generation the inferior would inevitably be killed off and the superior would remain —that is, *the fittest would survive.*"

So it was that the impact of the Malthusian idea on two richly stored and richly gifted minds flashed into existence the most brilliant and far-reaching conception in the history of all modern thought.

The writer of the present volume would not think of setting up a claim on behalf of the omnipotence of the cotton influence in the manifold directions where we find traces of it. It is only a single influence among the numerous causes of any important given effect, and the reason for tracing its ramifying course lies chiefly in the fact that cotton happens to afford a typical and fascinating example of those economic factors in history that have not received their due share of attention. No doubt Darwin and Wallace, without the intervention of Malthus, might have formulated that remarkable doctrine so closely associated with their names and so influential in the transformation of thought during the last half-century. But it happens that Malthus did influence them, and that Malthus, in a different economic environment from that of Rousseau and Lamarck, was led to his studies and conclusions by the results of the Industrial Revolution in England. What the incident illustrates is the interdependence of thought; and nothing in the history of science is more interesting than the manner in which social theory and biology have reacted one upon the other.

That distinguished biological writer, Professor J. Arthur Thomson of Aberdeen, believes that the two revolutions, French and English, one military and the other no less influential because bloodless, have expressed themselves through Lamarck and Darwin, respectively, more clearly than has ever been realized. "It was the former period, with its theories of society and of morals, which gave birth to the doctrine of Evolution; while the latter period, with its competitive industry, its resultant population question, etc., has found its expression in the doctrine of Natural Selection."[5]

Carlyle himself could not paint a more vivid portrait of competitive industrial warfare, nor Malthus show more clearly the baneful results of overcrowding, than the natural selectionist who tells us that

[5] Evolution: London, n. d.; pp. xi–xii.

any summer field, though mantled in softest green, is the scene of a struggle as widespread and ruthless as that of the fiercest human battlefield, and then stops there, as though that were the whole of the story. The life, even of plants, on any green sward, said a typical exponent of this doctrine a score of years ago, is one of unceasing toil, of crowding and jostling, where the weaker fall unpitied by the way, —"of starvation from hunger and cold, of robbery utterly shameless and murder utterly cruel."

Passing from plant life to bird life, the same author remarks that when we think of the hawk's talons buried in the breast of the wren, while the relentless beak tears the little wings from the quivering, bleeding body, our mood toward Nature is changed, and we feel like recoiling from a world in which such black injustice, such savage disregard for others, is part of the general scheme. "But," he continues, "as we look still further into the matter, we find that this hideous hatred and strife furnish the indispensable conditions for the evolution of higher and higher types of life. Increase in richness, variety, complexity of life is gained *only* by the selection of variations above or beyond a certain mean, and the prompt execution of a death sentence upon all the rest.—At all events, whenever the type is raised, it is through survival of the fittest, implying the destruction of all save the fittest."[6]

Any well informed contemporary biologist knows that this picture is grossly overdrawn, or, as might also be said, underdrawn, because it tells only half of the truth. It affords an apt illustration of the manner in which the doctrine of struggle and survival,

[6] J. Fiske, Through Nature to God: Boston, 1900; pp. 63–67 (Italics, the present writer's).

appropriated by way of Malthus from the most distressing social conditions modern England ever experienced, has overcolored the whole biological theory. Unfortunately, this exaggerated scientific conception, gripping the imagination of mankind as the final and complete expression of a natural and universal law, has reacted, in turn, by the sanction of accepted analogy, toward the perpetuation of those social conditions by which it was originally occasioned;[7] and we hear of a young American "captain of industry" justifying industrial monopoly by triumphantly pointing to the "American Beauty" rose, to produce one of which ninety-nine roses were lawfully nipped in the bud!

Biology has proceeded, since the days of Malthus and Darwin, to a closer and more truthful intimacy with the secrets of nature. It has now learned more of the comprehensive system of principles that govern the kingdom of life, including subordination and sacrifice. Who knows but that it may requite sociology for the suggestion of one law by the supplementary gift of another? Science may yet materialize the vision of Carlyle, and "every naked back of man be clothed," as he would phrase it, through a deeper consideration of the lilies. To this suggestive interaction of biology and social theory we may perhaps revert in the closing chapter of this volume.

[7] "Darwin's demonstration of evolution by means of the struggle for existence in the natural world was used to support the assumption that a similar struggle among civilized men was natural and therefore inevitable; and that all attempts to interfere with the conflict between the weak and the strong, the scrupulous and the unscrupulous, were foredoomed to disastrous failure."—Pollard's History of England, as cited, p. 233.

BOOK III

COTTON IN AMERICAN HISTORY: SECTIONAL EVOLUTION

CHAPTER 22

COLUMBUS AND CORTES

COLUMBUS, looking for India, found America; and the very first objects of native art that met his attention were made out of cotton. Every hammock swinging in a summer breeze bears witness to this, being the survival of an aboriginal invention which the great explorer found the Cubans using instead of beds,—cotton nets which they hung between trees and called *hamacas,* whence our English word. The people of the Bahamas brought gifts of cotton yarn in exchange for Castilian trinkets. Cuban women clothed themselves in cotton dresses. In a single house there were approximately 12,000 pounds of yarn on spindles, and there were also looms. In Cuba and Haiti and Guadaloupe even the idols were made of cotton, reminding one of the sacred associations of this plant among the ancient Hindus. When Fernando Magellan visited Brazil in 1520 he found Brazilians using mattresses stuffed with cotton lint.[1] In fact, the extensive Spanish explorations proved that the cultivation and manufacture of cotton had evolved independently on the South American continent, just as in India, reaching a notably high development in extremely remote times among the lordly peoples of Mexico.

When Cortes entered the city of Cholula in 1519 he

[1] Henry Lee, as cited, p. 84.

was especially struck with the costumes of the higher classes, who wore fine embroidered cotton mantles, similar to the Moorish cloak in both cloth and pattern.[2] Marching on to the great and romantic capital city, which stood buttressed and insulated in the middle of a huge salt lake, his soldiers discovered an imposing urban civilization that staggered them, as though they had suddenly stepped back across the centuries to Nineveh or Thebes.

From the lofty central temple, Montezuma, sacrificing to his gods, sent officers one day to conduct some of the leading Spaniards into his presence. Cortes wrote of this edifice as having a grandeur "which no human tongue can describe." Bernal Diaz, who was present, vividly depicts the scene. Montezuma, he says, took Cortes by the hand, and from the exalted summit of "this infernal temple" pointed out to him the different parts of the city, and its vicinity, all of which were commanded from that place. "Here we had a clear prospect of the three causeways by which Mexico communicated with the land, and of the aqueduct of Chapultepekue, which supplied the city with the benefit of water. We were struck with the numbers of canoes, passing to and from the main land, loaded with provisions and merchandise, and we could now perceive that in this great city, and all the others of that neighborhood which were built in the water, the houses stood separate from each other, communicating only by small drawbridges, and by boats, and that they were built with terraced tops. The noise and bustle of the marketplace below us could be heard almost a league off, and those who had been at Rome and Constanti-

[2] W. H. Prescott, History of the Conquest of Mexico: New York, 1844; vol. ii, p. 13.

nople said, that for convenience, regularity, and population, they had never seen the like."[3]

On their way to this royal reception, the Spaniards were particularly impressed with the elegant garb of their generous hosts. "The *tilmatli,* or cloak, thrown over the shoulders and tied round the neck, made of cotton of different degrees of fineness, according to the condition of the wearer, and the ample sash around the loins, were often wrought in rich and elegant figures, and edged with a deep fringe or tassel." The women wore skirts with highly ornamented borders, and over these, sometimes, loosely flowing robes, made of cotton, which was often of a delicate texture, richly dyed and embroidered.

Montezuma himself wore the girdle and the ample square cloak of his nation, made of the finest cotton, with the embroidered ends gathered in a knot around his neck. Whenever he deigned to walk his attendants strewed the ground with cotton tapestry, to prevent the imperial foot from the contamination of soil.[4] Diaz notes that "he had also much defensive armor of quilted cotton ornamented with feathers in different devices." Chief among the presents that he bestowed on his visitors were cotton dresses, enough to supply every man with a suit.[5]

In the market could be seen cotton piled up in bales, or made into quilted doublets and dresses, with such articles for domestic use as tapestry, curtains, coverlets, and hoods. Cortes, imitating the Mexicans, protected his own soldiers from hostile ar-

[3] Bernal Diaz del Castillo, The True History of the Conqnest of Mexico. Written in the year 1568; Maurice Keating, Translator: London, 1800; pp. 145–146.

[4] Prescott, as cited, p. 73.

[5] Prescott, as cited, p. 83.

rows by quilting their jackets with lint. He sent home to the Emperor Charles V cotton mantles, some all white, others mixed with white and black, or red, green, yellow, and blue; waistcoats, handkerchiefs, counterpanes, tapestries, and carpets of cotton, in which the colors of the cotton were extremely fine. From its fibers the Mexicans had learned to manufacture paper, and even to make up small cloths of it as a species of money. Explorers later than Cortes found the plant growing as far North as the country bordering the "Mishesepe" and its tributaries; de Vica, in 1536, discovering it in the territory now comprised within the States of Louisiana and Texas.[6]

The rich civilization of the Peruvian Incas also included a high development of the culture and manufacture of cotton.[7] Acquainted with the use of guano, these ancient farmers would excavate great tracts in the arid areas, deep enough to secure moisture, and then heavily fertilize their reclaimed sunken gardens, succeeding to such a degree in the scientific culture of the cotton plant that the Peruvian fiber is to this day exceeded in length only by Egyptian and sea-island products, while for strength and length of fiber combined it cannot be surpassed. Although, unlike the Mexicans, who used cotton exclusively, these Peruvians utilized the wool of alpacas, llamas, sheep, and other animals in the manufacture of clothing, they also produced colored cotton cloths worked in complicated and elegant patterns, Pizarro reporting that from time immemorial

[6] M. B. Hammond, The Cotton Industry: New York, 1897; p. 4.

[7] Clements R. Markham on "The Inca Civilization in Peru" in J. Winsor's Narrative and Critical History of America: Boston, 1889; vol. i, pt. ii, ch. iv.

the dress of the Inca had always been woven of cotton by the "virgins of the sun."

Even before the times of the Incas, tribes of "Chimu," inhabiting parts of the coast of Peru, erected temples and tombs and palaces, with furnaces for the smelting of metals, gateways constructed of enormous masses of stone, and aqueducts extending for hundreds of miles across the mountains and rivers. From their habit of interring with mummies all of the articles of ordinary daily use, it is possible to learn much of their customs; and numerous cotton garments have from time to time been exhumed, especially in the neighborhood of Ancon, showing a highly advanced knowledge of weaving.[8] Even spindles, with other implements used in spinning and sewing, have been recovered from the tombs of the Chimu, indicating, in the judgment of Mr. Henry Lee, among others, that the cultivation and manufacture of cotton in the so-called "New World" was "at least coeval with the similar use of it in India."

[8] The same, notes.

CHAPTER 23

COLONIAL LIFE

EXACTLY three hundred years, however, elapsed between the discovery of America by Columbus and the appearance of the cotton plant as an important item in North American life. It is only a little more than a century since cotton leaped suddenly into the national foreground, from which it has never receded. It came as though responsive to roaring British mills, to appease the fierce raiment hunger of England; it came as though magically summoned by the urgent genie of the Nick of Time; but no prophet, of even the most venturous imagination, could have foreseen the effect of this sorcerous plant on the woof of the national history, wherein it has woven a pattern so persistent and far-reaching and strange as to suggest the tampering hand of Pallas herself at the looms.[1]

In colonial times spinning and weaving figured always in the foreground of any picture of American domestic life, Priscilla being none the less attractive to the John Aldens of her day by reason of her use of the wheel, to excel in which was the pride of every lass and matron. The "spinning bee" became a popular social function, celebrated sometimes in the town hall, and again in the village manse; the women bringing with pride their wheels and flax for the contest, while cake and wine and tea were generously

[1] See Appendix B.

supplied by the gallant gentlemen who danced attendance on them.[2]

Flax mounted, in fact, to the dignity of a considerable item of export, so that Benjamin Franklin could testify before a committee of the House of Commons in 1766 that more than ten thousand hogsheads of flax-seed were annually exported from Philadelphia to Ireland, with probably an equal shipment from New York.

His questioners, who were considering the repeal of the Stamp Act, desired to ascertain whether the colonists could really clothe themselves without aid from England. Franklin, replying, alluded not only to the increasing manufacture of wool, in addition to linen, but said of the people in the populous State of Virginia that "their winters are short, and not very severe; and they can very well clothe themselves with linen and *cotton* of their own raising for the rest of the year."

The concluding questions and answers of this remarkable tourney of wit throw a vivid side-light on the independent temper of the times.

"What used to be the pride of the Americans?" —Franklin was questioned.

"To indulge in the fashions and manufactures of Great Britain," he answered.

"What is now their pride?" he was then asked.

"To wear their old clothes over again, till they can make new ones," he replied.[3]

The Virginia planter, George Washington, has left documents which illustrate these interesting opinions of Franklin. The records of his weaving establish-

[2] J. B. McMaster, History of the People of the U. S.: New York, 1892; vol. i, p. 62.

[3] J. N. Larned, History for Ready Reference, U. S., 1766: Springfield, 1895; vol. v, p. 3192 ff.

ment for 1767, the year after Franklin's examination, show that he manufactured clothing-goods for twenty-eight different persons besides himself and Mrs. Washington, making a total of 1,556 yards, of which about three hundred yards were of cotton, including "cotton striped, cotton-plain, cotton filled, cotton-birdeye, cotton Jumpstripe, and Cotton-India dimity;" while his summary of the business for 1768 [4] shows that he spun and wove for his own use (including his plantation) 815¾ yards of "linnen," 355¼ yards of woollen, 144½ yards of linsey, and forty yards of cotton—thus demonstrating his complete independence of England in the matter of clothing.

It is amusing nowadays to recall the attitude of these fathers of the Republic toward manufacture. Franklin, in a pamphlet written in 1760, said that "manufactures are founded in poverty.—No man who can have a piece of land of his own sufficient by his labor to subsist his family in plenty, is poor enough to be a manufacturer and work for a master."

The very word, as this last sentence shows, had a different connotation from that of its present usage, due to the fact that manufacture was still isolated and domestic, the factory system being as yet undeveloped.

Even Washington felt it necessary to apologize for his partiality to manufacture, saying in a letter to Lafayette in 1789: "Though I would not force the introduction of manufactures by extravagant encouragements, and to the prejudice of agriculture, yet I conceive much might be done in the way by

[4] U. B. Phillips, A Documentary History of American Industrial Society: Cleveland, 1910, vol. ii, p. 319 ff.

women, children, and others, without taking one really necessary hand from tilling the earth."[5]

In another letter written in the same year he reveals again the patriotic motives that enlisted his interest in home industry when he says: "No diminution in agriculture has taken place at the time when greater and more substantial improvements in manufactures were making than were ever before known in America.—I hope it will not be a great while before it will be unfashionable for a gentleman to appear in any other dress (except homespun). Indeed, we have already been too long subject to British prejudices. I use no porter or cheese in my family, but such as is made in America."[6]

[5] O. L. Elliott, The Tariff Controversy in the U. S.: Palo Alto, 1892; p. 40, note.

[6] Elliott, as cited, pp. 62–63.

CHAPTER 24

EARLY MANUFACTURE

To Alexander Hamilton, who was born on a West Indian cotton plantation, Americans owe the first pronounced argument for manufactures; his celebrated report to the House of Representatives in 1791 beginning with the words: "The expediency of encouraging manufactures in the United States, which was not long since deemed very questionable, appears at this time to be pretty generally admitted." Tench Coxe shares with Hamilton the honor of fathering the early interest in manufacturing progress, his position as assistant secretary of the Treasury, at Philadelphia, enabling him to give effective support to the policies of his brilliant associate, while of his own initiative he had already organized the "United Company of Philadelphia for Promoting American Manufactures."

This company secured and operated the first spinning-jenny seen in America, which was exhibited in Philadelphia in 1775, having been constructed according to the Hargreaves pattern by Christopher Tully. Coxe's company for a time employed four hundred women in the spinning and weaving of cotton, but the business subsequently passed into the hands of Samuel Wetherell, who used it for the more lucrative manufacture of wool.[1]

[1] J. L. Bishop, A History of American Manufactures from 1608 to 1860: Philadelphia, 1861; vol. i, pp. 383–410.

Practically all of the cotton used in the United States prior to this period was imported from the West Indies. It had found its way to New England in the first half of the seventeenth century. The earliest mention of ship building in Connecticut is connected with it; for the Colonial Records show that in 1640 the General Court declared: "It is thought necessary for the comfortable support of these plantations, that a trade in *cotton wooll* be sett uppon and attempted, and for the furthering thereof it hath pleased the Governor that now is to undertake the finishing and setting forth a vessel with convenient speed to those parts where the said comodity is to be had, if it be phesable."[2] John Winthrop said of his neighbors in 1643, "They are setting on the manufacture of linen and cotton cloth"; the women who delighted in flax finding that the same simple implements availed for the silky white fiber from the Indies. Weeden shows that the Connecticut people, moreover, took a leaf from the annals of Cortes, and, having learned in the Pequot War what Indian arrows could do, armored their pioneer soldiers in cotton-quilted corselets. Squaws were instructed in the new manufacture, the school at Martha's Vineyard providing "wheele cards and cotton woole to Imploy the Indian weemen" so early as 1661.[3]

Both Coxe and Hamilton not only held the opinion that cotton might be cultivated as a profitable commercial crop on American soil, but did everything in their power to promote its extensive introduction. It had been planted in Virginia in the first year of

[2] Cited by Bishop, i, pp. 49, 300.

[3] W. B. Weeden, Economic and Social History of New England, 1620–1789: Boston, 1890; vol. i, p. 201.

settlement (1607),[4] and in 1621 the "plentiful coming up" of seeds sown as an experiment became a subject of interest on both sides of the water.

Until the eighteenth century, however, cotton seems to have been planted in very small quantities, chiefly as a garden plant, for the sake of its delicate blossoms and the oddity of its beautiful fiber. But early in that century enough was raised in North Carolina to furnish one-fifth of the people with clothing,[5] and there are records of its sporadic cultivation for domestic use all through the century, one South Carolina planter devoting as much as thirty acres to this crop at the beginning of the Revolutionary War.[6]

The trouble with England quickened the popular interest in its possibilities; in 1775 the legislative assemblies of both South Carolina and Virginia exhorted the people to cultivate it; but on the other hand Swiss and German colonists in Georgia were warned by their trustees at home to desist from experimentation with cotton, as this might give umbrage to England.[7]

After the achievement of independence the industry made such headway that Jefferson wrote, in 1786: "The four southernmost States make a great deal of cotton. The poor are almost entirely clothed in it in winter and summer. In winter they wear shirts of it and outer clothing of cotton and wool mixed. In summer their shirts are linen, but

4 British State Papers, Colonial, vol. i, 15, i; Winder Papers, vol. i, pp. 3–4, cited by P. A. Bruce in Economic History of Va. in the 17th Century: New York, 1907; vol. i, p. 194, note.

5 Bulletin No. 33, as cited, p. 32.

6 W. B. Seabrook, Memoir on the Origin, Cultivation, and Uses of Cotton: Charleston, 1844; p. 9.

7 M. B. Hammond, as cited. p. 7.

the outer clothing cotton. The dress of the women is almost entirely of cotton manufactured by themselves, except the richer class, and even many of these wear a good deal of home spun cotton. It is as well manufactured as the calicoes of Europe. Those four States furnish a great deal of cotton to the States north of them, who cannot make as being too cold."[8]

In the same year Madison said to Tench Coxe at the Annapolis Convention that "there was no reason to doubt that the United States would one day become a great cotton-producing country";[9] while Hamilton had already taken the position that "several of the Southern colonies" might some day "clothe the whole continent."[10]

The industry stumbled, however, and made but slow progress at best, as the upland cotton plant was of a short-staple variety, characterized by the extreme stubbornness with which the lint adheres to its seed, so that in those times before the invention of the Whitney gin it took a full day's work to separate a single pound of the fiber for carding.

Very different, on the other hand, was the tractability of the long-staple imported variety, its lint being far less tenacious, so that the simple roller gin called the "churka," introduced from India, served its early purpose fairly well; while the quaint clumsy "bow," described on page 19, was also borrowed from India, and made to do service in cleansing.

When, finally, some of the Southern planters had

[8] Letter to Brissot de Warville, cited by M. B. Hammond, p. 13.
[9] Bishop, i, 355.
[10] In 1774 or '75, according to Carroll D. Wright, The Industrial Evolution of the U. S.: New York, 1902; p. 53.

undertaken the domestic production of this "sea-island" cotton (beginning in 1786),[11] the first cotton crops of noteworthy proportions appeared in the United States, reaching in three years an estimated output of a million pounds of lint, and at the end of five years, two millions. But the sea-island variety soon attained its maximum production, as it refused to grow outside of a narrowly circumscribed area,—being still confined to Southern sea-islands and a thin strip of land along the adjoining coast.

[11] Bishop, i, 355.

CHAPTER 25

THE DIS-UNITED STATES

We have now reached the most important year in the history of the cotton plant in America, if not in the world, the year 1793; when, by the ingenuity of a Yankee schoolmaster sojourning in Georgia, the stubborn and almost worthless short-staple fiber, which abounded in the uplands, was lifted from a negligible position in the domestic life of the South to become with astonishing suddenness the most important of national exports, and the chief source of supply for the ravenous markets of England, leading Macaulay to say: "What Peter the Great did to make Russia dominant, Eli Whitney's invention of the cotton gin has more than equaled in its relation to the power and progress of the United States."[1] But as we are considering the broad influence of cotton, the romantic and stormy career of Whitney may be deferred to a subsequent chapter, giving us time to indicate the course of a political revolution in which the skeins of this plant became involved with consequences quite as important, to say the least, as those of the Industrial Revolution in England. For there can be no question that the startling development of a novel and weighty economic factor had much to do with the new alinement that gradually arrayed the segregated States

[1] C. W. Burkett and C. H. Poe in Cotton: New York, 1906; p. 217.

into two clearly defined sections, with clashing convictions on vital matters of policy; how much, the reader will judge for himself. The facts will simply be marshaled so as to bear their own testimony.

So acute was the factional antagonism among the United States at the close of the Revolutionary War as to lead John Fiske to assert that the period of five years following the peace of 1783, and embracing the Constitutional Convention, was the gravest crisis in all the history of the American people. "The War of Secession was a terrible ordeal to pass through," he says; "but when one tries to picture what might have happened in this fair land without the work of the Federal Convention, the imagination stands aghast."[2] Certainly it cannot be too strongly insisted that the winning of the Revolutionary War did not establish the liberties of the American people; it merely cleared the path for their establishment. There was no American people except as united in a temporary warfare against a common enemy; this struggle ended, the colonies drifted back into factional bickerings and petty internecine warfare so acute and incessant that anarchy seemed the only logical outcome,—George III and Lord North and Thurlow confidently awaiting the issue. Even friendly Englishmen predicted that Americans must remain a disunited people until the end of time, and there were not wanting American citizens who saw the only hope of safety in a king.[3] The Confederation was nothing but a mere "league of friend-

[2] J. Fiske, The Critical Period of American History, 1783–1789: Boston, 1892; p. 262; see also pp. v. and 55.

[3] R. E. Thompson, The Hand of God in American History: New York, 1902; pp. 64–67. See also Allen Johnson, in Union and Democracy: Boston, 1915; p. 24.

ship," Congress lacking power to enforce its laws, as to impose taxes, and the bankrupt government being forced time and again to draw upon its foreign ministers for funds, discounting the drafts for cash, when there was not the slightest ground for supposing that the minister would have any funds. "He must go and beg the money. That was part of his duty as envoy,—to solicit loans without security for a government that could not raise enough money by taxation to defray its current expenses."[4]

Perhaps the most striking example of American powerlessness, resulting from the universal factionalism, is furnished by the plight of the Continental Congress, when, on one occasion during the seven years of its peripatetic history, it was actually chased from its quarters in Philadelphia by a handful of drunken soldiers demanding their pay, and forced to take refuge in the college buildings at Princeton. Congress skipped about from Philadelphia to Princeton, to Annapolis, to Trenton, to New York, until it became a common butt of ridicule; one editor, for example, writing in irony: "Verily the Lord shall make this government like unto a wheel, and keep it rolling back and forth betwixt Dan and Beer-sheba, and grant it no rest this side of Jordan."[5]

The point with which we are concerned at the moment is this: that the separatism responsible for such an unhappy condition was universal, sectionalism between North and South not yet having crystallized, but existing only as a dispassionate geographical fact somewhat accentuated by difference of interests, yet scarcely more positive than the an-

[4] Fiske, Critical Period, p. 156.
[5] Fiske, Critical Period, pp. 112–113, 271.

tagonism between Connecticut and New York, or New York and New Jersey, for example. The father of Gouverneur Morris expressly stipulated in his will that his son should not be educated in the colony of Connecticut, "lest he should imbibe in his youth that low craft and cunning so incident to the people of that country, which is so interwoven in their constitutions that all their art cannot disguise it from the world, though many of them under that sanctified garb of religion have endeavored to impose themselves on the world for honest men."[6]

Fiske gives equally laughable illustrations of the reprisals between New York, New Jersey, and Connecticut. "The city of New York, with its population of 30,000 souls, had long been supplied with firewood from Connecticut, and with butter and cheese, chickens and garden vegetables, from the thrifty farms of New Jersey. This trade, it was observed, carried thousands of dollars out of the city and into the pockets of detested Yankees and despised Jerseymen. It was ruinous to domestic industry, said the men of New York. Acts were accordingly passed, obliging every Yankee sloop which came down through Hell Gate, and every Jersey market boat which was rowed across from Paulus Hook to Cortlandt Street, to pay entrance fees and obtain clearances at the custom-house, just as was done by ships from London or Hamburg; and not a cart-load of Connecticut firewood could be delivered at the back-door of a country-house in Beekman Street until it should have paid a heavy duty. Great and just was the wrath of the farmers and lumbermen. The New

[6] J. H. Kirkland, Higher Education in the U. S. A.: Nashville, 1913; p. 6.

Jersey legislature made up its mind to retaliate. The city of New York had lately bought a small patch of ground on Sandy Hook, and had built a lighthouse there. This lighthouse was the one weak spot in the heel of Achilles where a hostile arrow could strike, and New Jersey gave vent to her indignation by laying a tax of $1,800 a year on it. Connecticut was equally prompt. At a great meeting of business men, held at New London, it was unanimously agreed to suspend all commercial intercourse with New York. Every merchant signed an agreement, under penalty of $250 for the first offense, not to send any goods whatever into the hated state for a period of twelve months."[7]

"A selfish habitude of thinking and reasoning," wrote one who styled himself Yorick, in the *New York Packet*, "leads us into a fatal error the moment we begin to talk of the interests of America. The fact is, by the interests of America we mean only the interests of that State to which property or accident has attached us." "Of the affairs of Georgia," Madison confessed in 1786, "I know as little as those of Kamskatska." Allen Johnson says that in order to find a historical parallel to the annals of this period, one must go back to the bickerings and jealousies of the states of ancient Greece.[8]

The only point on which some of the States seemed to agree had respect to their independence of any actual control by a common central authority; and since there was no lodestone to hold them in place, they jostled one another continually.

[7] Critical Period, pp. 146–147.
[8] Union and Democracy: Boston, 1915; p. 8.

CHAPTER 26

STATES-RIGHTS AND THE CONSTITUTION[1]

STATES-RIGHTS was not at first a distinctive Southern doctrine, as it afterwards pointedly became. On the contrary, the most acute opposition to the formation of the Union through creation of the Federal Constitution proceeded from Northern States such as New York and Rhode Island, while certain States of the South took a prominent part in bringing the Constitutional Convention to a successful issue, being generous not only in the initiation and execution of policies, but also in the surrender of individual rights. Maryland and Virginia successfully paved the way for the Convention. Virginia, besides furnishing a chairman in the person of Washington, a powerful foundation-builder in Edmund Randolph, and the chief craftsman of the great instrument in James Madison, had already distinguished herself by her cession of the huge Northwestern territory to the Union, while North Carolina in 1790 ceded the region since known as Tennessee; and South Carolina and Georgia, heavily concerned in the slave trade though they were, compromised with New England States in the Convention on a plan for the prohibition of a further importation of

[1] Chief authorities: J. Fiske, Critical Period, as cited; James Madison, Journal of the Federal Convention: Chicago, 1898 (reprinted from the edition of 1840); A. B. Hart, American History Told by Contemporaries: New York, 1908; vol. iii.

slaves after the year 1808, thus surmounting the chief obstacle in the way of federal union, after which progress became relatively easy.

On the other hand, several of the Northern States were so jealous of individual rights and so reluctant to make any material concessions as to endanger the formation of the Constitution time and again. Hamilton, brilliant and zealous as he was, had his vote negatived repeatedly by the two other delegates from New York, extreme and obstinate Anti-Federalists, who finally quit the Convention and went home disgusted. Rhode Island even refused to send delegates.

Other of the Northern States of course labored with conspicuous zeal and ability for the achievement of the great agreement, notably Pennsylvania, Connecticut and Massachusetts; but the point is, that radical opposition to the surrender of States-rights was at this time found in the North, while most of the Southern States persistently and patiently labored toward the construction of a Federal Constitution which involved a surrender of States-rights.

The factional dangers of the times are amply reflected in contemporary documents. Madison feared the "partition of the empire into rival and hostile confederacies." Hamilton gloomily demanded, in the Federalist,—"What indication is there of national disorder, poverty, and insignificance, which does not form a part of the dark catalogue of our public misfortunes?" The aged Franklin, despondent that so little progress had been made in the Convention after weeks of wrangling, proposed as a last resort that prayer be offered for divine interposition and assistance. Washington declared, with great solemnity: "It is too probable that no plan we propose will be adopted. Perhaps another dreadful conflict is to be sustained." Finally, after a weary struggle that had lasted from the 25th of May until the 17th of September, that instrument was at length complete which Gladstone called the greatest work ever struck off at any one time by the mind and purpose of man. Great it most certainly is; but its real greatness is enhanced by the fact that it was not struck off at a single blow by the unimpeded genius of calm statesmanship; it was built up from the slow accretions of a widely diversified colonial experience, and finally beat and hammered into shape by the arms of rough battling giants, in the heat of fierce factional jealousies. Franklin voiced the feeling of many delegates as the last members were signing, by pointing to a carved and gilded figure of the sun that may still be seen on the back of Washington's chair, and saying to those around him: "I have often and often, in the course of the session and the vicissitudes of my hopes and fears as to its issue, looked at that behind the President, without being able to tell whether it was rising or setting; but now at length, I have the happiness to know, that it is a rising, and not a setting sun"—while Washington sat with his head bowed in solemn meditation.

But, for all its vicissitudes, the Constitution had only been launched as yet; it had now to weather the storms of thirteen conventions before it could be christened as the true ship of State for the Union. This ratification struggle, lasting three years, proves conclusively that the doctrine of States-rights had not yet become a sectional issue, but was dispersed with impartiality among the dissident commonwealths. Delaware, a Southern State, was the first to ratify, and by a unanimous vote. In Pennsylvania the contest was sharp, violence being used to secure quorums, while pamphleteers sneered at Franklin as a dotard and branded Washington as a fool. Washington credited James Wilson, the Scotchman, with saving the Constitution. He carried Pennsylvania by stumping the State, the vote at length standing 46 to 23. New Jersey and Georgia followed unanimously, while Connecticut next ratified by 128 to 40. In Massachusetts the devotion to States-rights caused a serious struggle, which was not ended until Washington sent to Boston the solemn warning: "The Constitution or disunion are before us to choose from"—accompanied by the politic suggestion that "if the Constitution is our choice, a constitutional door is open for amendments." Hancock and Adams thereupon withdrew their objections, proposing a ratification with the accompanying recommendation that the instrument should subsequently be amended in important particulars; but, even so, their motion prevailed by the narrow margin of 187 to 168. Maryland was the next to confirm, 63 to 12; South Carolina followed with a vote of 149 to 73, and New Hampshire, the ninth State, made the union binding by a vote of 57 to 46.

Virginia, the most populous State, had divided on the Constitution in a prolonged debate, the opposition being led by such unquestioned patriots as Patrick Henry, Richard Henry Lee, and James Monroe. Although defended by Madison, Randolph, and Marshall, the Constitution would probably never have been ratified at all without the personal influence of Washington; even then, the vote stood 89 to 79.

But New York offered a still more stubborn resistance, which never yielded at all until news arrived from New Hampshire that the Union had at length become an accomplished fact, so that New York had to face the prospect of isolation should she refuse to sign. Except for Hamilton and his "Federalist" the decision would probably have been adverse in any event, ratification being at length secured by the bare majority of three votes, 30 against 27, the Constitution, besides being openly burned at Albany, receiving fierce denunciation as a "triple-headed monster," "as deep and wicked a conspiracy as ever was invented in the darkest ages against the liberties of a free people." It was, as John Adams said, "extorted from the grinding necessities of a reluctant people."

North Carolina stayed out of the Union until November, 1789, and Rhode Island did not come in until June of 1790. The doctrine of States-rights had not yet begun to be sectional. It was impartially shared by the North and South alike, with the pressure for it strongest in the North. We shall see that cotton localized it finally in the South.

NOTE. It would hardly be inaccurate to say that the friends of the Constitution would have been found between the coast and a line fifty miles west of it. West of the latter line lay the opposition. The States where ratification was easy were mainly commercial States. Of these, New Jersey had originally objected to the Articles of Confederation because they gave no protection to commerce; South Carolina's commerce was a far larger part of her wealth in 1788 than at any time since; Georgia was further influenced by her position as a frontier State, exposed to the powerful Southern Indian tribes, and anxious for protection by a strong Federal Government; and Maryland and Connecticut, having large and vague claims to territory in the Northwest, had solider hopes of justice from a firm Federal Government than from the Confederacy.

In the agricultural States ratification was difficult. Massachusetts was not then, as now, packed with manufactories. Her strength lay in agriculture, and her farmer delegates . . . held their ground obstinately.—Alexander Johnston, American Political History, 1763–1876: New York, 1913; p. 79.

According to John Adams, the Constitution was "the work of the commercial people in the sea-port towns, of the planters of the slave-holding States, of the officers of the Revolutionary army, and the property-holders everywhere." For a specific treatment of this subject, see C. A. Beard, An Economic Interpretation of the Constitution: New York, 1913.

CHAPTER 27

EARLY SLAVERY

SOUTH CAROLINA's able representatives in the Constitutional Convention had argued successfully for the recognition and protection of slaves, for economic reasons. Having regard to the rice and indigo crops, General Pinckney declared that so long as there remained one acre of swamp land uncleared in his native State, he would raise his voice against unduly restricting slavery, being thoroughly convinced that "the nature of our climate, and the flat, swampy situation of our country, obliges us to cultivate our lands with negroes; and that without them South Carolina would soon be a desert waste."[1] His cousin frankly said that South Carolina could never receive the plan should it prohibit the slave trade; but added significantly that "if the States be all left at liberty on this subject, South Carolina may perhaps, by degrees, do of herself what is wished."[2]

Coöperating, however, with the delegates from Georgia, and effecting a compromise with New England, Rutledge and the Pinckneys agreed to the prohibition of a further importation of slaves after the year 1808, but secured a slave law, in addition to a "three-fifths compromise,"—which provided that in counting the population for purposes of tax-

[1] Elliot's Debates (1876), iv: 263, cited by M. B. Hammond, p. 39.

[2] Madison's Journal, p. 578.

ation, or to determine representation in Congress, five slaves should be reckoned as three individuals. "I will confess," said General Pinckney, "that I had prejudices against the Eastern States before I came here, but I have found them as liberal and candid as any men whatever."[3]

But Virginia was not nearly so complaisant as New England on this question of slavery. Mason, in opposing the "bargain" between New England and the far South, denounced the slave trade as an "infernal traffic," which "discourages arts and manufactures.—Every master of slaves is born a petty tyrant," he said. "They bring the judgment of Heaven on a country. As nations cannot be rewarded or punished in the next world, they must be in this. By an inevitable chain of causes and effects, Providence punishes national sins by national calamities."[4]

Columbus himself had introduced slavery into America, by taking some of the Caribs into captivity and sending them back to Spain, afterwards dividing the entire island of Hispaniola into "repartimientos" for the purpose of exacting tribute in the guise of goods and severe personal labor.[5] From this there arose one of the most cruel and destructive systems of slavery that has ever been known.

But it was Sir John Hawkins, the English explorer, who introduced African slavery into Hispaniola,—bringing in three cargoes of negroes between 1562 and 1567, having founded on the Guinea coast a stockade where human chattels could be collected and held the year round. On his last voyage

[3] Fiske's Critical Period, p. 265.
[4] Critical Period, p. 264.
[5] J. Fiske, The Discovery of America: Boston, 1892; vol. ii, p. 432 ff.

he was accompanied by young Francis Drake, commanding the *Judith.*[6] It was from this West India traffic in negroes that slavery first spread into South Carolina.[7] But it had appeared in New York at an earlier date, under the Dutch; [8] and was introduced into Virginia in 1619.[9] The "Body of Liberties" adopted by the General Court of Massachusetts in 1641 provided for the existence of slavery in the case of "lawful captives taken in just wars, and such strangers as willingly sell themselves, or are sold to us," while prohibiting its further extension.[10] Goldwin Smith points out that although ships from New England took part in the slave trade, "the members of the religious commonwealth who made a murderous raid upon an African village on the Sabbath were brought to justice for their double crime.—Fortunately for New England, she had no industry like that of cotton, tobacco, or rice, in which slave labor could be profitably employed. Slaves do not make good husbandmen or seamen." [11]

[6] E. G. Payne, Voyages of the Elizabethan Seamen to America, ch. i; cited by Larned, vol. i, pp. 67–68.

[7] J. A. Doyle, The English in America: Virginia, Maryland, and the Carolinas, ch. xii; Larned, vol. iv, p. 2968.

[8] Larned, iv, 2920.

[9] Larned, v, 3630.

[10] Larned, iv, 2920.

[11] Goldwin Smith, The United States; an Outline of Political History: New York, 1899; p. 25. For slave trade of New England, see E. L. Bogart, The Economic History of the U. S.: New York, 1907; p. 121. Lincoln said, in 1854: "When Southern people tell us they are no more responsible for the origin of slavery than we are, I acknowledge the fact."—Complete Works: New York, 1894; vol. i, p. 187.

CHAPTER 28

THE SOUTH AGAINST SLAVERY

The first colonial legislation against slavery was enacted by Rhode Island in 1652, in order to check "the common course practised among Englishmen to buy negers." The Act provided that "no black mankind or white being forced by covenant, bond or otherwise shall be held to service longer than ten years," and that "that man that will not let them go free, or shall sell them any else where to that end that they may be enslaved to others for a longer time, hee or they shall forfeit to the Colonie forty pounds."[1]

It was left for Virginia, however, to be the first State to prohibit the further importation of negroes to be sold into slavery.[2] Under colonial rule this step had been often attempted, but as often thwarted by the British crown. Peter Fontaine wrote from Westover in 1757 that "our Assembly, foreseeing the ill consequences of importing such numbers amongst us, hath often attempted to lay a duty upon them which would amount to a prohibition, such as ten or twenty pounds a head, but no Governor dare pass such a law, having instructions to the contrary from the Board of Trade at home. By this means they are forced upon us, whether we will or not."[3] Lecky, the British historian, concedes that every at-

[1] Larned, as cited, vol. iv, p. 2642.
[2] Fiske, Critical Period, pp. 72, 74.
[3] Phillips's Documentary History, as cited, ii, 29.

tempt to prohibit or restrict that importation was rebuked and defeated by England.[4] Jefferson was strongly opposed to the slave trade, and included in his original draft of the Declaration of Independence a round denunciation of slavery, with a sharp thrust at George III for supporting it; but the denunciation was omitted because a majority of the members thought it inconsistent to hold George III responsible for a slave trade carried on by New England ship-masters for the benefit of the planters of the South. Jefferson boasts, however, that the Virginia legislature took up the subject again (1778), when free, and "in the very first session held under the republican government, passed a law for the perpetual prohibition of the importation of slaves."[5] In these same Notes on the State of Virginia he condemns slavery in the most emphatic language: "With what execration should the statesman be loaded, who, permitting one-half the citizens thus to trample on the rights of the other, transforms those into despots and these into enemies."

Washington more than once named it as among his "first wishes to see some plan adopted by which slavery, in this country, may be abolished by law."[6] Madison, as he himself writes in his Journal of the Federal Convention, "thought it wrong to admit in the Constitution the idea that there could be property in men."[7] Monroe, in the Virginia Convention, said: "We have found that this evil has

[4] W. E. H. Lecky, History of England in the 18th Century: New York, 1878–1890; vol. ii, ch. 5.

[5] Cited by Larned, iv, 2923.

[6] H. R. Helper, The Impending Crisis of the South: New York, 1857; p. 193.

[7] Journal, as cited, p. 610.

preyed upon the very vitals of the Union, and has been prejudicial to all the States, in which it has existed";[8] while Patrick Henry wrote: "It is a debt we owe to the purity of our religion, to show that it is at variance with that law which warrants slavery."[9]—And so on with other of the great elder Virginians.

But Virginia was not alone among the Southern States in its adverse judgment of slavery. Maryland followed her example in 1783 in prohibiting the further introduction of slaves and removing all restraints upon emancipation. North Carolina, like Virginia, sent delegates to the first Continental Congress who pledged their State not to import slaves and not to purchase them when imported by others; participating in the subsequent action of Congress that no slaves be imported into any of the thirteen United Colonies, and imposing through its own legislature in 1786 a fine of £5 per head on all negroes thereafter imported, so as to discourage the slave trade. The Rowan county committee of safety[10] and the convention of delegates at Newbern in 1774 adopted anti-slavery resolutions.[11] Georgia likewise, still farther to the South, signalized the opening of her colonial career by stringent opposition to slavery,[12] which renewed itself after the formation of the Union, Georgia prohibiting the further introduction of slaves, by constitutional provision, in 1798.[13] A member of the first Congress

[8] Helper, as cited, p. 200.

[9] Helper, as cited, p. 201.

[10] D. A. Tompkins, History of Mecklenburg County: Charlotte, 1903; vol. i, p. 86.

[11] Helper, as cited, p. 22.

[12] Larned, as cited, vol. ii, p. 1425.

[13] Alexander Johnston, American Political History, 1763–1876: Boston, 1912; vol. ii, p. 25.

declared: "Not a man in Georgia but wishes there were no slaves. They are a curse to the country." [14]

Ramsay's History shows that in 1774 a convention of South Carolina citizens "resolved that His Majesty's subjects in North America (without respect to color or other accidents) are entitled to all the inherent rights and liberties of his natural born subjects within the Kingdom of Great Britain"; [15] and we have already heard Charles Pinckney declare before the Constitutional Convention that if the States were left at liberty South Carolina might of her own accord stop the slave importation.[16] Lincoln frequently cites the remark of a later South Carolina congressman to the effect that when the Constitutional Convention was held, it was the belief of no man that slavery would long continue.[17]

While this Convention was deliberating in Philadelphia, Congress organized the Northwest territory that had been ceded by Virginia, and included in the ordinance a proviso that slavery should be shut out from all of the vast area northwest of the Ohio River; it being notable that this ordinance secured the unanimous concurrence of the States, with the exception of a single individual vote, which was cast by a Northern man. The Southern States were unanimous for it.[18]

14 McMaster, as cited, vol. ii, p. 359.
15 Cited by Helper, p. 228.
16 See page 138.
17 Complete Works, as cited, vol. i, pp. 268, 347, 480, 511, 516, 615.
18 Fiske, Critical Period, p. 205; Writings and Speeches of Daniel Webster: Boston, 1903; vol. x, p. 68.

CHAPTER 29

SOUTHERN SLAVERY DECLINES

THE unanimous Southern vote against the extension of slavery was cast in the year 1787; but six years later something happened. If it had not been for this overshadowing event and the enormous economic consequences that arose from it there can be little doubt that the compromise of the Constitution which provided that no slaves should be imported after 1808 would have been on all sides heartily accepted, and slavery eventually abolished from all the States, in the South and the North together. At the time the Constitution was adopted, New York, for example, had nearly as many slaves as Georgia, and New Jersey had as many as the much larger Southern territory of Kentucky; but their labor was not adapted to the climate and soil of the North, where a falling off could naturally be expected. What is far more important is the interesting fact that the three peculiar industries that had made negro slavery profitable to the South were now entering on a stage of rapid economic decline: indigo, rice, and tobacco.[1]

The decline of indigo was brought about largely by England. Impressed by Lord Sheffield's gloomy survey of American prospects, the British Government systematically sought to embarrass the new

[1] Sugar is negligible in this discussion because of its confinement to a very small area. See Report of 13th Census, vol. v, p. 685.

Republic by such measures as the prevention of the emigration of skilled laborers to America, or of the exportation of machinery; and, specifically, by ruining the important indigo industry through compelling the peasants of recently conquered Bengal to cultivate the indigo plant in great quantity. By the year 1790 Georgia and South Carolina had been entirely forced out of this lucrative business. Rice, from the fact of its necessary restriction to narrowly limited areas, required only a small body of labor; besides, its cultivation had greatly declined at the close of the Revolutionary War, the crop of 1783 being less than one-half of the average annual production before the war, and this staple never again approximating its former proportions.[2]

The superlative importance of tobacco in relation to slavery prior to 1793 is indicated by the fact that in 1790 there were 293,427 slaves in Virginia, a tobacco State, and only 29,264 in Georgia, which produced rice and sugar cane; while little Maryland, another tobacco State, contained almost as many as South Carolina; Virginia and Maryland together, the tobacco States, owning 296,463 slaves as against 246,177 for *all the other States of the South combined*, or nearly three-fifths of all the slaves in the Union.[3] But tobacco proved to be a tyrannous crop, as then cultivated, besides producing a rapid exhaustion of soil. An early planter thus plaintively wrote of his troubles:

"In Virginia and Maryland Tobacco is our Staple, is our All, and Indeed leaves no room for anything Else; It requires the Attendance of all our hands, and Exacts their utmost labour, the whole year

[2] M. B. Hammond, as cited, pp. 14–15, 39.
[3] For Slave Tables see Appendix F: 2a.

round; it requires us to abhor Communitys or townships, since a Planter cannot Carry on his Affairs without considerable Elbow room, within his plantation. When All is done, and our Tobacco sent home, it is perchance the most uncertain Commodity that Comes to Markett; and the management of it there is of such a nature and method that it seems to be of all other, most lyable and subject to frauds, in prejudice to the poor Planters."[4]

Jefferson, writing in 1781, said that the culture of tobacco "was fast declining at the commencement of this war," and that "it must continue to decline on the return of peace." His biographers say that as fast as the richness of the soil could be converted into tobacco it was sent to London and exchanged for fine mansions, heavy furniture, costly apparel, wines, fine horses, coaches and slaves. The soil was rapidly exhausted, the price of negroes always on the increase, and the price of tobacco always going downward.[5]

There can be little doubt, in view of the strong Southern sentiment against slavery—prior to 1793—and in view also of the apathy toward it resulting from the decline of the three crops which had been its mainstay and support, that all of the Southern States would have joined those of the North in giving up slavery, as they had repeatedly endeavored to do while still colonies, had it not been for the sudden apparition of the great cotton crop,[6]

[4] Documentary History, as cited, i, 282–283.

[5] W. E. Curtis, The True Thos. Jefferson: Philadelphia, 1901; p. 73.

[6] The Rev. Wm. Winterbotham wrote in 1795: "Cotton has been lately adopted as an article of culture in the Southern States; and as the prices of rice, tobacco, and indigo decline, it must be very beneficial."—Cited by A. B. Hart in American History Told by Contemporaries: New York, 1908; vol. iii, p. 67.

conjured by the genius of Whitney, and dwarfing to comparative insignificance all of the other Southern resources by the instant employment of the half-idle slaves, whose presence had begun to be felt as a burden. So far had the movement for the extinction of slavery proceeded that Tench Coxe wrote in 1794: "The separate American States (with one small exception) have abolished the slave trade, and they have in some instances abolished negro slavery; in others they have adopted efficacious measures for its certain but gradual abolition. The importation of slaves is discontinued and can never be renewed so as to interrupt the peace of Africa, or endanger the tranquillity of the United States."[7] A Southern historian of the cotton trade, and an apologist of slavery, wrote at a much later date (1863): "It is fortunate for the blacks, as well as the whites, that the cotton business sprang up, for the sons of Africa do not flourish in a state of freedom, and without the cultivation of the leading staple of commerce there would not have been sufficient occupation for them. The planters would have preferred to manumit their slaves, which, in fact, was done, rather than be encumbered with idle and superfluous hands."[8]

[7] Cited by Bogart, p. 119.

[8] G. McHenry, The Cotton Trade: 1863; cited by M. B. Hammond, p. 41.

CHAPTER 30

A STARTLING REVERSAL

Between 1790 and 1800, while the slave population fell off in the North, it disappointed all expectation by increasing nearly 33 per cent in the South. The next decade showed even a more startling divergence. The number of Southern slaves increased from 847,095 in 1800 to 1,163,854 in 1810, while the Northern slave population fell from 35,946 to 27,510. New York and Georgia, which had stood not far apart in 1790, now showed an enormous divergence: 15,000 in New York and 105,000 in Georgia, thousands of Northern slaves having flocked into the South in response to an economic summons.[1]

How powerful and sudden was this summons is sufficiently indicated by the fact that whereas in the year of Eli Whitney's invention the South produced only 10,460 bales (of 500 pounds gross weight) of ginned cotton, it produced 177,824 bales in 1810, of which it exported almost three-fourths, at 15½ cents a pound. The significance of these figures may be gathered from the following table [2] at a glance:—

[1] "The farmers of the Northern States were enabled to sell their slaves, who had become an expensive burden to them, to the cotton planters of the South."—M. B. Hammond, as cited, pp. 47–48.

[2] Based on U. S. Census Reports for number of slaves; and on Bulletin No. 131 of Department of Commerce for cotton statistics: Washington, 1915; p. 82. See Appendix F: 2a for slave figures for all the States, 1790–1860.

	1790	1793	1810
Slaves in New York	21,324	(Whitney invented	15,017
Slaves in Georgia	29,264	the gin)	105,218
Cotton production	3,138 bales	10,460 bales	177,824 bales
Cotton exports	379 "	3,565 "	124,116 "

During this same period, the commercial value of the African slave had trebled, and it continued to increase enormously. Hammond, after showing that the price of the best "field hands" grew from $200 in 1790 to $1,000 in 1850 and $2,000 in 1860, goes on to say: "It was cotton, and cotton alone, which was responsible for this increase in the value of slave property. In spite of the use of slaves in the tobacco fields and on the rice and sugar plantations, the number of slaves employed in the cultivation of all other crops than cotton in 1850 was only slightly in excess of the number of slaves in the United States in 1790, before the culture of the white staple had attained any importance. The natural increase among the blacks was almost entirely consumed by the cotton plantations, and even then the demand of the cotton planters was not satisfied. 'The great limitation in production' (of cotton) said De Bow, 'is labor.' For slave labor was considered at the South as the only kind which could be used in cultivating cotton. Everywhere in the slave region, in the border States as well as in the cotton belt, the value of the negro as a cotton cultivator determined the price for which he would sell. 'In estimating the market value of his labor, he was viewed for the time from the traders' point of view, or, as if the question were—What is he worth for cotton?' "[3] Frederick J. Turner says, in his "Rise of the New West," that "never in history, perhaps, was an economic force more influential upon the life

[3] M. B. Hammond, as cited, p. 52.

of a people.—This economic transformation resuscitated slavery from a moribund condition to a vigorous and aggressive life."[4] And Woodrow Wilson adds: "Before this tremendous development of cotton culture had taken place, slavery had hardly more than habit and the perils of emancipation to support it in the South: Southern life and industry had shaped themselves to it, and the slaves were too numerous and too ignorant to be safely set free. But when the cotton-gin supplied the means of indefinitely expanding the production of marketable cotton by the use of slave labor, another and even more powerful argument for its retention was furnished. After that, slavery seemed nothing less than the indispensable economic instrument of Southern society."[5]

Influenced by economic considerations, South Carolina in 1803 repealed its law against the further importation of slaves, cotton exports having grown in ten years from a million and a half pounds (in 1793) to more than thirty-five million pounds (in 1803). Other Southern States were influenced by similar considerations; Virginia and Maryland, for example, being enabled to recuperate from losses due to the decline of the tobacco industry by raising negroes, out of their own abundant supply, for the new Southern market, so that Professor Dew wrote in 1832: "Virginia is, in fact, a negro raising State for other States. She produces enough for her own supply, and six thousand for sale."[6] Four years later, when the adaptability of the Mississippi country to cotton culture had been fully demonstrated,

[4] The Rise of the New West: New York, 1906; pp. 48, 49.
[5] Division and Reunion: New York, 1909; p. 125.
[6] Cited by M. B. Hammond, p. 53.

Virginia sent 120,000 slaves in a single year into this new region,[7] where slavery as an adjunct to the cotton crop secured a firmer hold than in any other part of the country.

The South had thus been economically welded into a great unified section, with a common view-point and identical interests, while a similar process, due also in large measure to cotton, had been taking place in the North; factionalism among the States being in consequence replaced by sectionalism between two groups of States, so that two great sections were thus gradually arraying themselves on opposite sides in an economic and political struggle that resulted at last in war.

The following table[8] strikingly illustrates the changes in the character of the population that occurred in the South with the increasing production of cotton. The border States, some of which grew tobacco in large quantities, began, it will be noted, with a larger percentage of negroes than the cotton

PERCENTAGE OF NEGRO POPULATION IN THE TWO SETS OF SOUTHERN STATES FROM 1790 TO 1860

YEAR	COTTON STATES		BORDER STATES	
	Whites, %	Negroes, %	Whites, %	Negroes, %
1790	67.3	32.7	63.2	36.8
1800	66.7	33.3	63.8	36.2
1810	63.	37.	63.8	36.2
1820	61.2	38.8	64.6	35.4
1830	60.3	39.7	65.6	34.4
1840	59.2	40.8	68.8	31.2
1850	58.9	41.1	72.8	27.2
1860	58.6	41.4	76.9	23.1

[7] The same, p. 50.

[8] E. von Halle, Baumwollproduktion und Pflanzungswirtschaft in den Nordamerikanischen Südstaaten: Leipzig, 1897; Erster Teil: Die Sklavenzeit; p. 131.

States; but by 1860, just before the war broke out, this percentage was reduced by one-third, owing to the "draw" of the cotton industry; which shows, in the cotton States column, a negro percentage steadily climbing, while the reverse principle obtained with the whites, who decreased in the cotton territory while increasing in the States along the border.

The time has now come to tell the story of the American inventor who, by unconsciously responding to the enormous foreign demand for cotton arising from British inventions, created the new economic force in American history that had such far-reaching results.

CHAPTER 31[1]

WHITNEY IN GEORGIA

In the autumn of 1792 a young college graduate sailed from New York for Savannah, on his way to South Carolina to teach school. He had never seen a boll of cotton in his life. A year later he made the first cotton gin, which caused his great and generous rival in inventive genius, Robert Fulton, to class him among the three men who accomplished more for mankind than any other men of their times.

Prominent among the ladies on shipboard with Whitney when he left New York was the widow of the great Revolutionary general, Nathaniel Greene; a woman of quick thought and generous impulses, returning with her family to Mulberry Grove plantation after a summer spent in the North. During the tedious days of the long voyage, as the sailing ship tossed to the whim of the winds or lay almost becalmed in mid-ocean, a friendship ripened between the young Yale scholar and this wealthy Georgia matron, which profoundly influenced the world. It was purely platonic, to be sure; the lady shortly afterward married the man who became Whitney's

[1] Chief authorities, Chapters 31–33: Correspondence of Eli Whitney, edited by M. B. Hammond: *American Historical Review*, October, 1897; Memoir of Eli Whitney, by D. Olmsted: *American Journal of Science*, vol. xxi, 1832; Cotton and Cotton Oil, by D. A. Tompkins, Charlotte, N. C., 1901.

partner, Phineas Miller; but it brought to Eli Whitney fame and fortune, because it directly fostered his invention.

Mulberry Grove was the name of a great plantation (on the river near Savannah) that had been confiscated by the State of Georgia during the Revolution and afterward bestowed on General Greene for his gallant services. It was maintained in munificent style, with a retinue of fifty negro servants; and so pleased was Mrs. Greene with young Whitney that she invited him to make his first acquaintance with the South from the vantage ground of Mulberry Grove hospitality.

Mechanical ingenuity had been Whitney's bent from youth. Born on a Massachusetts farm—in Worcester County, December 8, 1765—he had early haunted the tool house. At the age of twelve, the story runs, his curiosity prompted him to take his father's watch to pieces, and his native ingenuity enabled him to put it together again without his father being any the wiser. When only fifteen or sixteen years old, he ended a nail famine of wartimes by setting up a nail factory of his own, with much profit to his hard-handed father. Overcoming many obstacles, he at length achieved the ambition of his youth by entering the freshman class of Yale College at the age of twenty-three and graduating four years later, just before going to Savannah.

The poetic side of his disposition, which had often betrayed itself during college days, must have been stirred profoundly by the charm of his new Southern home. Mrs. Greene's plantation had originally received its name from the profusion of mulberry trees peculiar to this favored locality. In the deep forests near by the gray drapery of moss-hung ancient oaks was relieved by the satin gleam of magnolia leaves, heavy with sweetness, or by the fronds of graceful palmettoes. In the shallow lonely bayou boomed the bull-frog, incredibly resonant, or the alligator bellowed out his louder bass; while bright against this dark background of sound could be heard the silver melodies of birds. "Every traveler expressed his pleasure in listening to the mocking-bird, which caroled a thousand several tunes, imitating and excelling the notes of all its rivals. The humming-bird, so brilliant in its plumage, and so delicate in its form, quick in motion, yet not fearing the presence of man, haunting the flowers like the bee gathering honey, rebounding from the blossoms into which it dips its bill, and as soon returning to renew its many addresses to its delightful objects; myriads of pigeons, darkening the air with the immensity of their flocks, and, as men believed, breaking with their weight the boughs of trees on which they alighted;"[2] the nimble squirrel, the sly raccoon, and the homely opossum, famed for the marsupial care of its young—these peopled the old Southern woods with abounding life, and filled them with deep charm.

But the chief center of interest was of course the broad plantations, spreading fertile acres in the sun. The marshes were reclaimed from barrenness by verdant fields of rice; on the dryer uplands rustled broad acres of Indian corn, yellow pumpkins gleaming like gold between the rows; while peas and potatoes and huge luscious watermelons abounded. At night, in front of their swarming cabins, the negroes would sit in a circle lit by a flam-

[2] Bancroft's History.

ing pine torch, one of their number being detailed by the overseer to prevent indolence and dozing, while they picked drowsily at the stubborn "vegetable wool" of the uplands, which, when once freed from its tenacious seeds, was adaptable to a far greater variety of uses than its restricted sea-island rival.

Such were the scenes that young Whitney encountered in Georgia at the close of the eighteenth century.

CHAPTER 32[1]

WHITNEY INVENTS THE GIN

DURING the time of Whitney's visit, Mulberry Grove entertained also a large party of army officers from Augusta and the "up country" who had served under General Greene in the war. Among them were Major Pendleton, Major Forsyth, and Major Bremen. These gentlemen happened to discuss the immense prosperity the South might enjoy if only a proper "gin" could be devised for the green-seed upland cotton. Roller gins, evolved from the Hindu "churka" (see page 19), had long been in existence for the sea-island variety, making the work of separation five times as expeditious as by hand; but these were entirely ineffectual with the short-staple fiber of the uplands.

With a woman's friendly enthusiasm, Mrs. Greene is said to have exclaimed:

"Gentlemen, apply to my young friend Mr. Whitney—he can make anything!"

She then showed the party some proofs of her visitor's cleverness, including a convenient embroidery frame that he had mended or made for her, and toys contrived for the children during the few days he had spent in the mansion. Whitney was thereupon called from his room, and the situation half humorously presented.

"I have accomplished my aim," said Mrs. Greene;

[1] See Chapter 31.

"Mr. Whitney is a very deserving young man, and to bring him into notice was my object."

How wide this notice was to extend lay beyond the power of her most friendly conjecture. Friendship had done its work; Whitney's energy and ingenuity were to do the rest.

A room was set apart in the basement as a workshop for this amateur inventor. With only the plantation tools he applied himself to his task, having even to draw his own wire. First he fixed wire teeth to a board, and managed, by pulling the cotton through the teeth, to leave the stubborn little woolly seeds behind. Then he reasoned that by applying these wire teeth to a cylinder the cotton could be rolled through with rapidity. By the addition of a rotating brush to clean the wire teeth free of the lint, the first Whitney gin was completed.

In a letter to his father Whitney described his experience as follows:

"I went from N. York with the family of the late Major General Greene to Georgia. I went immediately with the family to their Plantation about twelve miles from Savannah with an expectation of spending four or five days and then proceed into Carolina to take the school as I have mentioned in former letters. During this time I heard much said of the difficulty of ginning Cotton, that is, seperating it from its seeds. There were a number of very respectable Gentlemen at Mrs. Greene's who all agreed that if a machine could be invented which would clean the cotton with expedition, it would be a great thing both to the Country and to the inventor. I involuntarily happened to be thinking on the subject and struck out a plan of a Machine in my mind, which I communicated to Miller, (who is agent to the executors of Genl. Greene and resides in the family, a man of respectability and property) he was pleased with the Plan and said if I would pursue it and try an experiment to see if it would answer, he would be at the whole expense. I should lose nothing but my time, and if I succeeded we would share the profits. Previous to this I found I was like to be disappointed in my school, that is, instead of a hundred, I found I could get only fifty Guineas a year. I however held the refusal of the school until I tried some experiments. In about ten Days I made a little model, for which I was offered, if I would give up all right and title to it, a Hundred Guineas. I concluded to relinquish my school and turn my attention to perfecting the Machine. I made one before I came away which required the labor of one man to turn it and with which one man will clean ten times as much cotton as he can in any other way before known and also cleanse it much better than in the usual mode. This machine may be turned by water or with a horse, with the greatest ease, and one man and a horse will do more than fifty men with the old machines. It makes the labor fifty times less, without throwing any class of People out of business."

Having formed a partnership with Phineas Miller on the 27th of May, 1793, Whitney set out at once for New England, to further the plans of the firm. On the 20th of June he applied to the Government for a patent. Thomas Jefferson being Secretary of State, the petition duly came to his notice, and at once stirred his always insatiable interest. He wrote to Whitney as follows:

"As the State of Virginia, of which I am, carries on manufactures of cotton to a great extent, as I also do myself and as one of our greatest embarrassments is the cleaning of the cotton of the seed, I feel a considerable interest in the success of your invention, for family use. Permit me therefore to ask information from you on these points. Has the machine been thoroughly tried in the ginning of cotton, or is it yet but a machine of theory? What quantity has it cleaned on an average of several days, and worked by hand, and by how many hands? What will be the cost of one of them made to be worked by hand? Favorable answers to these questions would induce me to engage one of them to be forwarded to Richmond for me."

In a reply dated November 24, 1793, Whitney wrote to Jefferson as follows:

"It is almost a year since I first turned my attention to constructing this machine, at which time I was in the State of Georgia. Within about ten days after my first conception of the plan, I made a small though imperfect model. Experiments with this, encouraged me to make one on a larger scale; but the extreme difficulty of procuring workmen and proper materials in Georgia, prevented my completing the larger one until some time in April last. This, though much larger than my first attempt, is not above one third as large as the machines may be made with convenience.—The cylinder is only two feet two inches in length, and six inches diameter. It is turned *by hand*, and requires the strength of one man to keep it in constant motion. It is the stated task of one negro to clean fifty weight (I mean fifty pounds after it is seperated from the seed), of the green seed cotton per day."

Jefferson assured the inventor that a patent would be granted on the gin as soon as a model could be lodged in the Patent Office, but this transaction was not completed until after he had resigned his position as Secretary of State. On March 14, 1794, Whitney obtained his patent for a cotton gin consisting in spikes driven in a wooden cylinder, and having a slotted bar through which these spiked teeth pass, together with a brush to clear the spikes. It was signed by George Washington, President; Edmund Randolph, Secretary of State; and Wm. Bradford, Attorney.

Two years later—May 12, 1796—a resourceful and practical mechanic of Augusta, Hodgen Holmes by name, secured a patent for a valuable improvement on Whitney's cotton gin, consisting in the substitution of circular saws for wire teeth. Holmes's patent for the saw gin was signed by George Washington, President; Timothy Pickering, Secretary of State; and Chas. Lee, Attorney General. Both of the original records were destroyed in the Patent Office fire of 1836, but authentic copies certified by James Madison as Secretary of State in 1804, are on file in the court house at Savannah.

CHAPTER 33[1]

ELI WHITNEY VS. HODGEN HOLMES

CERTIFIED copies of the patents of Whitney and Holmes happen to be in Savannah because of prolonged litigation between Miller and Whitney on the one hand and numerous alleged trespassers on their rights on the other. The storm centered around Hodgen Holmes, whose cylinders were set with saws instead of spikes. Spikes had torn open the seeds and badly mangled the fiber, while the oil, oozing from out the crushed seeds, soon clogged the gin with moist lint; but all of these difficulties were alleviated by the simple substitution of saws, which cut the lint free without mangling the seeds, so that the original Whitney model was soon by way of being superseded. Instead of adopting the saw cylinder as an improvement by another inventor, Whitney attempted to claim for himself credit for the Hodgen Holmes device. An impartial examination of all the accessible original documents proves him and his partner Miller to have been in the wrong.[2]

[1] See Chapter 31.

[2] The curious reader is referred, for a complete survey of the necessary evidence in this interesting case, to Correspondence of Eli Whitney (M. B. Hammond, editor), in the *American Historical Review* for October, 1897; and to Cotton and Cotton Oil, by D. A. Tompkins: Charlotte, N. C., 1901, ch. ii, and appendix. In the Correspondence, compare especially the letter of Miller dated January 19, 1803, with Whitney's letters of September 11, 1793, and March 7 and October 15, 1803, and note the sharp inconsistencies touching the use of saws on the cylinders.

Whitney's fundamental mistake, out of which other troubles grew, was his attempt in conjunction with Miller to monopolize the whole cotton industry. Refusing to sell any gins, he demanded one out of every three pounds of lint as toll for their use, at a time when lint was selling at an average of thirty cents a pound. At other times he fixed a tax of two hundred dollars or more on every machine in use. As ginning immediately leaped to huge proportions, and as the country had not yet grown accustomed to "trusts," there were numerous protests against Whitney's system from a people who had just won their liberty. For example, Governor Jackson of Georgia in 1800 sent the legislature a message on this subject, from which the following extracts are taken.

"The two important States of Georgia and South Carolina," writes the Governor, "are made tributary to two persons who have obtained patents and who demand, as I am informed, $200.00 for the mere liberty of using a ginning machine, in the erection of which the patentees do not expend one farthing.—Monopolies are odious in all countries, but more particularly in a government like ours.—I do not doubt the power of Congress to grant these exclusive privileges, for the Constitution has vested them with it, but in all cases where they become injurious to the community, they ought to be suppressed, or the parties paid a moderate compensation for the discoveries from the Government granting the patent."

Governor Jackson then proposes that the two Carolinas and Tennessee should be invited to join Georgia in legislation to relieve the cotton States from oppression and at the same time provide fair remnneration for Eli Whitney. Notwithstanding Whitney's firm opposition, this object was finally accomplished in all of these States except Georgia, where Whitney's aggressive litigation interfered with satisfactory adjustment. It can be shown beyond question that he received in royalties $50,000 from South Carolina, at least $30,000 from North Carolina, and about $10,000 from Tennessee, making a total of $90,000.

The inventor was so vexed by his law suits, however, that he never could do justice to the South. During the course of a letter written in 1803 to Judge Josiah Stebbins (wherein he urges his friend to endeavor to remember that he had contemplated the use of saws from the beginning!) Whitney exclaims with some heat: "I have a set of the most Depraved villains to combat and I might almost as well go to *Hell* in search of *Happiness* as apply to a Georgia-Court for Justice."

While there can be no doubt, from the record, that Whitney was frequently the victim of grave injustice, it cannot be doubted on the other hand that he courted antagonism. It seems to be equally clear that Hodgen Holmes deserves a credit for the saw gin, in use to this day, which he is likely never to receive. All of the reference books attribute the saw gin to Whitney, and charge the South with unfairness. As a matter of fact, not only did he receive $90,000 from three States in addition to large private profits, but the courthouse in the very city where Hodgen Holmes lived contains a public tablet in commemoration of Eli Whitney's fame, and one of the most ardent tributes ever paid to his genius came from the lips of Judge Johnson in Georgia, during the trial in which Arthur Fort endeavored to push Holmes's patent too far, by claiming the invalidation of Whitney's patent altogether. A part of the decision, rendered for Whitney, is well worth reading, as its striking statements are altogether true.

"The cotton plant," said Judge Johnson, "furnished clothing to mankind before the age of Herodotus. The green seed is a species much more productive than the black, and by nature adapted to a much greater variety of climate. But by reason of the strong adherence of the fiber to the seed, without the aid of some more powerful machine for separating it, than any formerly known among us, the cultivation of it would never have been made an object. The machine of which Mr. Whitney claims the invention, so facilitates the preparation of this species for use, that the cultivation of it has suddenly become an object of infinitely greater importance than that of the other species ever can be.—With regard to the utility of this discovery, the court would deem it a waste of time to dwell long upon this topic.—From childhood to age it has presented to us a lucrative employment. Individuals who were depressed with poverty and sunk in idleness, have suddenly risen to wealth and respectability. Our debts have been paid off. Our capitals have increased, and our lands trebled themselves in value. We cannot express the weight of the obligation which the country owes to this invention. The extent of it cannot now be seen."

Speaking of Holmes's improvement, Judge Johnson said: "This is certainly a meritorious improvement in the mechanical process of constructing this machine.—Mr. Whitney may not be at liberty to use Mr. Holmes's iron plate; but certainly Mr.

Holmes's improvement does not destroy Mr. Whitney's patent right."

Whitney spent his later years in Connecticut, near the city of New Haven. Here, at the foot of East Rock, he erected machinery for the extensive manufacture of army guns, in which he had long been interested, and amassed a very large fortune. He died January 8, 1825, from an ailment which was probably the outcome of the long journeys he had made into Georgia—riding in an open "sulky" all the way, to prosecute his suits about the gin. The village of Whitneyville, now a part of Hamden, was named for him; but his real monument is the great invention that eventually cost him his life. It is remarkable that this cotton machine, by giving rise to the first American monopoly, involved New England and the South in a dispute of almost sectional proportions, and enticed its inventor from the quiet desk of the scholar to become a purveyor to warfare. The craftsman wove, as it proved, a tangled web; and his adventures held the seeds of prophecy.

CHAPTER 34

COTTON CHANGES THE SOUTH

NUMEROUS and rapid changes of various kinds took place in the South as a result of the new cotton industry. Ramsay's History of South Carolina, published in 1809, throws light on the nature of some of these changes. For example, cotton had by that time trebled the price of land suitable to its growth, —"and when the crop succeeds and the market is favorable, the annual income of those who plant it is double to what it was before the introduction of cotton." [1] Naturally, the agriculture of the South was profoundly affected; diversified crops giving way before the growing dominion of "King Cotton." In the year before the gin was invented, South Carolina exported Indian corn to the extent of nearly one hundred thousand bushels; but before Ramsay wrote his history maize had become an article of import.[2] The cultivation of other export crops speedily fell into decay, including tobacco and barley, flax, hemp, and silk. The farmers of the "up country," who had engaged successfully in the cultivation of cereals without the use of slave labor to any appreciable extent, now joined forces with tide-water planters in the all absorbing interest of the new industry, since the gin had made upland cotton

[1] David Ramsay, The History of South Carolina from Its First Settlement in 1670, to the Year 1808: Charleston, 1809; vol. ii, p. 214.

[2] The same, p. 218.

profitable as well as the sea-island crop; and labor conditions were so vitally affected that the negro population soon overshadowed the white in the "up-country," where, in 1790, the whites had outnumbered the blacks four to one.

Perhaps the most striking economic change that the new industry effected in the South after the re-introduction of slavery was the speedy abandonment of manufactures. Not only was the negro as unfitted for mechanical occupation as he was deft in the manipulation of cotton, but what was the use of nerve-racking investment in elaborate and costly machinery when a land-owner could reap ten per cent net profit from a few negroes and mules and a bushel or two of the magical cotton seed? And yet the South had unusual manufacturing facilities, such as almost inexhaustible iron and coal fields lying near the shores of an abundant water supply, suitable alike for power and for easy transportation. Before the domination of cotton culture due advantage had been taken of these facilities; the census of 1810 (according to Mr. D. A. Tompkins)[3] showing that the manufactured products of Virginia, the Carolinas and Georgia exceeded in variety and value those of all the New England States, with New York thrown in for good measure, while Mr. Victor S. Clark[4] has shown from the same census that more homespun cotton manufactures existed in Virginia, South Carolina and Georgia than in the thirteen other States and territories combined, more flax was spun in Virginia than in any other State, and throughout the South a general activity was mani-

[3] American Commerce, Its Expansion: Charlotte, 1900; pp. 111, 125.

[4] In The South in the Building of the Nation; J. C. Ballagh, editor: Richmond, 1910.

fest in these and allied pursuits. But, for the reason already suggested, manufacture soon fell into decay; the Piedmont region being still dotted with the moldering ruins of iron works and other mills that bear witness to the overwhelming power of the new agricultural absorption. The soil, the climate and the cheap labor were all favorable to agriculture, and particularly to cotton planting, says Mr. Tompkins;[5] and as the people could easily and comfortably live by this occupation alone, they did not care to engage in manufacturing or anything similar. All the work was done by slaves, and agriculture was the only work for which they were fitted. The capital of the people consisted of slaves, and that was a form of capital that could not be invested except in one department of labor. One of the chief reasons for the peaceable prosperity of the South was the freedom from agitators and struggles between labor and capital, caused by conditions wherein labor and capital were one and the same.

Ramsay points out the interesting fact that the farmer without slaves engaged heartily in the production of the early cotton crops, and even attributes to the novel pursuit a distinctly moralizing influence. He says: "The cultivation of the former great staples, particularly rice and indigo, required large capitals. They could not be raised to any considerable purpose but by negroes. In this state of things poor white men were of little account otherwise than as overseers. There were comparatively few of that intermediate and generally most virtuous class which is neither poor nor rich. By the introduction of the new staple the poor became of value, for they generally were or at least might be elevated to this

[5] History of Mecklenburg County, as cited; p. 100.

middle grade of society. Land suitable for cotton was easily attained, and in tracts of every size either to purchase or rent. The culture of it entailed no diseases; might be carried on profitably by individuals or white families without slaves, and afforded employment for children whose labor was of little or no account on rice or indigo plantations. The poor having the means of acquiring property without the degradation of working with slaves, had new and strong incitements to industry. From the acquisition of property the transition was easy to that decent pride of character which secures from low vice, and stimulates to seek distinction by deserving it. As they became more easy in their circumstances, they became more orderly in their conduct. The vices which grew out of poverty and idleness were diminished. In estimating the value of cotton, its capacity to excite industry among the lower classes of people, and to fill the country with an independent industrious yeomanry, is of high importance. It has had a large share in moralizing the poor white people of the country."[6]

[6] History of South Carolina, vol. ii, pp. 448–449.

CHAPTER 35

COTTON AFFECTS NEW ENGLAND [1]

New England was quick to improve the new manufacturing opportunities provided by the Southern production of cotton. The beginning of the factory system had occurred in 1786, under the patronage of Hugh Orr, of Bridgewater, after an unsuccessful attempt had been made at Worcester, in 1780. Tench Coxe, always alert for the encouragement of domestic manufacture, and dissatisfied with the crude spinning-jenny of Christopher Tully (see page 122), had contrived to secure brass models of the Arkwright inventions, which were effecting an industrial revolution in England; but the British Government jealously guarded the novel machinery, and, strictly enforcing its laws against the exportation of models, seized Coxe's trinkets and made way with them; whereupon Mr. Orr instructed the Barr brothers, two Scotch employees familiar with the English spinning system, to reproduce the British devices. The result was a series of three machines for carding, sizing, and spinning, built at a cost of £187, and duly set up in the Orr works at East Bridgewater, where they were visited by thousands. The Massachusetts legislature granted the Barr brothers a bounty of £200 and six tickets in the state lottery "as a reward for their ingenuity in forming

[1] Chief authority: G. S. White, Memoir of Samuel Slater: Philadelphia, 1836.

those machines, and for their public spirit in making them known to the Commonwealth." In the following year a British sailor, Thomas Somers, secured a grant of £20 from the legislature, which was deposited in Mr. Orr's keeping for the construction of an Arkwright water-frame, duly set up as "the State Model," and visited, among others, by the quaker, Moses Brown, of Providence, who subsequently became the friend and patron of Samuel Slater. An unsuccessful attempt was made by Daniel Anthony to duplicate the Arkwright machinery at Providence, Almy A. Brown taking over the apparatus, which Slater was soon to pronounce worthless.

The first permanent cotton factory of New England was erected of brick on the Bass River at Beverly, Massachusetts, in 1787-'88, John Cabot and Joshua Fisher being the principal managers. George Washington, the Virginia weaver, gives an interesting account of this first cotton mill to be built in the United States, in the diary of his journey through New England in 1789:

"In this manufactory, they have the new invented spinning and carding machines. One of the first supplies the warp, and four of the latter, one of which spins eighty-four threads at a time by one person. The cotton is prepared for these machines by being first (lightly) drawn to a thread on the common wheel. There is also another machine for doubling and twisting the threads for particular cloths; this also does many at a time. For winding the cotton from the spindles and preparing it for the warp, there is a reel which expedites the work greatly. A number of looms (fifteen or sixteen) were at work with spring shuttles, which do more than double work. In short, the whole seemed perfect and the cotton stuffs which they turn out excellent of their kind; warp and filling both cotton."

Washington also visited the "Hartford Woollen Manufactory," which had been established in 1788 by thirty-one merchants, found it "going on with spirit," and on the occasion of his first speech to Congress wore a broadcloth suit presented by the owners of the mill.[2] While neither this factory nor the cotton mill at Beverly were commercially successful, the New Englanders persisted in their determination to be independently clothed, so that by the year 1810 nearly every township had its carding and fulling mill. The carded wool was delivered to households for spinning and weaving, after which it was returned to the mill for fulling and dressing. North says that in Vermont alone, in 1810, 1,040,000 yards of cloth and flannel were woven by families and dressed in these mills.[3]

Samuel Slater, whom Andrew Jackson called "the father of American manufactures," found a receptive environment when he came to New England from England in 1789, with models of the Arkwright machinery in his brain only, and set up his successful Pawtucket factory the next year, just in the nick of time for the flood of "vegetable wool" from the South. Four years after Whitney's invention there were four cotton factories in operation; five years later there were fifteen, with 20,000 spindles; the manufacture leaping to four times that number of spindles by 1811, and to half a million by the year 1815, employing $40,000,000 capital, 100,000 workmen, and paying $15,000,000 in annual wages.[4]

[2] Bishop, as cited, vol. i, p. 418.
[3] North, as cited, pp. 465–466.
[4] Bishop, as cited, vol. ii, p. 214.

The large majority of these factories were in New England, where the predisposition of the people was furthered by investment in the new industry of capital released from shipping interests through the results of the Embargo and the British blockade. In addition to the huge Southern exports of raw cotton, which leaped to such enormous volume immediately after the invention of the gin, the South was able also to feed these new mills of New England, providing 500 bales for domestic manufacture in 1800, doubling that quantity in five years, bringing it up to 10,000 bales by 1810, and to 90,000 bales in 1815, by which time the capital invested in the combined cotton and woolen manufacture amounted to fifty-two million dollars. The New England cotton industry was driven toward its climax of development through the introduction of the power-loom in 1814 by Francis C. Lowell, who for the first time assembled in one building the several processes of spinning and weaving, establishing at Waltham "the first complete factory in the world."

Thus the Industrial Revolution in England cooperated with an unexampled cotton production in America to bring about the political revolution of the United States. The South, becoming suddenly rich and solidified through the sale to British mills of its huge slave-produced crop, abandoned manufacture to become an enormous plantation. New England, on the other hand, having succeeded at last in acquiring possession of the machinery that had revolutionized England, took enough of the new Southern crop to keep its spindles profitably busy, and led the rest of the North in the development of manufacturing enterprise. Two great sections emerged, more and more socially divergent through the ramifying influences of slavery, and with opposed economic interests due largely to the fact that while one section farmed a certain plant, the other manufactured it. From these opposed interests arose divergent political policies, the South, now conscious of its strong solidarity, alining itself on the side of free trade and States-rights, while the manufacturing North preferred protection and became the defender of the Union. The Great Controversies that ensued, which were really the intellectual fighting out of the war, were all concerned with the extension of national territory, which involved slavery simply because slavery was involved in the extension of cotton lands. But Arachne had overreached herself. Enmeshing as she did four million slaves in her web, the human race could not look on passionless and indifferent. And so the war was fought, to prove that cotton is *not* king, and to suggest to the future that instead of permitting himself to become embroiled by economic forces in destructive warfare, man must rise to an intelligent understanding and a rational control of these forces, and be the master of his own social destiny.

BOOK IV

COTTON IN AMERICAN HISTORY: THE GREAT CONTROVERSIES

CHAPTER 36[1]

PROTECTION AND FREE TRADE; ANOTHER REVERSAL

SINGULARLY enough, before the development of the cotton industry the South had inclined toward protection, while New England favored free trade. Although the Virginians, Jefferson and Madison, originally extolled the virtues of a free interchange of commodities, they united in 1793 in the advocacy of vigorous measures of protection directed against England; and so zealous a convert did Madison become to Hamilton's economic doctrine, that in laying before Congress the treaty of peace in 1815 he called attention to the "unparalleled maturity" attained by manufactures, and "anxiously recommended this source of national independence and wealth to the prompt and constant guardianship of Congress."

The Protective Tariff of 1816 was introduced by Lowndes of South Carolina, and ably defended by Calhoun, who declared that manufactures produced an interest strictly American, and "calculated to bind the widely separated Republic more closely together, greatly increasing mutual dependence and intercourse." Through the signature of Madison this Tariff became a law. In fact, the Southern cotton growers were among the first and chief beneficiaries of the original protective Act passed by the very first Congress in 1789, through a provision advocated by Tench Coxe that imposed a duty of three cents a

[1] Chief authority: O. L. Elliott, as cited.

pound on cotton of foreign growth, which manufacturers were then importing from Brazil and the West Indies instead of using the sea-island home product. Only John Randolph of Virginia had the penetration to discern that the South-fostered Tariff of 1816 would work an economic hardship on the South. "The agriculturist," he said, "has his property, his lands, his all, his household goods to defend. Upon whom bears the duty on coarse woollens and linens and blankets, upon salt and all the necessaries of life? Upon poor men and upon slaveholders!"

New England, represented by Daniel Webster, opposed the Protective Tariff of 1816. Goldwin Smith says that there is nothing better on the side of free trade than some of Webster's early speeches.[2] "This 'favorite American policy,' sir," said Webster in Congress, combating Clay, "is what America has never tried, and this odious foreign policy is what we are told foreign states have never pursued. Sir, that is the truest American policy which shall most usefully employ American capital and American labor, and best sustain the whole population. With me it is a fundamental axiom that is interwoven with all my opinions that the great interests of the country are united and inseparable, that agriculture, commerce, and manufactures will prosper together or languish together, and that all legislation is dangerous which proposes to benefit one of these without looking to consequences which may fall on the others. I know it would be very easy to promote manufactures, at least for a time, but probably only for a short time. If we might act in disregard of other interests we could cause a sudden transfer of capital and a violent change in the

[2] The United States, as cited, p. 186.

pursuits of men. We could exceedingly benefit some classes by these means; what then would become of the interests of others?"

This was in 1816. When the Tariff enacted in that year came up for revision in 1824 Webster was still opposed to it, denying the necessity for increased protection to manufactures, and disputing its adequacy, if granted, to the relief of the country where distress prevailed. But in 1828, when the "Tariff of Abominations" was proposed, he frankly changed front; while Calhoun also had swung squarely about, appearing now as a strenuous foe of protection. The two powerful debaters were opposed to each other, indeed, just as in 1816; but now each was standing in the other's shoes, having completely reversed their positions, each opposing what he had formerly defended, and supporting the side he had previously opposed. Webster's own words explain his reversal:

"New England, sir, has not been a leader in this policy (of protection). The opinion of New England up to 1824 was founded in the conviction that, on the whole, it was wisest and best, both for herself and others, that manufactures should make haste slowly.—When, at the commencement of the late war, duties were doubled, we were told that we should find a mitigation of the weight of taxation in the new aid and succor which would be thus afforded to our own manufacturing labor. Like arguments were urged, and prevailed, but not by the aid of New England votes, when the tariff was afterwards arranged, at the close of the war in 1816. Finally, after a whole winter's deliberation, the act of 1824 received the sanction of both Houses of Congress and settled the policy of the country. What, then, was New England to do?—Was she to hold out forever against the course of the Government, and see herself losing on one side, and yet make no effort to sustain herself on the other? No, sir. Nothing was left to New England, after the act of 1824, but to conform herself to the will of others. Nothing was left to her, but to consider that the government had fixed and determined its own policy; and that policy was *protection.*"[3]

Senator Lodge, in his biography of Webster, offers this comment:—"The speech which he made on this occasion is a celebrated one, but it is so solely on account of the startling change of position which it announced.—Opinion in New England changed for good and sufficient business reasons, and Mr. Webster changed with it. Free trade had commended itself to him as an abstract principle, and he had sustained and defended it as in the interest of commercial New England. But when the weight of interest in New England shifted from free trade to protection Mr. Webster followed it."[4]

Calhoun was neither better nor worse. Both of them simply swung true to the economic interests of their respective constituencies.[5]

[3] Writings and Speeches: Boston, 1903.

[4] H. C. Lodge, Daniel Webster: Boston, 1895; pp. 165, 167.

[5] Free trade became a leading economic interest of the South not only because the huge export business in cotton made it desirable to load the empty ships with cheap foreign supplies for the return voyage, but also because the need of all kinds of manufactured articles was greatly intensified by the decline of Southern manufacture due to absorption in cotton cultivation (see pp. 169–170). As Ashley says, Southern political leaders began about this time to be convinced that the policy of protection was undermining the interests of the South, while building up those of the North at the expense of the slave States. High tariffs, they said, were valuable only for manufacturing districts. "Naturally, in South Carolina and some other States there was a growing sentiment that the Constitution did not give Congress the right to pass a tariff which protected one section only."—R. L. Ashley, American History: New York, 1914; pp. 305–306.

CHAPTER 37

NEW ENGLAND AND THE SOUTH

THE shifting of this New England "weight of interest" of which Senator Lodge speaks was from commerce and transportation to manufacture. The War of 1812 had lamed the carrying power of New England, and forced her away from shipping investments deeper and deeper into the manufacturing opportunities provided by English invention of cotton machinery on the one hand and by Southern production of cotton on the other. In 1816, when Webster opposed protection, there was a capital of only about $52,000,000 [1] invested in textile manufacture, of which much still lay in the South. In 1828, when he reversed his position, this capital had probably doubled,[2] and had become localized in and about New England.[3] Massachusetts led with 260 mills and factories, representing an investment of thirty million dollars; Rhode Island followed with 150 mills, employing thirty thousand operatives; New Hampshire supported sixty cotton mills, 300 tanneries, 200 bark factories, and ten paper mills; Vermont manufactured copper, iron, and wool; New York was engaged in diversified industries, while New Jersey had gone largely into the cotton and wool manufacture, and in one county of Pennsyl-

1 Bishop, as cited, ii, 214.

2 Bishop, ii, 357, 360; and J. B. McMaster, in Cambridge Modern History, vii, 375.

3 Bogart, as cited, p. 149.

vania there were 157 mills and factories, with 4,000 weavers earning a livelihood in the city of Philadelphia alone.[4]

If we anticipate a little, we find that by the year 1830 the United States was second only to England in the amount of cotton consumed in manufacture, while the constantly increasing localization of this industry is shown by the fact that by the year 1840 three-fourths of all American cotton goods were produced by New England mills.[5]

These figures indicate an immense change from the census of 1810, which showed the South to be the leading manufacturing section of the country (see page 169). But while Southern manufactures had declined, agriculture, denoting preëminently the cultivation of cotton, had made progress no less amazing than the advance of New England manufacture. Figures showing the economic position of the South at the time of the great Tariff struggle are strikingly displayed in Wilson's valuable work entitled "Division and Reunion." Of the total value of exports of all kinds from the United States in 1829, amounting to $55,700,193, the South furnished $34,072,655 in cotton, tobacco, and rice. The contribution of the South appears still more striking if it be compared with the total value of the agricultural exports only, which was a little under $44,000,000. Three-fourths of the agricultural exports of the country, in short, came from the South; and very nearly three-fifths of *all* the exports. The value of the exports of manufactured articles reached only about $6,000,000. High duties on hemp and flax, on wool, on lead and iron, meant that those who contributed most to the external com-

[4] McMaster, as just cited. [5] Bogart, as cited, p. 149.

merce of the country were to have their markets restricted for the benefit of those who contributed very little. The total value of the exports of cotton was $26,575,311; that of cotton manufactured goods exported, only $1,258,000. It seemed evident that the South was to suffer almost in direct proportion as other sections of the country gained advantage from tariff legislation.[6] Being inhibited from domestic manufacture by the incapacity of her labor supply, as well as by the more lucrative opportunities of agriculture, the South faced the double disaster, should the "Tariff of Abominations" be enacted, of the further restraint of that foreign trade on which her prosperity depended, and of taxation for the benefit of New England by precisely the amount of the duty rates.

McMaster says: "The real purpose of the proposed tariff was to force capital into channels in which it could not naturally flow, and to produce a ruinous change in the pursuits of the Southern people.—Of the 600,000 bales of cotton sold annually, two-thirds were sent to foreign countries, which sent in return almost every manufactured article used in the South. The duties contemplated would therefore fall with especial severity on the South, and were in the nature of a tax on the industry of one part of the country for the benefit of the manufactures of another."[7]

The bill of 1828 originated in the agitation of the woolen manufacturers of New England, being chiefly designed to favor that branch of industry, and suggesting on a small scale the political struggle occasioned by the two rival fibers in England (See Book

[6] Wilson, as cited, p. 50.
[7] Cambridge Modern History, vii, 376.

II). It was called the "Tariff of Abominations," says W. G. Sumner, "on account of the number of especially monstrous provisions which it contained."[8] McMaster, in fact, says that the bill was reported with the expectation that it never would pass. "Indeed, it was carefully prepared to invite defeat, for in 1828 a President was to be elected; and each party, fearing to pass the bill, sought to throw the odium of defeat on the other. But the bill, with all its excessive duties on raw materials and imported manufactures, passed both Houses of Congress, and was accepted by the President."[9] John Randolph caustically remarked that it "referred to manufactures of no sort or kind except the manufacture of a President of the United States."[10]

[8] Andrew Jackson as a Public Man: Boston, 1883; ch. ix; cited by Larned, iv, 3071.

[9] Cambridge Modern History, vii, 377.

[10] A. B. Hart, Formation of the Union: New York, 1909; p. 258.

CHAPTER 38

COTTON EXPORTS AND THE TARIFF

South Carolina, as Wilson points out, was entitled to be spokesman for the South in opposition to the "Tariff of Abominations," her exports at this period reaching the sum of $8,175,586,—figures exceeded only by the values of New York and Louisiana, and, by a few thousands, by those of Massachusetts.[1] Anti-tariff meetings were at once held throughout the South, and the ships in Charleston harbor flew their flags at half mast. Senator Hayne informed the Charleston Chamber of Commerce "that the rich manufacturers of the North originated the bill, in order that they might secure a monopoly of the home market and enhance their profits; and that nothing but a firm remonstrance from the planting States could prevent the ruin of the South." Whereupon the Charleston Chamber sent to Congress a remonstrance denouncing the proposed tariff as "unjust and unconstitutional."

"Have you," asked another memorial, "ascertained beyond the possibility of deception how far the patience of the people of the South exceeds their indignation, and at what precise point resistance may begin and submission end?"[2]

[1] Division and Reunion, p. 50.
[2] Cambridge Modern History, vii, pp. 376–378.

Governor Hamilton, in response to numerous petitions, appointed a day of fasting, humiliation, and prayer. How tensely the sectional lines were drawn is shown by the fact that in the presidential election which now took place, in all the States south of the Potomac River Adams failed to receive a single electoral vote, while throughout New England Jackson received but one. The election of Jackson was acclaimed by the South, whose spokesman in the person of John C. Calhoun now advanced the argument known as the South Carolina Exposition, declaring the tariff laws of 1828 to be unconstitutional, oppressive, and unequal, and calling a state convention in order to "decide in what manner they ought to be declared null and void within the limits of the State, which solemn declaration would be obligatory on our own citizens."

This document set forth the declaration that there was a permanent dissimilarity between the South and the rest of the Union, since the Southern States were "staple States," exclusively devoted to agriculture, and destined always to remain so because of their "soil, climate, habits, and peculiar labor," whose advantage could never coincide with the advantage of the majority of the States in respect of the commercial policy of the country. The Federal Constitution being a "compact," it is within the power of a minority State to veto the legislation in question, and suspend its operation. Nevertheless, it is inexpedient to adopt measures of suspension at once; time should be allowed for "further consideration and reflection, in the hope that a returning sense of justice on the part of the majority, when they came to reflect on the wrongs which this and the other staple States have suffered and are suffering, may repeal the obnoxious and unconstitutional Acts, and thereby prevent the necessity of interposing the veto of the State."[3]

In the same year (1828) Georgia instructed her governor, should the tariff law not be repealed, to appoint delegates to a convention of the Southern States in order "to deliberate upon and devise a suitable mode of resistance to that unjust, unconstitutional, and oppressive law," while Mississippi and Virginia adopted similar measures.[4]

To such a pitch had the sectional-economic controversy mounted; and, following as it did the Missouri Compromise of 1820, this tariff agitation developed swiftly into the great debates that found their ultimate determination in civil war. The South, instead of being foremost for the Union as at the time of the Constitutional Convention, was now becoming the lusty exponent of States-rights, although Calhoun was not yet prepared to go as far as Josiah Quincy went (see page 194) in pressing this point to its issue.

General Jackson proved a strong friend of the Union, and paid little heed to the logic or persuasiveness of his colleague, Vice-President Calhoun. When, shortly after his inauguration, a representative from South Carolina, in calling on Jackson, asked whether he had any commands for his friends in South Carolina,

"Yes, I have," he replied; "please give my compliments to my friends in your State, and say to them that if a single drop of blood shall be shed there in opposition to the laws of the United States, I will hang the first man I can lay my hand on en-

[3] Wilson, Division and Reunion, p. 57.
[4] Cambridge Modern History, vii, pp. 380–381.

gaged in such treasonable conduct, upon the first tree I can reach."[5]

Later, he denounced Nullification as "incompatible with the existence of the Union" and called on the South Carolinians to yield.—"The laws of the United States must be executed. I have no discretionary power on the subject,—my duty is emphatically pronounced in the Constitution. Those who have told you that you might peacefully prevent their execution deceived you.—Their object is disunion, and disunion by armed force is treason."[6]

In 1832 Congress undertook to return substantially to the Tariff of 1824. But before this action of Congress could become effective, and after the threatening exchange of wrathful proclamations and counter-proclamations between Jackson and Governor Hayne, Clay succeeded (1833) in the passage of a compromise measure, based on a horizontal rate, which placated South Carolina while it "saved the protective principle" and maintained the rights of the Union. The Force Bill of Jackson, intended for the execution of the former obnoxious tariff laws by military power, if necessary, now became a dead letter: whereupon South Carolina repealed her ordinance nullifying the tariff laws, but at the same time "saved the principle" of States-rights by passing another ordinance nullifying the moribund Force Bill!

It seems already quite evident that even the deft compromises of the highly ingenious Clay cannot long weave together the raveling threads of a Union between two sections whose main object in the yield-

[5] Division and Reunion, p. 172.
[6] Division and Reunion, p. 61.

ing of policy is the salvation of contradictory principles.

NOTE. The extent to which cotton now dominated the commerce of the South may be gathered from the humorous "impressions of a traveler" printed in the *Courier* of Augusta, Ga., Oct. 11, 1827:

"A plague o' this Cotton.

"When I took my last walk along the wharves in Charleston, and saw them piled up with mountains of Cotton, and all your stores, ships, steam and canal boats crammed with and groaning under, the weight of Cotton, I returned to the Planters' Hotel, where I found the four daily papers, as well as the conversation of the boarders, teeming with Cotton! Cotton!! Cotton!!! Thinks I to myself, 'I'll soon change this scene of cotton.' But, alas! How easily deceived is short-sighted man! Well, I got into my gig and wormed my way up through Queen, Meeting, King and St. Philip's streets, dodging from side to side, to steer clear of the Cotton waggons, and came to the New Bridge Ferry. Here I crossed over in the Horse-boat, with several empty cotton waggons, and found a number on the other side, loaded with cotton, going to town. From this I continued on, meeting with little else than cotton fields, cotton gins, cotton waggons—but 'the wide, the unbounded prospect lay before me!' I arrived in Augusta; and when I saw cotton-waggons in Broad-street, I whistled! but said nothing!!! But this was not all; there was more than a dozen tow boats in the river, with more than a thousand bales of cotton on each; and several steam-boats with still more. And you must know, that they have cotton warehouses there covering whole squares, all full of cotton; and some of the knowing ones told me, that there were then in the place from 40,000 to 50,000 bales. And Hamburg (as a negro said) was worser, according to its size; for it puzzled me to tell which was the largest, the piles of cotton or the houses. I now left Augusta; and overtook hordes of cotton planters from North Carolina, South Carolina, and Georgia, with large gangs of negroes, bound to Alabama, Mississippi and Louisiana; 'where the cotton land is not worn out.'—I crossed over to Mobile in a small steam boat loaded up to the top of the smoke-pipe with cotton. This place is a receptacle monstrous for the article. Look which way you will you see it; and see it moving; keel boats, steam boats, ships, brigs, schooners, wharves, stores, and press-houses, all appeared to be full; and I believe that in the three days that I was there, boarding with about one hundred cotton factors, cotton merchants, and cotton planters, I must have heard the word cotton pronounced more than 3,000 times.

"From Mobile I went to New Orleans in a schooner, and she was stuffed full of cotton.—I don't know how many hundred thousand bales of cotton there were in New Orleans; but I was there only six days, in which time there arrived upwards of 20,000 bales,—and when we dropped out into the stream in a steam-boat, to ascend the river, the levee for a mile up and down, opposite the shipping, where they were walking bales on end, looked as if it was alive.—From New Orleans to the mouth of Tennessee River, we passed about thirty steam-boats, and more than half of them laden with cotton.—I passed to Nashville; and on my way saw an abundance of cotton and cottonfields.—They calculate on 40 or 50,000 bales of cotton going from Nashville this season.—After seeing, hearing, and dreaming of nothing but cotton for seventy days and seventy nights, I began to anticipate relief. For, on the route I took, whether by night or by day or by stage or by steam boat, wake up when or where you would, you were sure to hear a dissertation on cotton."—Cited in Documentary History (as cited), pp. 283–288.

CHAPTER 39

THE CONSTITUTIONAL DILEMMA †

THE fact that the Constitution was a complex of compromises [1] had begun to bear fruit very soon after its adoption. The great instrument offered plenty of handles for disgruntled statesmen or States that might wish to assert individual liberty against the prerogatives of Union. Madison, in spite of his firm stand for the rights of the Union in the Constitutional Convention of 1787 joined with Jefferson in 1798 in the preparation of Resolutions aimed at Federalist policies. These Resolutions not only formulated the "compact" theory of government, afterwards developed by Calhoun and enunciated also by Hayne, but even anticipated Calhoun's doctrine of Nullification. Declaring the Constitution to be a compact to which the States were parties, and that "each party has an equal right to judge for itself as well of infractions as of the mode and measure of redress," they denounced certain statutes as "not law—void and of no effect;" while the Kentucky Resolutions of 1799, prepared by Jefferson, asserted that "the several States who formed the Constitution, being sovereign, independent, have the unquestionable right to judge its infractions; and a nullification by those sovereigns of all un-

† See also chapters 51–54.

[1] See Alexander Johnston, American Political History, 1763–1876: New York, 1912; vol. ii, pp. 101 ff, 337.

authorized acts done under color of that instrument, is the rightful remedy."[2]

But Nullification and Secession had not at that early time become a localized doctrine; New England, when the need arose, did not hesitate to conjure their spectral wraith from the vasty deeps of the Constitutional oracle. As spokesman for Massachusetts in opposing the admission of Louisiana in 1811 Josiah Quincy said in the House of Representatives: "I am compelled to declare it as my deliberate opinion, that, if this bill passes, the bonds of this union are, virtually, dissolved; that the States which compose it are free from their moral obligations, and that as it will be the right of all, so it will be the duty of some, to prepare, definitely, for a separation: amicably, if they can; violently, if they must."[3]

Just as there is no indication that the Virginia and Kentucky Resolutions were deemed treasonable when they were passed, or that they even seem to have shocked the public feeling of the day, so on this occasion the House of Representatives saw nothing in Quincy's speech to warrant a reprimand. Two years later (1813) when Massachusetts was opposing the war with England, Quincy became spokesman before the state legislature to the effect that "it is not becoming a moral and religious people to express any approbation of military or moral exploits which are not immediately connected with the defense of our sea-coast and soil;" and in the following year the Massachusetts legislature received a report which adopted almost literally the word-

[2] See Hart's Formation of the Union, p. 171.

[3] Alexander Johnston, American Orations; Studies in American Political History: New York, 1906; vol. i, p. 182.

ing of Madison's Virginia Resolutions of 1798.—"Whenever the national compact is violated, and the citizens of the State oppressed by cruel and unauthorized laws, this legislature is bound to interpose its power and wrest from the oppressor his victim."[4]

Hart says that in 1814 "the time seemed to have arrived when the protests of New England against the continuance of the war might be made effective. The initiative was taken by Massachusetts, which, on October 16, voted to raise a million dollars to support a state army of 10,000 troops, and to ask the other New England States to meet in convention."[5]

This Hartford Convention in its formal report declared that the Constitution had been violated and that "States which have no common umpire must be their own judges and execute their own decisions." "Behind the whole document," says Hart, "was the implied intention to withdraw from the Union" if Congress refused to meet the New England demands. No one knows what would have happened had not the deputies who were to present this virtual ultimatum to Congress been checked by the declaration of peace.

Discussing the subject of state sovereignty and the right of secession, Goldwin Smith[6] has aptly said: "The Constitution was on this point a Delphic oracle. Its framers had blinked the question of state sovereignty, as they had compromised on that of slavery. They trusted to time, and had slavery been out of the way, time would have done the work." It is easy to understand the alarm of

[4] Cited in Hart's Formation of the Union, p. 216.
[5] Hart, as just cited, p. 217.
[6] As cited, p. 248.

the aged Jefferson when the silenced question of slavery suddenly became politically clamorous in 1820, disturbing the peace of Monroe's administration, as Jefferson said, "like a fire-bell in the night." In a letter to John Holmes, dated April 22, 1820, he wrote:

"I had for a long time ceased to read newspapers, or pay any attention to public affairs, confident they were in good hands, and content to be a passenger in our bark to the shore from which I am not distant. But this momentous question, like a fire-bell in the night, awakened and filled me with terror. I considered it at once as the knell of the Union.—A geographical line, coinciding with a marked principle, moral and political, once conceived and held up to the angry passions of men, will never be obliterated, and every new irritation will mark it deeper and deeper."[7]

[7] Cited by Elliott, pp. 234–235, note.

CHAPTER 40

THE STRUGGLE FOR FRESH COTTON LANDS

While the acquisition of the Louisiana territory in 1803 had far more than doubled the area of the slave system, and in fact more than doubled the area of the United States, it evoked little controversy on the subject of slavery, as was the case also when Louisiana sought admission as a State in 1811. Josiah Quincy's speech on the latter occasion seems to have been prompted not by antagonism to slavery so much as by his resentment at the prospect of mixing the "rights and liberties and property of this people into 'hotch-pot' with the wild men on the Missouri" and with the "race of Anglo-Hispano-Gallo Americans who bask on the sands in the mouth of the Mississippi."[1] Alexander Johnston, however, is probably correct in his statement that the Congress of 1803–'05, which impliedly legitimated the domestic slave trade to Louisiana, and legalized slavery wherever population should extend between the Mississippi and the Rocky Mountains, should rightfully bear the responsibility for all the subsequent growth of slavery, and for all the difficulties in which it involved the South and the country.[2]

Directly out of this Act of Congress grew the *Missouri Compromise* of 1820, the *Compromise of* 1850, and the *Repeal of the Missouri Compromise*

[1] A. Johnston, Orations, as cited; i, 198.
[2] The same, ii, 8.

in 1854, which, with the *Admission of Texas* in 1845, occasioned the series of great Congressional debates that preceded the Civil War.

It is only fair to the Congress of 1803–'05 however, to bear in mind that at the time of the Louisiana acquisition its enormous effect on the extension of slavery was not understood,[3] for the simple reason that the availability of the Mississippi Valley for cotton cultivation was not yet appreciated.[4] While some cotton had been raised in the Louisiana territory before its purchase by the United States, this plant was then regarded as the peculiar pet of the uplands, and it was not until during the "twenties" that the discovery was made of the rich adaptability of prairie lands and river bottoms to the successful production of cotton on an enormous scale. In 1811 this region raised but five million pounds of cotton; ten years later its product was sixty million pounds; and in 1826 its fields were white with a crop of over one hundred and fifty million pounds.[5] "By the side of the picture of the advance of the pioneer farmer," says Turner, "must be placed the picture of the Southern planter crossing the forests of Western Georgia, Alabama, and Mississippi, or passing over the free State of Illinois to the Missouri Valley, in his family carriage, with servants, packs of hunting dogs, and a train of slaves, their nightly camp-fires lighting up the wilderness where so recently the Indian hunter had held possession."[6]

Freely the slaves were poured in from the old

[3] J. F. Rhodes, History of the U. S. from the Compromise of 1850: New York, 1906; i, 28.

[4] Hammond's Cotton Industry, as cited, p. 50.

[5] The Rise of the New West: New York, 1906; p. 94.

[6] The same, p. 92.

South—250,000 in a single year—and by the year 1830 the Western country had outstripped the seaboard States in the production of cotton. "Soon thereafter a capital of $55,000,000 was applied to the cultivation of cotton lands in the new States, within three years; and during that same brief period the output of cotton in these States was almost doubled." W. B. Hammond [7] thinks that the expanding geographical distribution of slaves and of cotton cultivation affords the most striking evidence of the close connection of the two institutions that can be had; the lines for the gradual spread of slavery over the map coinciding almost exactly with those suitable for the extension of cotton: as if this plant-king were literally leading the human captives in his train. Between 1830 and 1850 the slave population of Maryland decreased and that of Virginia remained stationary, while, as Rhodes points out, Louisiana more than doubled, Alabama nearly trebled, and Mississippi almost quintupled their number of slaves.[8]

Naturally, the desire for new cotton lands had much to do with the Southern movement for the acquisition of additional national territory, and as negroes were deemed to be absolutely essential to the successful cultivation of this great money crop, every Congressional discussion about new lands inevitably became a slavery controversy. The desire of Southern planters for fresh lands was greatly intensified by the shiftless and unscientific character of slave agriculture, which resulted, notwithstanding the fact that cotton exhausts the soil less than any other of the great staples, in a rapid wearing

[7] The Cotton Industry, p. 59.
[8] As cited, i, 315.

out of the lands where it was grown, without rotation, one year after another. Undoubtedly this economic argument influenced the South in favoring the admission of Texas; and probably the same consideration, in spite of the rhetorical denial of Toombs, was influential in the movement for the purchase of Cuba, which led Seward to his gruff remark in the Senate: "The Cuba bill is the question of slaves for the slave-holders." Rhodes thinks that if Cuba had been acquired, no doubt can exist that it would have been admitted into the Union as one or more slave States.[9]

However this may be, there can be no question whatever that it was the extension of the national territory that occasioned the increasingly bitter debates centering around the years 1820, 1845, 1850, and 1854, which, in their turn, brought about a development of increasingly divergent political theories on subjects of vital importance. The first debate, which startled the prophetic vision of Jefferson and produced the "Missouri Compromise," afforded the first clear demarcation between the two sections. To clarify the Congressional action which had accompanied the acquisition of the huge Louisiana country, a literal geographical and political dividing line was now drawn westward from the southern boundary of Missouri, admitted as a slave State with the proviso that in no other part of the territory acquired from France in 1803 north of 36° 30′ should there be slavery or involuntary servitude. The Northern States, although they had not opposed the admission of the Southern district centering around New Orleans as slave territory in 1812, now resisted the admission of the Northern district cen-

[9] As cited, ii, 350–352.

tering around St. Louis as the slave State of Missouri; but their resistance was countered by the ingenuity of Thomas of Illinois and the strategic manipulation of Clay, Maine being at the same time admitted as a free State so as to maintain equilibrium.

The maintenance of a geographical "balance of power" henceforth became a matter of vital concern to the South, which began to recognize its profound estrangement from the North, and the consequent conclusion that only by an equalized Congressional representation could it hope for the preservation of its interests.

NOTE. Professor Turner, in his Rise of the New West (page 47) presents a valuable table which shows both the enormous increase in the cotton crop during the period under consideration, and also its extension into the fresh cotton lands:

COTTON CROP

(In million pounds)

	1791	*1801*	*1811*	*1821*	*1826*	*1834*
South Carolina	1.5	20.	40.	50.	70.	65.5
Georgia	.5	10.	20.	45.	75.	75.
Virginia		5.	8.	12.	25.	10.
North Carolina		4.	7.	10.	10.	9.5
Total	*2.*	*39.*	*75.*	*117.*	*180.*	*160.*
Tennessee		1.	3.	20.	45.	45.
Louisiana			2.	10.	38.	62.
Mississippi				10.	20.	85.
Alabama				20.	45.	85.
Florida					2.	20.
Arkansas					.5	.5
Total		*1.*	*5.*	*60.*	*150.5*	*297.5*
Grand Total	*2.*	*40.*	*80.*	*177.*	*330.5*	*457.5*

CHAPTER 41

SOUTHERN NATIONALISM

This recognition of sectional estrangement from the North coöperated with the economic tendency in favor of land expansion to produce a Southern sentiment toward nationalism in the direction of the West. Cotton had much to do with the building of the first railroad using an American locomotive in the regular service—the South Carolina railway, connecting Charleston with the head of navigation on the Savannah River (begun in 1830, completed in 1833), for the purpose of deflecting the raw material from its course down the river to Savannah, and for the further ambitious purpose of strengthening connections with the West. The road was extended to Augusta, then to Atlanta and Chattanooga under the name of the "Western and Atlantic;" and finally the "Charleston and Memphis" was built from Chattanooga to Memphis, whereupon a through train was run over the entire line, carrying a company of Memphis and Charleston citizens and also a barrel of water from the Mississippi River, which was emptied into the bay of Charleston to symbolize the future connections of commerce.[1] General Hayne, the great colleague of Calhoun and antagonist of Webster, was deeply interested in promoting the construction of a through line from Charleston to Cincinnati, with the expectation that

[1] Tompkins, American Commerce, as cited, pp. 113–114.

by deflecting the immense tide of export commerce from Pittsburgh and the Middle West down the Ohio to Cincinnati and thence by rail to Charleston, this port could be lifted from its already notable standing among American cities to a position second to none.

While this Cincinnati project has only succeeded within recent years, a great Western traffic was built up by the early railroads, which stimulated the extension of cotton culture and in return reduced the cost of Southern living through a plentiful supply of Western "hog and hominy." From 1845 to 1860 the South built more miles of railroad than the New England and Middle States together, and expended over $60,000,000 on mills and factories. In Alabama there was "a sort of frenzy" over railroads in the middle of the 'fifties.

Water traffic also developed. In the lower South, as Brown says, the steamboats, plying all the navigable rivers, enlivening the forests with their steam calliopes, and brightening the lowlands at night with their brilliant cabin lights, were the chief representatives of modern methods of transportation. Cotton was hauled from the plantation to the nearest river bluff, the bales went sliding down an incline to the waiting steamboat, and so passed on to Mobile, New Orleans, Boston, Liverpool. The planter perhaps followed his crop as far as Mobile or New Orleans, made a settlement with his agent, enjoyed his annual outing, and returned with his supplies for another year, not neglecting a proper provision for the fortnight's feasting and jollity at the approaching Christmastide.[2] As for South

[2] W. G. Brown, The Lower South in American History: New York, 1902; pp. 36–37.

Carolina and the West, so early as 1826 there were ten steamboats plying between Charleston and the towns of Columbia, Cheraw, Georgetown, Hamburg, Augusta, and Savannah, having an average capacity of six hundred cotton bales, thus extending the facilities of the railroads and tending to make the South independent of the North Atlantic States by a system of free trade with the West.

Wilson writes of this period with keen insight: "Southern politicians, indeed, were busy debating sectional issues; but Southern merchants presently fell to holding conventions in the interest of the new industrial development. These conventions spoke very heartily the language of nationality; they planned railways to the Pacific; they invited the co-operation of the Western States in devising means for linking the two sections industrially together; they hoped to be able to run upon an equality with the other sections of the country in the race for industrial wealth. But in all that they said there was an undertone of disappointment and of apprehension. They wished to take part, but could not, in what was going forward in the rest of the country. They spoke hopefully of national enterprise, but it was evident that the nation of which they were thinking when they spoke was not the same nation that the Northern man had in mind when he thought of the future of industry."[3]

Even in its influence in behalf of a Southern nationalism, cotton pointed westward, and thereby lent itself to a further estrangement between South and North.

[3] Division and Reunion, as cited, p. 164.

CHAPTER 42

TEXAS AND THE WILMOT PROVISO

THE second great sectional struggle occurred twenty-five years after the Missouri Compromise, in connection with the admission of Texas in 1845. No particular stir was occasioned by the admission in the same year of Iowa and Florida, which maintained the equilibrium theory, as had been the case with Michigan and Arkansas in 1836. But to admit Texas would be "to add to the area of slavery an enormous territory, big enough for the formation of eight or ten States of the ordinary size, and thus to increase tremendously the political influence of the Southern States and the slave-holding class. For this the Northern members of Congress were not prepared."[1] John Quincy Adams led a Northern body of opinion to the effect that the annexation of Texas would bring about and fully justify a dissolution of the Union, while William Lloyd Garrison met hearty applause when he proposed in Boston that Massachusetts should actually secede. On the other hand, "Texas or disunion" was the rallying cry of Southern extremists, who, under the conditions to which cotton culture had now advanced, regarded the Garrison program of abolition as "nothing less than a proposal to destroy, root and branch, the whole industry of that section."

Texas came in as a cotton State in December, but

[1] Wilson, Division and Reunion, p. 143.

in August of the following year David Wilmot, of Pennsylvania, perpetuated and heightened the controversy by his famous "Proviso," offered as rider to an appropriation bill, *to exclude slavery and involuntary servitude, except for crime, from any additional territories that might be acquired from Mexico.*

While the Wilmot Proviso merely adopted the phraseology of the Ordinance of 1787 (for the government of the Northwest Territory), this is sixty years later; and nothing could better illustrate the political evolution that had taken place during that period than the treatment accorded to this measure in the Senate. Calhoun promptly met it by a series of resolutions asserting in substance that Congress lacked the power to prohibit slavery in a territory, and that the attempted exercise of such power would violate the Constitution and lead to a subversion of the Union. Both the Proviso and these resolutions failed of passage, as Calhoun had probably expected. His prescience of the waning power of the South, however, inclined him to immediate aggression. In a private letter written during the year he said:

"Instead of shunning, we ought to court the issue with the North on the slavery question.—We are now stronger relatively than we shall be hereafter, politically and morally.—Had the South, or even my own State, backed me, I would have forced the issue on the North in 1835, when the spirit of abolitionism first developed itself to any considerable extent. It is a true maxim, to meet danger on the frontier, in politics as well as war. Thus thinking, I am of the impression, that if the South act as it ought, the Wilmot Proviso, instead of proving to be the means of successfully assailing us and our peculiar institution, may be made the occasion of successfully asserting our equality and rights, by enabling us to force the issue on the North. Something of the kind was indispensable to rouse and unite the South."[2]

Calhoun was not writing of war; he was seeking to force the issue politically, as his words indicate; and thus, by averting war, to preserve the Union. The last great struggle to this end took place three years later between him and Webster, in connection with Clay's famous Compromise of 1850. Calhoun and Webster were both devoted to the Union, although they grasped opposite horns of the Constitutional dilemma of States-rights and centralized sovereignty. Clay, no less a friend of the Union than they, had succeeded marvelously with compromise measures for twenty years, but this was to be his last victory. It was a conflict of giants, involving the most intense human interest, and also setting forth with consummate skill—in the great speech of Webster on "The Constitution and the Union"—the effect which the innocent cotton plant had wrought towards the sundering of the States.

The Wilmot Proviso came up again and again. The principle involved was successfully applied to the organization of the Oregon territory in 1848, after great wrangling, but promised such interminable dissension with regard to California and New Mexico that Clay, in the January of 1850, proposed his last and most inclusive compromise. "California and New Mexico"—comprising at that time not only these sections as now defined, but also Nevada, Utah, and Arizona, with parts of Colo-

[2] Cited by Larned, vol. v, p. 3381.

rado and Wyoming—were to be exempt of any national regulation as to slavery, thus avoiding offense in either direction, although California had already adopted a non-slavery constitution; and it was thought that New Mexico would do likewise, which proved to be true; while the free-soilers were to be placated by prohibiting the slave trade in the District of Columbia, and the Border States appeased by the enactment of a stricter fugitive slave law.

Thus Clay, with the dignity of years upon him, arose from his seat in the Senate Chamber, and, "waving a roll of papers, with dramatic eloquence and deep feeling, announced to a hushed auditory that he held in his hand a series of resolutions proposing an amicable arrangement of all questions growing out of the subject of slavery."[3]

From January until September the great dialectic struggle continued, centered about the Wilmot Proviso, which would not down. Clay made his chief defense of his own measure in July, declaring with a sincere if somewhat florid eloquence his absolute devotion to the Union.—"I believe from the bottom of my soul that the measure is the reunion of this Union. I believe it is the dove of peace, which, taking its aërial flight from the dome of the Capitol, carries the glad tidings of assured peace and restored harmony to all the remotest extremities of this distracted land.—I owe a paramount allegiance to the whole Union—a subordinate one to my own State."[4]

[3] F. W. Seward, Seward at Washington: New York, 1891; ch. xvi, cited by Larned, v, 3383.

[4] A. Johnston, American Orations, as cited, ii, pp. 210, 218.

CHAPTER 43[1]

1850: CALHOUN SPEAKS

PROFESSING an equal devotion to the Union, Calhoun held an opinion directly opposed to Clay's on the question of paramount allegiance. His position is best expressed in the last speech he delivered, that of March 4, 1850, when the debate had reached its grand climax. "Long battle with disease had wasted his frame, but, swathed in flannels, he crawled to the Senate Chamber to utter his last words of warning to the North, and to make his last appeal for what he considered justice to his own beloved South."[2] Too feeble for the task of delivering his speech, he explained that "his friend, the Senator behind him, would read it for him." Dr. White draws a graphic picture of the scene: "While Mason was reading there was a deep silence. Webster and Clay sat like statues. Many of the Senators were moved to tears. There was a great hush among the people in the galleries as the last appeal for peace between North and South was heard from the noble Carolina Senator."[3]

The speech is a model of that severe and compact logic in which Calhoun was a master. Taking as his great theme the question, "How can the Union

[1] Chief authority: Johnston's American Orations, as cited, ii, 123–160, and notes.

[2] Rhodes, i, 127.

[3] H. A. White, in Library of Southern Literature: Atlanta, 1908; vol. ii, p. 679.

be preserved?" he says that in order to answer this we must first know what has endangered the Union; and answers, that it is the almost universal discontent pervading the Southern States. Inquiring as to the cause of this discontent, he finds it in the belief of the Southern people "that they cannot remain, as things now are, consistently with honor and safety, in the Union." Proceeding next to the causes of this general belief, he reaches his favorite equilibrium doctrine, and furnishes some interesting figures. When the Constitution was ratified there was nearly a perfect equilibrium between the two sections, "which afforded ample means to each to protect itself against the aggression of the other"—a population of 1,997,899 in the North, and of 1,952,072 in the South, with an almost equal representation in the electoral college and the two Houses of Congress. But now, by the census of 1840, the North is shown to have a population of 9,728,920, while the South has only 7,334,437; the North having a majority of two in the Senate, forty-eight in the House, and fifty in the electoral college, which majority will be so augmented, "should the effort now made to exclude the South from the newly acquired territories succeed," as to give forty Northern senators to twenty-eight Southern—thus "effectually and irretrievably destroying the equilibrium which existed when the Government commenced."

Calhoun then goes on to say that had this destruction been the operation of time, without the interference of Government, the South would have no reason to complain; but it was caused by discriminatory legislation, including laws that affected slavery and the tariff. He also complains of the meddlesome mischief wrought by fanatical abolitionists, and shows the fearsome signs of the times, implied in such facts as the sundering of the great religious denominations by sectional cleavage. Coming at length to his important original question, "How can the Union be saved?" he declares that the South "has no compromise to offer but the Constitution;" let its provisions concerning fugitive slaves be faithfully fulfilled, and let it be amended so as to "restore to the South, in substance, the power she possessed of protecting herself, before the equilibrium between the sections was destroyed by the action of this Government.—It is time, Senators, that there should be an open and manly avowal on all sides, as to what is intended to be done. If the question is not now settled, it is uncertain whether it ever can hereafter be. If you, who represent the stronger portion, cannot agree to settle on the broad principle of justice and duty, say so; and let the States we both represent agree to separate and part in peace. If you remain silent, you will compel us to infer by your acts what you intend. In that case, California will become the test question. If you admit her, under all the difficulties that oppose her admission, you compel us to infer that you intend to exclude us from the whole of the acquired territories, with the intention of destroying, irretrievably, the equilibrium between the two sections. We would be blind not to perceive in that case, that your real objects are power and aggrandizement, and infatuated, not to act accordingly.

"I have now, Senators, done my duty in expressing my opinions fully, freely and candidly, on this solemn occasion. In doing so I have been governed by the motives which have governed me in all the stages of the agitation of the slavery question since its commencement. I have exerted myself, during the whole period, to arrest it, with the intention of saving the Union, if it could be done; and if it could not, to save the section where it has pleased Providence to cast my lot, and which I sincerely believe has justice and the Constitution on its side."

When the address was finished, says Dr. White,[4] the members of the Senate crowded around Calhoun to take him by the hand and congratulate him. He walked forward and stood for a few moments near the clerk's desk and there held an earnest talk with his two great friends, Daniel Webster and Henry Clay. Von Holst dramatically adds that when, supported on the shoulders of two of his friends, he tottered out of the Senate Chamber, the doors that shut behind him closed on the second period of the history of the Union under the Constitution, in which the Star of the South had mounted to the Zenith.[5] On the seventh of March, three days later, Calhoun, with the dew of death upon him, crept back within the Senate Chamber to hear the immortal reply of Webster, of which Rhodes says: "It is the only speech in our history which is named by the date of its delivery, and the general acquiescence in this designation goes to show that it was a turning point in the action of Congress, in popular sentiment, and in the history of the country."[6]

[4] As cited.
[5] Cited in Johnston's Orations, ii, 386–387.
[6] Rhodes, i, 144.

CHAPTER 44

1850: WEBSTER[1] ANSWERS CALHOUN

WEBSTER, profoundly concerned, like Calhoun, for the preservation of the menaced Union, and also clearly conscious of the strength of Calhoun's constitutional position, threw himself with his almost superhuman ability into this attempt to save the Union, by making every concession consistent with justice, and by recommending to his Northern colleagues reliance upon natural laws for preventing the further extension of slavery, rather than national laws like the mooted Wilmot Proviso, which would only produce deeper irritation and danger. F. W. Seward,[2] an eye-witness, thus describes Webster's demeanor in speaking:

"He rose from his seat near the middle of the Chamber, wearing his customary blue coat with metal buttons, and with one hand thrust into the buff vest, stood during his opening remarks, as impassive as a statue; but growing slightly more animated as he proceeded. Calm, clear and powerful, his sonorous utterances, while they disappointed thousands of his friends at the North, lent new vigor to the 'Compromisers,' with whom, it was seen, he would henceforth act."

Webster began by saying:

"I wish to speak to-day, not as a Massachusetts

[1] Chief authority, Webster's Writings and Speeches: Boston, 1903; vol. x.

[2] Cited by Larned, v, 3384.

man, nor as a Northern man, but as an American. The imprisoned winds are let loose. The East, the North and the stormy South combine to throw the whole sea into commotion, to toss its billows to the skies, and disclose its profoundest depths. I have a part to act, not for my own security or safety, for I am looking out for no fragment upon which to float away from the wreck, if wreck there must be, but for the good of the whole, and the preservation of all. I speak to-day for the preservation of the Union. 'Hear me for my cause.' "

Perhaps the most brilliant period of the address occurs near the close, when, referring to Calhoun's suggestion of peaceable secession, Webster exclaimed:

"Sir, your eyes and mine are never destined to see that miracle. The dismemberment of this vast country without convulsion! The breaking up of the fountains of the great deep without ruffling the surface! Who is so foolish, I beg everybody's pardon, as to expect to see any such thing? Sir, he who sees these States, now revolving in harmony around a common center, and expects to see them quit their places and fly off without convulsion, may look the next hour to see the heavenly bodies rush from their spheres, and jostle against each other in the realms of space, without causing the wreck of the universe."

But Webster had been profoundly wrought upon by those points of Calhoun's speech that drew their cogency from the principles of legality and justice; moreover, he realized fully the sincere seriousness of the Carolinian, who, he knew, hardly exaggerated the danger of disunion in the South. Therefore, he took a position adverse to the insertion of a Wilmot

Proviso or anything like it in the ordinance for the organization of new territory.

"I would put in no Wilmot Proviso for the mere purpose of a taunt or a reproach," said he; "I would put into it no evidence of the votes of a superior power, exercised for no purpose but to wound the pride, whether a just and a rational pride, or an irrational pride, of the citizens of the Southern States."

He even pointed out, in reply to Calhoun's doctrine of equilibrium, that new slave States might be legally carved from the immense area of Texas. He went so far as to favor a strict administration of the fugitive slave laws; and he denounced the abolitionists in a context that warrants quotation:—

"I cannot but see what mischief their interference with the South has produced. And is it not plain to every man? Let any gentleman who entertains doubts on this point recur to the debates in the Virginia House of Delegates in 1832, and he will see with what freedom a proposition made by Mr. Jefferson Randolph for the gradual abolition of slavery was discussed in that body. Every one spoke of slavery as he thought; very ignominious and disparaging names and epithets were applied to it. The debates in the House of Delegates on that occasion, I believe, were all published. They were read by every colored man who could read, and to those who could not read, those debates were read by others. At that time Virginia was not unwilling or afraid to discuss this question, and to let that part of her population know as much of the discussion as they could learn. That was in 1832. As has been said by the honorable member from South Carolina, these Abolition societies commenced their course of action in 1835. It is said, I do not know how true it may be, that they sent incendiary publications into the slave States; at any rate, they attempted to arouse, and did arouse, a very strong feeling; in other words, they created great agitation in the North against Southern slavery. Well, what was the result? The bonds of the slaves were bound more firmly than before, their rivets were more strongly fastened. Public opinion, which in Virginia had begun to be exhibited against slavery, and was opening out for the discussion of the question, drew back and shut itself up in its castle. I wish to know whether anybody in Virginia can now talk openly as Mr. Randolph, Governor McDowell, and others talked in 1832, and sent their remarks to the press? We all know the fact, and we all know the cause; and everything that these agitating people have done has been, not to enlarge, but to restrain, not to set free, but to bind faster, the slave population of the South."

Webster admonished Calhoun, in turn, that the South was not without blemish in violence of language and action; and then went on to agree with him that slavery was at the root of the dissension that threatened the Union with destruction. He pointed out what has already been shown in this book, that at the time of the formation of the Constitution the South, no less than the North, had inclined to the abolition of slavery; and in tracing the cause of the change that had occurred, advanced the argument which lay at the heart of his speech, and at the same time bears such peculiar relation to our subject as to warrant the closest attention.

CHAPTER 45[1]

DANIEL WEBSTER ON THE POWER OF COTTON[2]

"THERE was, if not an entire unanimity," said Webster, "a general concurrence of sentiment running through the whole community, and especially entertained by the eminent men of all parts of the country (concerning early slavery). But soon a change began, at the North and the South, and a difference of opinion showed itself; the North growing much more warm and strong against slavery, and the South growing much more warm and strong in its support. Sir, there is no generation of mankind whose opinions are not subject to be influenced by what appears to them to be their present emergent and exigent interests. I impute to the South no particularly selfish view in the change which has come over her. I impute to her certainly no dishonest view. All that has happened has been natural. It has followed those causes which always influence the human mind and operate upon it. What, then, have been the causes which have created so new a feeling in favor of slavery in the South, which have changed the whole nomenclature of the South

[1] See Chapter 44.

[2] No apology should be necessary for such a long citation from this famous speech, in view of the surprising fact that even such excellent works as Johnston's American Orations omit the very heart of Webster's argument, which summarized the growth of the cotton industry. For additional evidence of the importance attached by Webster himself to COTTON as the heart of his argument (which is otherwise really inexplicable), see Appendix E.

on that subject, so that, from being thought and described in the terms I have mentioned and will not repeat, it has now become an institution, a cherished institution, in that quarter; no evil, no scourge, but a great religious, social, and moral blessing, as I think I have heard it latterly spoken of? This, I suppose this, sir, is owing to the rapid growth and sudden extension of the COTTON [3] plantations of the South. So far as any motive consistent with honor, justice, and general judgment could act, it was the COTTON interest that gave a new desire to promote slavery, to spread it, and to use its labor. I again say that this change was produced by causes which must always produce like effects. The whole interest of the South became connected, more or less, with the extension of slavery. If we look back to the history of the commerce of this country in the early years of this government, what were our exports? Cotton was hardly, or to a very limited extent, known. In 1791 the first parcel of cotton of the growth of the United States was exported, and amounted only to 19,200 pounds.[4] It has gone on increasing rapidly, until the whole crop may now, perhaps, in a season of great product and high prices, amount to a hundred millions of dollars. In the years I have mentioned, there was more of wax, more of indigo, more of rice, more of almost every article of export from the South, than of cotton. When Mr. Jay negotiated the treaty of 1794 with England, it is evident from the twelfth article of the

[3] This typographical emphasis is copied from Webster's works.

[4] Seybert's Statistics, p. 92. A small parcel of cotton found its way to Liverpool from the United States in 1784, and was refused admission, on the ground that it could not be the growth of the United States (Note in Webster's Works).—See *Navigation Laws* cited at close of Chapter 9.

treaty, which was suspended by the Senate, that he did not know that cotton was exported at all from the United States.

"Well, sir, we know what followed. The age of cotton became the golden age of our Southern brethren. It gratified their desire for improvement and accumulation, at the same time that it excited it. The desire grew by what it fed upon, and there soon came to be an eagerness for other territory, a new area or new areas for the cultivation of the cotton crop; and measures leading to this result were brought about rapidly, one after another, under the lead of Southern men at the head of the Government, they having a majority in both branches of Congress to accomplish their ends. The honorable member from South Carolina observed that there has been a majority all along in favor of the North. If that be true, sir, the North has acted either very liberally and kindly, or very weakly; for they never exercised that majority efficiently five times in the history of the Government, when a division or trial of strength arose. Never. Whether they were outgeneraled, or whether it was owing to other causes, I shall not stop to consider; but no man acquainted with the history of the Union can deny that the general lead in the politics of the country, for three-fourths of the period that has elapsed since the adoption of the Constitution, has been a Southern lead.

"In 1802, in pursuit of the idea of opening a new cotton region, the United States obtained a cession from Georgia of the whole of her Western territory, now embracing the rich and growing States of Alabama and Mississippi. In 1803 Louisiana was purchased from France, out of which the States of

Louisiana, Arkansas, and Missouri have been framed, as slave-holding States. In 1819 the cession of Florida was made, bringing in another region adapted to cultivation by slaves. Sir, the honorable member from South Carolina thought he saw in certain operations of the Government, such as the manner of collecting the revenue, and the tendency of measures calculated to promote emigration into the country, what accounts for the more rapid growth of the North than the South. He ascribes that more rapid growth, not to the operation of time, but to the system of government and administration established under this Constitution. That is matter of opinion. To a certain extent it may be true; but it does seem to me that if any operation of the Government can be shown in any degree to have promoted the population, and growth, and wealth of the North, it is much more sure that there are sundry important and distinct operations of the Government, about which no man can doubt, tending to promote, and which absolutely have promoted, the increase of the slave interest and the slave territory of the South. It was not time that brought in Louisiana; it was the act of men. It was not time that brought in Florida; it was the act of men. And lastly, sir, to complete those acts of legislation which have contributed so much to enlarge the area of the institution of slavery, Texas, great, and vast, and illimitable Texas, was added to the Union as a slave State in 1845; and that, sir, pretty much closed the whole chapter, and settled the whole account."

Webster then stated what he intended as the main proposition of his speech—"that there is not at this moment within the United States, or any territory of the United States, a single foot of land, the character of which, in regard to its being free territory or slave territory, is not fixed by some law, and some irrepealable law, beyond the power of the action of the Government."

This he argued with considerable length as to Texas. Coming at last to the crucial question of California and New Mexico, he said:

"I hold slavery to be excluded from those territories by a law even superior to that which admits and sanctions it in Texas. I mean the law of nature, of physical geography, the law of the formation of the earth. That law settles forever, with a strength beyond all terms of human enactment, that slavery cannot exist in California or New Mexico. Understand me, sir; I mean slavery as we regard it; the slavery of the colored race as it exists in the Southern States. California and New Mexico are Asiatic in their formation and scenery. They are composed of vast ridges of mountains, of great height, with broken ridges and deep valleys. The sides of these mountains are entirely barren; their tops capped by perennial snow. There may be in California, now made free by its constitution, and no doubt there are, some tracts of valuable land. But it is not so in New Mexico. What is there in New Mexico that could, by any possibility, induce anybody to go there with slaves? There are some narrow strips of tillable land on the borders of the rivers; but the rivers themselves dry up before midsummer is gone. All that the people can do in that region is to raise some little articles, some little wheat for their tortillas, and that by irrigation. And who expects to see a hundred black men cultivating tobacco, corn, cotton, rice, or anything else, on lands in New Mexico, made fertile only by irrigation? I look upon it, therefore, as a fixed fact, to use the current expression of the day, that both California and New Mexico are destined to be free, free by the arrangement of things ordained by the Power above us. I have, therefore to say, in this respect also, that this country is fixed for freedom, to as many persons as shall ever live in it, by a less repealable law than that which attaches to the right of holding slaves in Texas; and I will say further, that, if a resolution or a bill were now before us, to provide a territorial government for New Mexico, I would not vote to put any prohibition into it whatever. Such a prohibition would be idle, as it respects any effect it would have upon the territory; and I would not take pains uselessly to reaffirm an ordinance of nature, nor to reënact the will of God."

In short, Webster answered Calhoun's political explication of the growth of divergence between the two sections with an economic argument: the introduction of cotton had caused the South to recede from its early opposition to slavery; slavery had extended with the growth of the cotton States, and now there was no more cotton territory left. Therefore, in his effort to preserve the Union, he pleaded for the *status quo,* and endorsed Clay's Compromise.

CHAPTER 46

THE END OF AN EPOCH

THE Congressional struggle had not yet reached the stage of contention as to whether slavery should continue to exist in the States where it was already established; the question was just one of extension. Webster's fresh and brilliant economic argument, backed by his immense influence, had a tremendous effect. He himself considered this speech the most important effort of his life. His eulogists assert that it postponed the decisive conflict until the superiority of the North over the South, in population and material resources, was overwhelming. Had it not been for the terrible blundering of Douglas in 1854, this postponement might possibly have been protracted until some wise and kindly genius like Lincoln could have accomplished the emancipation of the slaves without war; for the speech expressed the quintessence of sanity, in spite of mistakes in some minor particulars.[1] As Rhodes says, it "produced a wonderful sensation; none other in our annals had an immediate effect so mighty and striking.—His moral and intellectual influence in the free States was greater than that of any man living, for the people had confidence that his gigantic intellect would discover the right, and that his intellectual honesty would compel him to follow it. The country has listened to but two men on

[1] See Chapter 74.

whose words they have hung with greater reverence than those of Webster. The intellectual force and moral greatness of Washington and of Lincoln were augmented by their high office and the gravity of the existing crises. When the first excitement had subsided, the friends of Webster bestirred themselves, and soon testimonials poured in, approving the position which he had taken. The most significant of them was the one from eight hundred solid men of Boston [presumably "cotton whigs"], who thanked him for 'recalling us to our duties under the Constitution,' and for his 'broad, national and patriotic views.'—It is frequently said that a speech in Congress does not alter opinions; that the minds of men are determined by set political bias or sectional considerations. This was certainly not the case in 1850. Webster's influence was of the greatest weight in the passage of the compromise measures, and he is as closely associated with them as is their author. Clay's adroit parliamentary management was necessary to carry them through the various and tedious steps of legislation. But it was Webster who raised up for them a powerful and much needed support from Northern public sentiment. His argument could not legally be impugned. —It is probable that the matured historical view will be that Webster's position as to the application of the Wilmot Proviso to New Mexico was statesmanship of the highest order." [2]

The abolitionists, however, were angered. Theodore Parker compared the speech with the treason of Benedict Arnold.[3] Emerson wrote: "He is a man who lives by his memory; a man of

[2] Rhodes, i, 149, 152, 156–157.
[3] See note at end of this chapter.

the past, not a man of faith and hope. All the drops of his blood have eyes that look downward, and his finely developed understanding only works truly and with all its force when it stands for animal good; that is, for property."[4] Whittier wrote a threnody of "Ichabod":

So fallen! So lost! the light withdrawn
  Which once he wore.
The glory from his gray hairs gone
  Forevermore.

. . .

Let not the land once proud of him
  Insult him now,
Nor brand with deeper shame his dim
  Dishonored brow.

. . .

Of all we loved and honored naught
  Save power remains;
A fallen angel's pride of thought
  Still strong in chains.

All else is gone; from those great eyes
  The soul has fled;
When faith is lost, when honor dies,
  The man is dead.

Then pay the reverence of old days
  To his dead fame;
Walk backward with averted gaze
  And hide his shame.

The free-soilers were not without able spokesmen in Congress, of whom Seward was chief; and the Compromise was not finally effected before he was

[4] Cited in Johnston's Orations, ii, 398.

heard from. Two years previously he had created a profound sensation at Cleveland by declaring: "Slavery can be limited to its present bounds; it can be ameliorated; it *can* and *must* be abolished, and you and I can and must do it." Four days after Webster's famous speech he arose in his place in the Senate and sounded the note of aggression in the challenging phrase, *"a higher law"*—asserting that slavery must yield "to the salutary instructions of economy and to the ripening influences of humanity." Around this "higher law doctrine" the Abolition movement now began to crystallize, having as its object not the mere limitation of slavery to its foothold already obtained, but its utter extirpation. The stage was setting for new scenes, and we have reached the end of an epoch. Calhoun died on the last day of March, 1850, "stricken at heart, as it must have seemed to all who observed him closely, because forced in those last days to see with his keen eye of prophecy what the years to come must inevitably bring to pass."[5] Two years later Clay and Webster followed him.

NOTE.—Parker could occasionally be very effective as a satirist. In his "Anti-Slavery Scrap Book" (now in the Boston Public Library) may be found "Another Chapter in the Book of Daniel," written for the New York *Tribune* apropos of the capture of "Shadrach" [a fugitive slave]. The bitter allusions to Webster make this lampoon very interesting.

"Now it came to pass in the latter days that Daniel was King over all the children of Jonathan, which had waxed many and fat in the land. And by reasons which the prophet detaileth not, Daniel's head was turned and he went after strange gods."

Then comes an account of Daniel's gradual surrender to these gods of the Southernites, followed by several very telling paragraphs about "the great city of the Northernites which lieth to the eastward on the seashore as thou goest down to the old country, and it is called Boston."

"And in that city there was a street called Milk, peradventure

[5] Woodrow Wilson in Cambridge Modern History, vii, 418. See also Division and Reunion, p. 174.

because it is the dwelling place of so many of the babes and sucklings of commerce, and also another called State, wherein be the priests' offices and the temples of their chief gods.

"For in that city they did worship many strange gods whereof the chief was called Money, an idol whose head was of fine gold, the belly of silver, and legs of copper; but second thereto was another notable idol called Cotton.

"Unto this latter they did sacrifice and build him high places and factories by the brooks that run among the hills, and bowed down and worshiped him, saying, 'Cotton help us! Cotton help us!'

"Then they held a meeting and cried out, 'Great is Cotton of the Bostonians. There is no god but Money, no lord but Cotton, no king but Daniel, nothing better than riches, and no justice but only the laws of Daniel.' Then said they, 'We be a great people.'"

After which comes a description of the capture of Shadrach, "a servant in an inn," whom they "took away from his frying pans and his skillets and his ovens and his gridirons and his spits," but whom, none the less, the Lord delivered, "whereupon the worshipers of Money and of Cotton fell down on their faces and wept sore, and they said, 'Alas for us, the Lord has triumphed, and Cotton has fallen down. Lo, Daniel will hate us and will make a proclamation and send a message and the Southernites will be upon us and take away our hope of a tariff. We will be all dead men.' And their hearts became as a dog's heart when he barketh but knoweth not whom he may bite."—Mary C. Crawford, Romantic Days in Old Boston: Boston, 1912; p. 211.

CHAPTER 47

"COTTON IS KING"

THE mad action of Douglas in 1854 justified Seward's subsequent prediction of "the irrepressible conflict," which it undoubtedly hastened, by repealing the Missouri Compromise altogether—something that the Southerners had never dreamed of obtaining, and that threw the country into a passionate uproar of excitement. Almost immediately the Burns case flared up in Boston, and it took 1,140 Federal soldiers with muskets loaded, backed by a field piece loaded with grape-shot, to enforce the fugitive slave law against mobs led by such men as Higginson, Phillips, and Parker.[1] "Bloody Kansas" became an actual battle-ground in the physical contention over slavery, Northern and Southern settlers vying for mastery in the settlement of Kansas and Nebraska, now that the decision as to slavery was to be left to the popular vote. By the irony of fate, Kansas was to retaliate on Virginia in 1859, through the strange and sinister raid of "Ossawotomie Brown." Judges like Taney and writers such as Mrs. Stowe were fanning the fires in the North, from one side and the other, while the South was stirred to its depths by the expectation of Northern invasion, and inspired by the belief that it must fight for its hearth-stones. The threads of the gigantic drama became inextricably tangled and

[1] Rhodes, 1, 500–506.

confused, so that now this and now that line has been seized upon as the clue to the mazes of this terrible war; but the complicated pattern is after all a web of Arachne's own weaving. Shuttled back and forth through labyrinths of political and emotional disputation flew on either side the economic arguments, arresting the attention of the thoughtful as a source of relief from the passionate confusion of the times. In the South there appeared in 1855 a book by an anonymous writer, entitled, "Cotton is King; or, Slavery in the Light of Political Economy." Subsequently the author declared himself as David Christy, of Cincinnati; and, associated with other writers, produced so late as 1860 a bulky volume of pro-slavery arguments whose bare titles indicate the character and number of protagonists that cotton had drawn to its defense.

Besides Christy's original work on "Cotton is King," this book includes a treatise on "Liberty and Slavery: or, Slavery in the Light of Moral and Political Philosophy,"[2] by Albert Taylor Bledsoe, LL.D., professor of mathematics in the University of Virginia; "The Bible Argument: or, Slavery in the Light of Divine Revelation," by Thornton Stringfellow, D.D., of Richmond; a chapter on "Slavery in the Light of Social Ethics," by Chancellor Harper, of South Carolina; one on "Slavery in the Light of Political Science," comprising the famous Clarkson Letters, by James Henry Hammond, formerly Governor of South Carolina and

[2] "Had the Northern and Western States been subjected to the same climatic and economic conditions, there is little doubt that . . . they would have completely shared the moral views of their Southern brethren. Men are what conditions make them, and ethical ideals are not exempt from the same inexorable law of environment."—E. R. A. Seligman, The Economic Interpretation of History: New York, 1912; p. 128.

then United States Senator; a dissertation on "Slavery in the Light of Ethnology," by Samuel A. Cartwright, M.D., of Louisiana, who also wrote a chapter on "The Education, Labor and Wealth of the South"; a treatise on "Slavery in the Light of International Law," by President Elliott, of the Planters' College of Mississippi; and two by Charles Hodge, D.D., of Princeton, New Jersey, entitled respectively "The Fugitive Slave Law" and "The Bible Argument on Slavery." But all of these diverse pro-slavery arguments are properly marshaled under the title of the opening chapter, "Cotton is King; or, Slavery in the Light of Political Economy," the original nucleus around which the larger compendium was assembled.

The viewpoint of David Christy, the Northern author of "Cotton is King," is well expressed in the preface to this edition of 1860:

The negro is to American politics what cotton is to European manufactures and commerce—the controlling element. As the overthrow of American slavery, with the consequent suspension of the motion of the spindles and looms of Europe, would bring ruin upon millions of its population; so the dropping of the negro question, in American politics, would at once destroy the prospects of thousands of aspirants to office. In ninety-nine cases out of a hundred, the clamor against slavery is made only for effect; and there is not now, nor has there been at any other period, any intention on the part of political agitators to wage actual war against the slave States themselves."

CHAPTER 48

"THE IMPENDING CRISIS"

As Christy, from the North, produced the most notable argument in behalf of slavery, so Hinton Rowan Helper, a Southern man, produced the chief economic argument against it, in a book called "The Impending Crisis of the South: How to Meet It," published in 1857 in New York.

Helper, whose name originally was Helfer, was a native of Rowan County, North Carolina; a member of the "poor white" class, befriended in youth by Mr. Michael Brown,[1] a merchant of the town of Salisbury. Subsequently taking up his home in the North and studying practical economics for practical purposes, when "Cotton is King" first appeared Helper was able to answer it with considerable spirit and ability.

"The truth is," he says, "that the cotton crop is of but little value to the South. New England and Old England by their superior enterprise and sagacity, turn it chiefly to their own advantage. It is carried in their ships, spun in their factories, woven in their looms, insured in their offices, returned again in their own vessels, and, with double freight and cost of manufacture added, purchased by the South at a high premium."[2]

Touching on a tender spot with no light finger, Helper violently exclaims:

[1] The author's maternal grandfather.
[2] Crisis, p. 54.

"Reader! would you understand how abjectly slave-holders themselves are enslaved to the products of Northern industry? If you would, fix your mind on a Southern 'gentleman'—a slave breeder and human-flesh monger, who professes to be a Christian! Observe the routine of his daily life. See him rise in the morning from a Northern bed, and clothe himself in Northern apparel; see him walk across the floor on a Northern carpet, and perform his ablutions out of a Northern ewer and basin. See him uncover a box of Northern powders, and cleanse his teeth with a Northern brush; see him reflecting his physiognomy in a Northern mirror, and arranging his hair with a Northern comb. See him dosing himself with the medicaments of Northern quacks, and perfuming his handkerchief with Northern cologne. See him referring to the time in a Northern watch, and glancing at the news in a Northern gazette. See him and his family sitting in Northern chairs, and singing and praying out of Northern books. See him at the breakfast table, saying grace over a Northern plate, eating with Northern cutlery, and drinking from Northern utensils. See him charmed with the melody of a Northern piano, or musing over the pages of a Northern novel. See him riding to his neighbors in a Northern carriage, or furrowing his lands with a Northern plow. See him lighting his segar with a Northern match, and flogging his negroes with a Northern lash. See him with Northern pen and ink, writing letters on Northern paper, and sending them away in Northern envelopes, sealed with Northern wax, and impressed with a Northern stamp. Perhaps our Southern 'gentleman' is a merchant; if so, see him at his store, making an unpatriotic use of his time in the miserable traffic of Northern gimcracks and haberdashery; see him when you will, where you will, he is ever surrounded with the industrial products of those whom, in the criminal inconsistency of his heart, he execrates as enemies, yet treats as friends. His labors, his talents, his influence, are all for the North, and not for the South; for the stability of slavery, and for the sake of his own personal aggrandizement, he is willing to sacrifice the dearest interests of his country."[3]

Helper's book circulated in immense quantities throughout the North, where great piles of it "might be seen on the counter of every book-store, news-depot, and newspaper stand." Rhodes says: "'Uncle Tom's Cabin' was full of burning indignation at the wrong done the slave, and John Brown sacrificed his life willingly for him; while Helper, though he had the prejudices of his class against the black, made a powerful protest against the institution in the name of the non-slaveholding white."[4]

"The Impending Crisis" created a sectional stir in Congress, a Virginia member declaring any one who assisted in the propagation of such writings to be unfit to live; while in the South it could be circulated only by stealth. The Southern feeling against it, while due largely to its unnecessary bitterness, was stimulated by the strength of its economic argument against slavery. It was perfectly true, as Helper claimed, that slavery had turned the South into a great cotton plantation, while the North had developed a large diversity of crops and an amazing system of manufactures. It is also true that the increasing disparity in population of which Cal-

[3] Crisis, 355–356.

[4] Rhodes, ii, 419, 428.

houn complained in the Senate (see page 210) was not due to legislation, as Calhoun had believed, but to slavery; the immigrants who had begun to pour in from Europe being unwilling to compete with slave labor or to associate with it. Even the native population drifted away westward and northward. "The census of 1860 was to show that there were in South Carolina only 277,000 white persons born within her borders, while 193,000 born within the State were living in other parts of the country. North Carolina had kept only 634,000 out of 906,000; and Virginia only 1,000,000 out of 1,400,000. Immigrants did not come down into those fertile valleys; and the great plantations, with their crowding, docile slaves, thrust out even those of native stock whose homes had been there."[5] Woodrow Wilson characterizes North and South respectively as the section which commerce, industry, migration, and immigration had expanded and nationalized, and the section which slavery and its attendant social institutions had kept unchanged and separate.

[5] W. Wilson, Cambridge Modern History, vii, 415. See also Division and Reunion, p. 163.

CHAPTER 49

SENATOR HAMMOND ON THE POWER OF COTTON [1]

THE voice of the South was articulate in the national councils, after the tongue of Calhoun had been stilled, most typically and with the greatest distinction in the speeches of Senator Hammond of South Carolina. His son, Major Harry Hammond, says: "Opposed to slavery in the abstract, opposed to the reopening of the African slave trade, opposed to the extension of slavery by propagandism in this country, he defended the peculiar domestic slavery of the South against the denunciations of Abolitionists from all quarters, asserting that they denounced a thing of which they knew absolutely nothing—nay, which did not even exist." Senator Hammond's historic speech of the fourth of March, 1858, is peculiarly suited for the close of these final chapters on the Great Controversies, which were soon to be silenced by the more clamorous voices of war.

Incited by such arguments as those of Helper, but more immediately by a speech of Seward the day before, in which the threat had been made "to take this Government from unjust and unfaithful hands and place it in just and faithful hands," Senator Hammond combined in his speech an economic panegyric on the South with a ringing exposition of her part in the making of the nation, that sounded like a defiant valedictory—as indeed it was.

[1] Chief authority: Printer's proofs of J. H. Hammond's speeches, courteously furnished by Major Harry Hammond.

After discussing the admission of Kansas and touching on some of the general resources of the South, Senator Hammond put the pith of his economic argument into the following words:

"The strength of a nation depends in a great measure upon its wealth, and the wealth of a nation, like that of a man, is to be estimated by its surplus production. You may go to your trashy census books, full of falsehood and nonsense—they tell you, for example, that in the State of Tennessee, the whole number of house servants is not equal to that of those in my own house, and such things as that. You may estimate what is made throughout the country from these census books, but it is no matter how much is made if it is all consumed. If a man possesses millions of dollars and consumes his income, is he rich? Is he competent to embark in any new enterprise? Can he build ships or railroads? And could a people in that condition build ships and roads or go to war? All the enterprises of peace and war depend upon the surplus productions of a people. They may be happy, they may be comfortable, they may enjoy themselves in consuming what they make; but they are not rich, they are not strong. It appears, by going to the reports of the Secretary of the Treasury, which are authentic, that last year the United States exported in round numbers $279,000,000 worth of domestic produce, excluding gold and foreign merchandise re-exported. Of this amount $158,000,000 worth is the clear produce of the South, articles that are not and cannot be made at the North. There are then $80,000,000 worth of exports of products of the forest, provisions, and breadstuffs. If we assume that the South made but one-third of these, and I think that is a low calculation, our exports were $185,000,000, leaving to the North less than $95,000,000.

"In addition to this, we sent to the North $30,000,000 worth of cotton, which is not counted in the exports. We sent to her seven or eight millions worth of tobacco, which is not counted in the exports. We sent naval stores, lumber, rice, and many other minor articles. There is no doubt that we sent to the North $40,000,000 in addition; but suppose the amount to be $35,000,000, it will give us a surplus production of $220,000,000. But the *recorded* exports of the South now (1858) are greater than the whole exports of the United States in any year before 1856. They are greater than the whole average exports of the United States for the last twelve years including the two extraordinary years of 1856 and 1857. They are nearly double the amount of the average exports of the twelve preceding years. If I am right in my calculations as to $220,000,000 of surplus produce, there is not a nation on the face of the earth, with any numerous population, that can compete with us in produce *per capita*. It amounts to $16.66 per head, supposing that we have twelve million people. England, with all her accumulated wealth, with her concentrated and educated energy, makes but sixteen and a half dollars of surplus production per head. I have not made a calculation as to the North, with her $95,000,000 surplus; admitting that she exports as much as we do, with her eighteen millions of population it would be but little over twelve dollars a head. But she cannot export to us and abroad exceeding ten dollars a head against our sixteen dollars. I know well enough that the North sends to the South a vast amount of the productions of her industry. I take it for granted that she, at least, pays us in that way for the thirty or forty million dollars worth of cotton and other articles we send her. I am willing to admit that she sends us considerably more; but to bring her up to our amount of surplus production; to bring her up to $220,000,000 a year, the South must take from her $125,000,000; and this, in addition to our share of the consumption of the $333,000,000 worth introduced into the country from abroad, and paid for chiefly by our own exports. The thing is absurd; it is impossible; it can never appear anywhere but in a book of statistics."

The Senator, sure of his premises, now proceeded to draw the conclusion that the South could never have war.

"With an export of $220,000,000 under the present tariff, the South organized separately would have $40,000,000 of revenue. With one-fourth the present tariff she would have a revenue adequate to all her wants, for the South would never go to war; she would never need an army or a navy, beyond a few garrisons on the frontier and a few revenue cutters. It is commerce that breeds war. It is manufactures that require to be hawked about the world, that give rise to navies and commerce. But we have nothing to do but to take off restrictions on foreign merchandise and open our ports, and the whole world will come to us to trade. They will be too glad to bring and carry for us, and we never shall dream of a war. Why, the South has never yet had a just cause of war. Every time she has drawn her sword it has been on the point of honor, and that point of honor has been mainly loyalty to her sister colonies—and sister States, who have ever since plundered and calumniated her.

"But if there were no other reason why we should never have war, would any sane nation make war on cotton? Without firing a gun, without drawing a sword, should they make war on us we could bring the whole world to our feet. The South is perfectly competent to go on, one, two or three years without planting a seed of cotton. I believe that if she was to plant but half her cotton, for three years to come, it would be an immense advantage to her. I am not so sure but that after three years' entire abstinence she would come out stronger than ever she was before, and better prepared to enter afresh upon her great career of enterprise. What would happen if no cotton was furnished for three years? I will not stop to depict what every one can imagine, but this is certain: England would topple headlong and carry the whole civilized world with her, save the South. No, you do not dare to make war on cotton. No power on earth dares to make war upon it. Cotton *is* King."

CHAPTER 50

THE SOUTH'S VALEDICTORY[1]

SENATOR HAMMOND'S emphasized use of Christy's phrase immediately gave it universal currency, and sent it running through the world of commerce to this day. Another phrase, "mud-sill," has given added fame to his speech. After showing how the cotton crop had recently saved the North from financial ruin, he claimed that the greatest strength of the South, after all, was not financial, but social; "arising from the harmony of her political and social institutions." Speaking to this point, he continued thus in defense of Southern slavery:

"In all social systems there must be a class to do the menial duties, to perform the drudgery of life. That is, a class requiring but a low order of intellect and but little skill. Its requisites are vigor, docility, fidelity. Such a class you must have, or you would not have that other class which leads progress, civilization, and refinement. It constitutes the very mud-sill of society and of political government, and you might as well attempt to build a house in the air, as to build either the one or the other, except on this mud-sill. Fortunately for the South, she found a race adapted to that purpose to her hand. A race inferior to her own, but eminently qualified in temper, in vigor, in docility, in capacity to stand the climate, to answer all her pur-

[1] See Chapter 49.

poses. We use them for our purpose, and call them slaves. We found them slaves by the 'common consent of mankind,' which, according to Cicero, '*lex naturæ est:*' the highest proof of what is Nature's law. We are old-fashioned at the South yet; it is a word discarded now by 'ears polite;' I will not characterize that class at the North by that term; but you have it; it is there; it is everywhere; it is eternal."

After an expansion of this idea and an interchange of taunts with the other side, the Senator uttered the eloquent peroration that may well serve as the South's defiant valedictory to the Union in whose building she had taken such large share:

"Transient and temporary causes have thus far been your preservation. The great West has been open to your surplus population, and your hordes of semi-barbarian immigrants, who are crowding in year by year. They make a great movement, and you call it progress. Whither? It is progress; but it is progress towards Vigilance Committees. The South have sustained you in a great measure. You are our factors. You bring and carry for us. One hundred and fifty millions dollars of our money passes annually through your hands. Much of it sticks; all of it assists to keep your machinery together and in motion. Suppose we were to discharge you; suppose we were to take our business out of your hands; we should consign you to anarchy and poverty. You complain of the rule of the South: that has been another cause that has preserved you. We have kept the Government conservative to the great purposes of Government. We have placed it, and kept it, upon the Constitution—and that has been the cause of your peace and prosperity. The Senator from New York says that it is about to be at an end; that you intend to take the Government from us; that it will pass from our hands. Perhaps what he says is true; it may be; but do not forget—it can never be forgotten—it is written on the brightest page of human history—that we, the slaveholders of the South, took our country in her infancy, and, after ruling her for sixty out of the seventy years of her existence, we shall surrender her to you without a stain upon her honor, boundless in prosperity, incalculable in her strength, the wonder and the admiration of the world. Time will show what you will make of her; but no time can ever diminish our glory or your responsibility.''

Senator Hammond, whatever may be thought of his general argument, did not overstate the immense commercial preëminence to which cotton had by this time ascended. The Report on Commerce and Navigation for the year ending June 30, 1859,[2] shows that of all products of the forest and of agriculture the North exported goods to the value of $45,305,541, as against $193,399,618 from the South, of which $161,434,923 must be set to the credit of cotton. Tested from the standpoint of national manufactures, regardless of exportation, cotton shows a similar striking importance; its value as a manufactured product in 1860 being $115,681,774, as against $73,454,000 for wool, and an almost equal amount for forged, rolled, wrought, and cast iron taken together.

Thus cotton had immeasurably enriched the country, North and South, since the year (1784) when eight bags were seized on an American vessel at

[2] See Appendix F:2b.

Liverpool, upon the ground that it could not have been grown in North America, and therefore the existing navigation laws must have been violated.[3] No account can be taken in these figures of the enormous stimulus which the invention of the series of cotton machines exercised in the manufacture of wool and in numerous other directions. But the price which America paid for the introduction and use of cotton was sectionalism, slavery, and war.

[3] See Webster's note to 7th of March Speech, page 218.

CHAPTER 51

SECESSION AND FACTIONALISM

PRECEDING chapters have traced the course by which the haphazard factions of the early American Union finally gravitated into two great groups, or sections, ready for collision. The thirteen original States, after the welding influence of a common cause had ceased to bind them, were like so many shots poured out on the floor—utterly wanting cohesion; but, long before 1861, and with augmented number and power, they had been molten into two hostile masses, arrayed for the propulsion of battle. The question of slavery, at length fiercely sectional, had become so through the cotton influence. The dogma of States-rights, at last jealously and distinctively Southern, had once been held in the North quite as tenaciously as by the South.

So also was it with the doctrine of Secession. As long as this remained only an abstract question, disentangled from practical implications, the right of a State to secede had been supported by academic argument on both sides of the Mason and Dixon line, and supported earnestly. Even Abraham Lincoln had said: "Any people anywhere being inclined and having the power have the right to rise up and shake off the existing government, and form a new one that suits them better. This is a most valuable, a most sacred right—a right which we hope and believe is to liberate the world. Nor is this right confined to cases in which the whole people of an existing government may choose to exercise it. Any portion of such people that can may revolutionize and make their own of so much of the territory as they inhabit."[1]

The slave power had no more bitter and persistent enemy than John Quincy Adams, yet Jefferson Davis himself could not have argued more forcibly for the expediency of disunion than did this former President of the United States at the semi-centennial "Jubilee of the Constitution" held in New York City in 1839:

"If the day should ever come (may Heaven avert it!)" he said, "when the affections of the people of these States shall be alienated from each other, when the fraternal spirit shall give way to cold indifference, or collisions of interest shall fester into hatred, the bands of political association will not long hold together parties no longer attracted by the magnetism of conciliated interests and kindly sympathies; and far better will it be for the people of the disunited States to part in friendship from each other than to be held together by constraint. Then will be the time for reverting to the precedent which occurred at the formation and adoption of the Constitution, to form again a more perfect union by dissolving that which could no longer bind, and to leave the separated parts to be reunited by the law of political gravitation to the center."[2]

Later, as a member of Congress, John Quincy Adams (on January 21, 1842), created an uproar by actually offering a petition from citizens of Haver-

[1] In his speech in the House of Representatives, Jan. 12, 1848: Lincoln's Works, as cited, vol. i, p. 105. See also Goldwin Smith in The United States; an Outline of Political History: New York, 1899; p. 248.

[2] C. F. Adams, Studies Military and Diplomatic: New York, 1911.

hill, Massachusetts, praying the House "immediately to adopt measures peaceably to dissolve the union of these States," because of the incompatibility between free and slave-holding communities. We have already noted the speech delivered by Josiah Quincy in 1811 (see page 194). On that occasion, however, no reprimand was administered; but in 1842 the question had become so embittered that Adams was accused of a "high breach of privilege, a contempt offered to this House, a direct proposition to the Legislature and each member of it to commit perjury, and involving necessarily in its execution and its consequences the destruction of our country and the crime of high treason." [3]

Adams was not alone among the Abolitionists in his attitude as to "incompatibility." Wendell Phillips said of the South in 1861: "Here are a series of States, girdling the Gulf, who think that their peculiar institutions require a separate government. They have a right to settle that question without appealing to you or me;" while William Lloyd Garrison, frankly confessing that the Constitution established slavery, had blasphemed that idol, calling it an agreement with hell and a covenant with death, and at last publicly burning it on the Fourth of July, 1854, at Framingham, in Massachusetts [4]—the State which in 1814 had proposed not only to secede from the Union, but also to fight it (see page 195). Writing to Lafayette of the War of 1812, Jefferson quaintly said that four of the Northern States were attached to the Union only as inanimate objects might be attached to a living man. Alexander John-

[3] J. T. Morse, Jr., J. Q. Adams: Boston, 1895; pp. 281–283.

[4] Oliver Johnson, Wm. Lloyd Garrison and His Times: Boston, 1880; pp. 336, 348. See also Rhodes, ii, 57.

ston has written, indeed, that almost every State in the Union has "in turn declared its own sovereignty, and denounced as almost treasonable similar declarations in other cases by other States." [5]

[5] Cited by H. W. Elson in his History of the United States: New York, 1904; page 626, note.

CHAPTER 52

SECESSION AND THE CONSTITUTION *

THE cause of this singular historical paradox inheres in the familiar fact that the Constitution of the United States is really a complex of compromises; the reconciliation of its doctrine of state freedom with that of a central sovereignty being in the abstract as difficult as the analogous theological puzzle of free will as related to the Divine sovereignty. Reverting to the Constitutional struggle of 1787, Professor Gordy has said, in his work on "Political Parties": "The convention framed a Constitution by the adoption of which thirteen peoples imagining themselves still independent and sovereign, really acknowledged themselves to be but parts of a single political whole. But they made this acknowledgment unconsciously. They continued to think of themselves as sovereigns, who indeed permitted an agent to exercise some of their functions for them, but who had not abdicated their thrones. If the Constitution had contained a definite statement of the actual fact; if it had said that to adopt it was to acknowledge the sovereignty of the one American people, no part of which could sever its connections from the rest without the consent of the whole, it would probably have been rejected by every State in the Union."[1]

* See also Chapter 39.

[1] Cited by C. F. Adams in Studies Military and Diplomatic: New York, 1911; p. 211, note.

Henry Cabot Lodge has said practically the same thing in his Life of Webster: "When the Constitution was adopted by the votes of States at Philadelphia, and accepted by the votes of States in popular conventions, it is safe to say that there was not a man in the country, from Washington and Hamilton, on the one side, to George Clinton and George Mason, on the other, who regarded the new system as anything but an experiment entered on by the States, and from which each and every State had the right peaceably to withdraw, a right which was very likely to be exercised."[2]

The late Charles Francis Adams, a Union soldier as well as a distinguished historical scholar, comments on these views in his valuable book of "Military Studies" and gives his own opinion as follows: "When the Federal Constitution was framed and adopted,—an indissoluble Union of indestructible States,—what was the law of treason?—to what or to whom, in case of final issue, did the average citizen owe allegiance? Was it to the Union or to his State? As a practical question, seeing things as they then were,—sweeping aside all incontrovertible legal arguments and metaphysical disquisitions,—I do not think the answer admits of doubt. If put in 1788, or indeed at any time anterior to 1825, the immediate reply of nine men out of ten in the Northern States, and of ninety-nine out of a hundred in the Southern States, would have been that, as between the Union and the State, ultimate allegiance was due to the State.—From 1788 to 1861, in case of direct and insoluble issue between sovereign State and sovereign Nation, every man was not only free to decide, but had to decide the question of ultimate alle-

[2] Daniel Webster, as cited, pp. 176–177.

giance for himself; and, whichever way he decided, almost equally good grounds in justification thereof could be alleged. The Constitution gave him two masters. Both he could not serve; and the average man decided which to serve in the light of sentiment, tradition and environment. Of this I feel as historically confident as I can feel of any fact not matter of absolute record or susceptible of demonstration."[3]

[3] Studies Military, etc., pp. 212, 215.

CHAPTER 53

WAS SECESSION TAUGHT AT WEST POINT?

MR. ADAMS, having "looked up the matter with the utmost care," confirms the widespread belief that Rawle's "View of the Constitution" was used as a text-book at West Point when Robert E. Lee and Jefferson Davis were students there. In spite of denials by General J. W. Latta and others, testimony on this question seems to be almost conclusive, including not only the published opinions of officials of the Military Academy, but the declarations of Generals Fitzhugh Lee and Dabney H. Maury, based on their personal experience as former students.[1] But even some of those who question its actual use by Robert Lee as a text-book assert that Rawle's "View of the Constitution" was undoubtedly in use at the Academy during a part of the time he was a student there; as, for example, Mr. Gamaliel Bradford, Jr.[2] Rawle himself was a member of the Philadelphia bar during the sittings of the Constitutional Convention of 1787, and afterwards rose to "the foremost rank of American legal luminaries in the first third of the nineteenth century," being the principal author of the revised code of Pennsylvania. A pronounced friend of the Union, he nevertheless taught in his text-book as follows:

[1] R. Bingham, Sectional Misunderstandings: Pamphlet reprinted (with important preface) from *N. A. Review* for September, 1904.

[2] Lee the American: Boston, 1912; p. 33. See also A. Johnston, American Political History, as cited, p. 293 ff.

"If a faction should attempt to subvert the Government of a State for the purpose of destroying its republican form, the national power of the Union could be called forth to subdue it. Yet it is not to be understood that its interposition would be justifiable if a State should determine to retire from the Union" (page 289). "It depends on the State itself whether it will continue a member of the Union. To deny this right would be inconsistent with the principle on which all our political systems are founded, which is, that the people have in all cases the right to determine how they shall be governed" (page 289). "The States may then wholly withdraw from the Union" (page 290). "If a majority of the people of a State deliberately and peacefully resolve to relinquish the republican form of government, they cease to be members of the Union" (page 292). "The secession of a State from the Union depends on the will of the people of such State" (page 295). "This right must be considered an ingredient in the original composition of the general government, and the doctrine heretofore presented in regard to the indefeasible nature of personal allegiance is so far qualified in respect to allegiance to the United States" (page 289).[3]

[3] See also pages 296, 297, 298, A View of the Constitution of the United States of America, William Rawle: Philadelphia, 1825.

CHAPTER 54

COTTON LOCALIZES SECESSION

It seems as clear as day that the doctrine of Secession did not become exclusively Southern and sectional until the Great Controversies drove it over to the Southern alinement. As with the questions of States-rights and slavery, so also in this case the far-reaching influence of the huge cotton industry wove its potent political spell. Cotton made the South a free trade section and the North protective; cotton lured the South back to slavery; cotton drove the South to seek the annexation of new lands for its plentiful production, and to insist on the maintenance of slave labor on those lands in order to produce it; cotton drove the South to an extreme States-rights position in those great Congressional struggles in which the efforts for territorial expansion became inextricably involved; and cotton at last drove the South to translate extreme States-rights into the terms of Secession, while the North step by step lined up on the opposite side of all these questions, which at first had not been sectional at all.

BOOK V

COTTON IN AMERICAN HISTORY: THE CIVIL WAR

CHAPTER 55

COTTON AND THE SINEWS OF WAR

SENATOR HAMMOND'S famous speech of the fourth of March, 1858 (see Chapters 49, 50) was not only the South's valedictory to the Union, it was also the South's declaration of economic independence. "Cotton is king" became such a feverish watchword on Southern lips that the more cautious citizens warned the public, when hostilities seemed to be imminent, not to "attach to it the power imputed of old to an incantation, and indulge in vague and, perhaps, extravagant notions of its efficiency." [1] Jefferson Davis, in his inaugural address as President of the provisional Confederate Government, at Montgomery,[2] mentioned at once the chief economic hope of the South and its only fear, in the following striking sentences:

"An agricultural people—whose chief interest is the export of a commodity required in every manufacturing community, our true policy is peace and the freest trade which our necessities will permit. It is alike our interest, and that of all those to whom we would sell and from whom we would buy, that there should be the fewest practicable restrictions upon the interchange of commodities.—This common interest of the producer and consumer can only be interrupted by an exterior force, which

[1] Cited by E. von Halle in Baumwollproduktion, vol. ii, p. 230.
[2] Feb. 18, 1861.

should obstruct its transmission to foreign markets —a course of conduct which would be as unjust toward us as it would be detrimental to the manufacturing and commercial interests abroad."[3]

Jefferson Davis was talking to England when he uttered those sentences: reminding England of its dependence on the South for the staple of its leading industry, promising England the coveted policy of free trade, and warning England of the mischief which the North might inflict on its interests by a possible blockade. His reminder and his promise were diplomacy of the highest order, and his warning proved to be prophecy. So great was his faith in the incantation, "Cotton is king," that after his prophecy had been fulfilled he expected the blockade to bring about automatically recognition from England, which was the substance of the thing chiefly hoped for. Mrs. Davis writes in her biography that "the President and his advisers looked to the stringency of the English cotton market, and the suspension of the manufactories, to send up a ground swell from the English operatives, that would compel recognition.—Foreign recognition was looked forward to as an assured fact."[4] Schwab says that in the Montgomery Convention of 1861 the sentiment already prevailed that a stoppage of the supply of cotton would soon bring the commercial nations, especially the North and Great Britain, to terms, and an embargo upon that staple was looked upon with favor.[5] And the correspondent of the London *Times*, writing from Montgomery, said: "They

[3] Library of Southern Literature, as cited, vol. iii, pp. 1268, 1270.

[4] C. F. Adams, Charles Francis Adams: Boston, 1900; pp. 162–163.

[5] J. C. Schwab, The Confederate States of America: New York, 1901; p. 250.

firmly believe that the war will not last a year.—They believe in the irresistible power of cotton, in the natural alliance between manufacturing England and France and the cotton-producing slave States, and in the force of their simple tariff."[6]

Visiting Charleston, Dr. Russell found the same faith. A merchant, pointing to the wharf laden with cotton bales, exclaimed: "Look out there! There's the key will open all our ports, and put us into John Bull's strong-box as well." "Rhett is also persuaded," Russell wrote, "that the Lord Chancellor sits on a cotton bale."[7] The Southerners agreed with one of the characters of Thucydides in believing that war is not merely an affair of arms, but of money, which gives to arms their use. Theodore Price has recently expressed the opinion that without cotton it is entirely improbable that the war would ever have been fought, and that it is extremely doubtful whether the Confederate States would have seceded had they not felt that because of England's dependence on American cotton they could rely upon her support, and on British disregard of the teachings of John Bright.[8] M. B. Hammond, another expert, says that had it not been for the reliance which the architects of the "Great Rebellion" placed on cotton as a means of obtaining revenue, it is doubtful if the war would have been undertaken. He quotes DeBow, the great war-time economist of the South, as saying to his people, of cotton: "To the slaveholding States, it is the great source of their power and their wealth, and the main security for their peculiar institutions.—Let us teach our children to hold

[6] Adams, as just cited, 162.
[7] Cited by Rhodes, iii, 416. See p. 40 of this volume.
[8] The *Outlook:* New York, March 28, 1914; p. 720.

the cotton plant in one hand and a sword in the other, ever ready to defend it as the source of commercial power abroad, and, through that, of independence at home."[9]

[9] The Cotton Industry, as cited, pp. 64, 257.

NOTE.—When the war broke out, the South paid instantly a very heavy penalty for her absorption in cotton cultivation at the expense of manufactures. As Ashley says, "The South had large natural resources, but they were undeveloped. She had not attempted to manufacture what she needed, for she had exported almost everything she produced to Europe or to the North, and purchased usually from the North even many necessities of life. At the beginning of the war, she did not have enough factories to supply her people with clothing and shoes. There were no powder plants, no factories for making cannon or small arms, no shipyards. Rolling-mills and iron foundries were uncommon. Railways were not particularly plentiful in the South, but they had been equipped with Northern rails and supplied with Northern locomotives and cars. In short the South was entirely dependent on the outside world, to which she had given her cotton and other products for the articles she needed."—R. L. Ashley, as cited, p. 386.

CHAPTER 56

THE COTTON FAMINE IN ENGLAND

Mr. Charles Francis Adams, already quoted on another subject, wrote for the "American Statesmen" series of biographies a sketch of his father, who, bearing the same name, represented the United States in England during the war. The preparation of this biography led Mr. Adams to a careful study of the Cotton Famine resulting in Great Britain from the blockade which Mr. Davis had predicted; and his opinion is therefore entitled to great weight. Mr. Adams says:

"The European cotton famine of 1861–63, at the time a very momentous affair, is now forgotten; yet upon it hung the fate of the American Union.[1]—The story of that Lancashire Cotton Famine of 1861 to 1864 has never been adequately told in connection with our Civil War. Simply ignored by the standard historians, it was yet the Confederacy's fiercest fight, and its most decisive as well as far-reaching defeat. A momentous conflict, the supremacy of the Union on the ocean hung on its issue; and upon that supremacy depended every considerable land operation: the retention by the Confederacy of New Orleans, and the consequent control of the Mississippi; Sherman's march to the sea; the movement through the Carolinas; the operations before Petersburg; generally, the maintenance of the Confederate

[1] Charles Francis Adams: Boston, 1900; pp. 265–266.

armies in the field. It is in fact no exaggeration to assert that both the conception and the carrying out of every large Union operation of the war without a single exception hinged and depended on complete national maritime supremacy. It is equally indisputable that the struggle in Lancashire was decisive of that supremacy. As Lee himself admitted in the death agony of the Confederacy, he had never believed it could in the long run make good its independence 'unless foreign powers should, directly or indirectly, assist' it in so doing. Thus, strange as it sounds, it follows as a logical sequence that Lee and his Army of Northern Virginia were first reduced to inanition, and finally compelled to succumb, as the result of events on the other side of the Atlantic, largely stimulated by a moral purpose over which they could exert no control. The great and loudly trumpeted cotton campaign of the Confederacy was its most signal failure; and that failure was decisive of the war." [2]

Many foreign students of Confederate history are strongly inclined to think, with Mr. Adams, that the blockade was the paramount cause of Southern defeat. As an example, we may translate the opinion of "Nauticus," writing in his famous year-book for 1900.[3]

"The blockade of the South," says this able authority, endorsing Admiral Porter,—"i.e., the sea-power of the North, contributed more to the down-

[2] Studies Military and Diplomatic: New York, 1911; pp. 317–318.

[3] Beiträge zur Flotten-Novelle; von Nauticus: Berlin, 1900; pp. 113–114. For an extended German account of the blockade, see E. von Halle, as cited, Zweiter Teil: Sezessionskrieg und Rekonstruktion (Leipzig, 1906); pp. 146–229. A study of Die Baumwollhungersnot in Lancashire is given in the same volume, pp. 256–265.

fall of the South than all other military operations put together. That is to say, the South, with its revenues, was wholly dependent on freedom of export for its land products, such as cotton, sugar, tobacco, etc., and its war supplies, besides machinery, wheat, peas, and potatoes, it had to obtain from outside. Through the gradually expanded blockade on all the coasts of the South (roundly, 3,000 sea-miles in length), which was vigorously carried out by means of 313 steamers and 105 sailing vessels, the sea traffic of the South was as good as wholly cut off; at all events, the blockade sufficed more and more to break altogether the power of resistance of the brave Southern army.—Want and misery everywhere was the frightful work of the blockade, which prepared and accomplished the defeat of the South."

Many American judgments to the same effect might be cited, of which perhaps the most recent from an authoritative Northern pen has been expressed by Professor George W. Kirchwey, as follows: "The exhaustion of the South, which, in the last analysis, gave the North the victory in our own Civil War, was mainly due to the effectiveness of our blockade and the thoroughness with which we acted on the principle of making war by starvation."[4]

Even a brief review of the facts of the Cotton Famine in England will give point to these impressive opinions. According to the London *Times* of September 19, 1861,[5] English cotton manufacture had grown to such enormous proportions as to support one-fifth of the entire population, with an annual pay-roll of $55,000,000. Over a thousand million pounds of cotton were consumed every year, pro-

[4] Editorial article in Los Angeles *Times*, Feb. 5, 1915.

[5] Cited by Rhodes, iii, 503, note.

ducing for exportation 2,800,000,000 yards of cloth and nearly 200,000,000 pounds of twist and yarn. There were 2,650 factories, of which 2,195 were localized in Lancashire County and on the borders of its two Southern neighbors; these factories containing over 30,000,000 spindles and 350,000 looms run by a 300,000 horse power, and employing nearly half a million operatives, of whom 56 per cent were females.—Before the close of the year 1862, 485,454 of the inhabitants of Lancashire were recipients of organized charity!

The cause of this swift and appalling catastrophe is not far to seek. A vast population in a limited area was dependent for its daily bread on the cotton industry. During the year 1860 America furnished 84 per cent. of the entire European supply of cotton, and during 1862 only 7 per cent, while the increased imports from India had not yet had time to alleviate the situation even measurably, and the demand for cotton in the Northern States had meanwhile become so intense that Liverpool actually re-exported 52,000 bales to the United States in 1862, so that the net receipts from America were less than 1,000 bales a week, as against 78,000 bales in 1860.[6]

And yet, in a way, the English market had been protected from disaster. Short crops in the United States had long ago led Lancashire to fear a cotton famine, and to organize in 1858 a "Cotton Supply Association," with an object identical with that of the British Cotton Growing Association of the present day (see chapter LXXIII); so that the production of India, Egypt, and Brazil had been stimulated, India alone furnishing England with 563,000 bales in 1860. At Christmas of that year the mills were

[6] Ellison, as cited, p. 93.

running four months behind their supply, investors were rejoicing in a return of 35 per cent on their capital, and operatives happy with the highest wages ever received. Moreover, America in 1860 produced its record crop, which the Southern planter marketed with unusual haste on account of the threats of trouble, England taking 1,650,000 bales before the war broke out. The British market was glutted to such an extent that many of the mills actually shut down in 1861, and prices remained practically stationary. The blockade, when it came, was laughed at as "a paper blockade," and indeed it seemed to be so, for it is estimated that 3,127,568 bales were exported during the year ending August 31, 1861. Mill owners even longed for an effective blockade to relieve the glut of the market. As to the duration of the war, they probably accepted the views conveyed by Seward to the distinguished son of Lancashire, John Bright, in September, 1861. "Tell him," Seward wrote to Charles Sumner, who was then in England, "the American question is not half so difficult of solution as he thinks. The rebellion is already arrested. Henceforward it will drag, languish, perish; that it owes all the success it attained to the timidity, hesitation, and indirect favor of British statesmen and the British press; that our interest in regard to it is Great Britain's interest—nothing different.—We shall soon see the war successful."[7]

The blockade was made effective during the latter half of 1861, and with such immediate pinching results that the English Christmas of that year was very different from the Christmas preceding; leading the London *Times* of December 27 to say:

[7] Cited by Rhodes, iii, 524, note.

"Christmas comes this year on a country bright with sun and frost, but on a people oppressed with a national loss and threatened with a formidable war. Already closed mills and short time have given some part of our population an earnest of what they may hereafter expect; already speculation is more careful than it has been for many years, and the somber appearance of our churches and chapels last Sunday portends a bad season next spring."

The same paper said a fortnight later: "There should have arrived by this time at the Southern ports of America, for shipment to England, from 500,000 to 1,000,000 bales of last year's cotton crop. By the latest estimate it was calculated that not 1,000 bales had been sent down, and it was known indeed that small stocks of cotton remaining over from the preceding year's crop had been removed from the ports to the interior of the country." [8]

During the first half of 1862, only 11,500 bales reached England from America, less than a hundredth of the quantity for the same period of the year preceding. Half of the Lancashire spindles were idle, and the price had jumped to thirteen pence a pound. In August it went up to twenty pence, and in the following month to half a crown.

A midsummer issue of the *Saturday Review* gives a vivid picture of the crisis at its height: "The cotton famine is altogether the saddest thing that has befallen this country for many a year. There have been gloomy times enough before this. We have seen Ireland perishing from actual starvation, and England half ruined from commercial distress. War and rebellion have taken their turn among the

[8] Cited by Rhodes, iii, 526–527, notes.

troubles from which a great nation can scarcely expect to be long free. But in the worst of our calamities there has seldom been so pitiable a sight as the manufacturing districts present at this moment.''[9]

By the close of that awful year the resources of organized charity for the relief of Lancashire pauperism had been exhausted, and alms were trickling in from Australia, Canada, India, and even China. Nearly a quarter-million operatives were entirely out of work, while only 121,129 were working full time, and, as already noted, 485,454 people were receiving alms, comprising 24.1 per cent of the entire population affected. Richard Cobden wrote from Lancashire in November to a friend in Staffordshire: ''Few people can realize the appalling state of things in this neighborhood. Imagine that the iron, stone, and coal were suddenly withheld from Staffordshire, and it gives you but an imperfect idea of what Lancashire, with its much larger population, is suffering from the want of cotton; it reverses the condition of the richest county in the kingdom, and makes it the poorest. A capitalist with £20,000 invested in buildings and machinery, may be almost on a par with his operatives in destitution, if he be deprived of the raw material which alone makes his capital productive.—Unhappily the winter is upon us to aggravate the sufferings of the working people.''[10] The London *Times* of December 31 said: ''The memory of the year which ends this day will hereafter be chiefly associated with the American war and its consequences at home. No crisis in modern times has been so anxiously watched, nor has any Euro-

[9] Rhodes, iv, 84, note.

[10] J. Morley, The Life of Richard Cobden: Boston, 1890; pp. 580–581.

pean war or revolution so seriously threatened the interests of England."[11]

This was the final climax of the famine. George McHenry was too late in 1863 with his book on "The Cotton Trade," addressed to the people of England in behalf of the Confederacy, and as an apology of slavery. The machinery of the mills had been adjusted to Surat or Indian cotton, of which 1,179 bales came in during the year, together with increased supplies from Egypt, Turkey, and Brazil. In 1864 the supplies from India proved sufficient to meet the demand, and the weekly number of applicants for alms was reduced to 135,000. Surat cotton was very unpopular, however, being short, harsh, brittle, and dirty, requiring much harder work than the American staple, and at one-third less than normal wages; so that many of the operatives preferred to be treated as paupers. Hammond cites reports that the word "Surat" became an odious epithet in Lancashire, so that a firm of brewers brought a libel suit to recover damages for having been maligned as "Surat brewers;" and John Bright used to tell a story of a church-going operative who once interrupted his pastor's prayer for increased cotton supplies, with the fervent ejaculation, "Amen, O Lord! *but not Shoorat!*"[12]

In 1865 the famine ended, having cost the British cotton trade in the neighborhood of $350,000,000, not including about $20,000,000 expended by the public in alms. Many mill owners, says Ellison, regained a part of their losses, but a large number lost nearly

[11] E. D. Fite, Social and Industrial Conditions in the North during the Civil War: New York, 1910; p. 19, note.

[12] G. M. Trevelyan, The Life of John Bright: Boston, 1913, p. 318, note.

everything they were worth, while many were reduced to bankruptcy.

John Bright, always an active friend of the Union, was astute enough to write to Sumner, during the height of the famine: "This country is passing through a wonderful crisis, but our people will be kept alive by the contributions of the country. I see that some one in the States has proposed to send something to our aid. If a few cargoes of flour could come, say 50,000 barrels, as a gift from persons in your Northern States to the Lancashire working men, it would have a prodigious effect in your favor here." [13] Three relief ships accordingly came out from New York to Liverpool, laden with bread, meat, and flour; a gift which, coming as it did from "those involved in the real agony of war to those for whom that war had occasioned distress, passing though sharp, was neither unnoticed nor barren of results."

[13] The same, p. 309.

CHAPTER 57

THE COTTON FAMINE IN FRANCE

THE Cotton Famine occasioned no real distress in New England, although curtailing, of course, the operation of the mills. As Hammond points out, there was plenty of employment in the army and in the government work shops for all industrious men, while the women readily found employment in the woolen mills, which the Cotton Famine and the government demand together caused to be unusually active. In Lowell, where the largest proportion of the cotton mills were idle, the deposits in the savings banks largely increased during the war.[1]

One result of the scarcity of cotton in the North appeared in various suggestions of a substitute, including a grandiloquent plan set out by an official of the Geological Survey for introduction of the perennial Peruvian variety, as follows:

"The period is not very remote when hedges, most efficient as fences, shall yield annual dividends of cotton; ornamental trees, blending the useful with the beautiful, shall repay ten-fold their cost and culture; when the rugged heights of the Hudson, the plains of New Jersey, the fertile valleys of the Keystone State, and the undulating prairies of the great West shall gleam in the sunlight, white as the winter drift, with generous pods of democratic cotton."[2]

[1] Hammond's Cotton Industry, p. 265.

[2] Cited by Hammond's Cotton Industry (p. 260) from Hunt's *Merchants' Magazine*, xlvi, 272.

Next to England, France suffered most from the Famine; consuming as she did 240,000,000 pounds annually, as against a thousand millions in England and 364,000,000 in America. Practically all of the French supply was American. When this was suddenly cut off, 300,000 people in one district were made absolutely destitute, subsisting, according to report, "by roaming at night from house to house, and demanding, rather than asking, alms;" while at Rouen, out of 50,000 operatives 30,000 were "laid off," and in the surrounding country only one-fifth of the hand weavers had work.

It was at this juncture that Louis Napoleon attempted to intervene. This versatile monarch had already evinced keen interest in American affairs. His troops were in Mexico, endeavoring to restore the prestige of the Latin race in the Western Hemisphere by setting a European monarch on the throne: Maximilian. The Confederacy, presuming no doubt on his lack of enthusiasm for the Government of the United States, had sent Commissioner Slidell to see him. In July, 1862, Slidell offered him a hundred thousand bales of cotton (worth in Europe at that time twelve and a half million dollars) if he would send his men-of-war and break the blockade. After considerable rumination, and influenced, undoubtedly, by the sad results of the Cotton Famine in France, the Emperor decided to interpose by calling on Russia and England to join him in the so-called task of "mediation." "My own preference," he said to Slidell, "is for a proposition of an armistice of six months; this would put a stop to the effusion of blood, and hostilities would probably never be resumed. We can urge it on the high grounds of humanity and the interest of the whole civilized world;

if it be refused by the North, it will afford good reason for recognition, and perhaps for more active intervention."[3]

Russia, "our only well-wisher in Europe," promptly declined to act with Napoleon. On the decision of England rested the fate of the war. It was at this critical juncture that our American minister wrote: "A word from the Prime Minister, suggesting that the time had arrived for recognition [of the Confederacy], would meet with unanimous response in the affirmative." Such was at one time the feeling in England against the Union and in behalf of the South.

[3] Verified by Rhodes, iv, 346. For an extremely interesting account of Napoleon in Slidell's own words, see Proceedings of Mass. Hist. Soc'y, May, 1914; p. 379.

CHAPTER 58

NAPOLEON'S FAILURE

NOTHING gives a clearer idea of the chances that favored Napoleon's plans for interference than extracts from the letters written to Charles Sumner in December, 1861, by Richard Cobden, who, like Bright, was an earnest friend of the Union, although at one time himself engaged in the cotton trade.

"From all that I hear from France," he says, "the trade of that country is dreadfully damaged, and I feel convinced the Emperor would be supported by his people if he were to enter into alliance with England to abolish the blockade and recognize the South. The French are inconvenienced in many ways by your blockade, and especially in their relations with New Orleans, which are more important to them in exports than to us.—I am not justifying any interference on the part of Europe; but it is a fearful thing to have the whole civilized world undergoing privations and sufferings which they lay at the door of the North, thus making it the interest of their governments to interfere with you.—The state of modern society, where you have millions of laborers in Europe depending for the means of employment on a regular supply of raw materials brought from another continent, to say nothing of hundreds of millions of capital invested on the same dependence, will necessitate a change in the law of blockade and other belligerent rules.—The recognition of the independence of the South, and the forcing of the blockade, will come to be viewed, about next March, as a matter of life and death by many millions of people in Europe, and as a question of high political urgency by the most powerful governments of the world.—We in England have ready a fleet surpassing in destructive force any naval armament the world ever saw, exceeding greatly the British navy in the great French war in 1810. This force has been got up under false pretenses. There is always a desire on the part of governments to use such armaments, by way of proving that they were necessary. France was the pretense, and now we have plenty of people who would be content to see this fleet turned against you."[1]

English feeling had been significantly indicated by a proclamation of the belligerency of the Confederacy within a month of the outbreak of the war; which so excited Secretary Seward that he was inclined to challenge a general European combat, in the singular belief that "the presence of a foreign foe alone can reconcile the disintegrated States," and "all the hills of South Carolina would pour forth their population to the rescue."[2] "Great Britain," he wrote to his wife, "is in great danger of sympathizing so much with the South, for the sake of peace and cotton, as to drive us to make war against her as the ally of the traitors." Later in the year a war with England was indeed very narrowly averted in consequence of the unwarranted seizure by a United States officer of the two outward bound European commissioners of the Confederacy, Slidell and Mason, from the British steam-packet *Trent*. Thirty thousand English

[1] Cited by Rhodes, iii, 529, 531, notes, and 535.
[2] Cited in Charles Francis Adams, p. 184.

troops were immediately despatched to Halifax, and ships hastily loaded with ammunition and artillery; but Lincoln saved the life of the nation by disavowing this seizure, and releasing Messrs. Mason and Slidell, who proceeded to Europe. It was the latter who, coöperating with Mason, in London, from his own headquarters in Paris, later almost succeeded in the scheme for Napoleonic intervention.

But in the British Government a diversity of sympathy developed. The premier, Lord Palmerston, had said to Minister Adams, immediately on his arrival in London: "We do not like slavery, but we want cotton, and we dislike very much your Morrill tariff." Earl Russell, the Secretary for Foreign Affairs, now inclined strongly toward the South. In the May of 1862 he had said: "Thousands are now obliged to resort to the poor-rates for subsistence, owing to this blockade, yet Her Majesty's Government have not sought to take advantage of the obvious imperfections of this blockade, in order to declare it ineffective. They have, to the loss and detriment of the British nation, scrupulously observed the duties of Great Britain to a friendly State."[3] But in the autumn of that year he wrote to Lord Palmerston: "I agree with you, the time is come for offering mediation to the United States Government, with a view to the recognition of the independence of the Confederates. I agree further that, in case of failure, we ought ourselves to recognize the Southern States as an independent State."[4]

The feeling of the Chancellor of the Exchequer, Mr. Gladstone, may be gathered from his famous

[3] Jefferson Davis, The Rise and Fall of the Confederate Government: New York, 1881; p. 344.

[4] Charles Francis Adams, as cited.

speech at Newcastle, made in the autumn of 1862, when the Cotton Famine was at its height, and just at the time when Louis Napoleon was pressing for armed intervention.

"There is no doubt," Gladstone said, amid the cheering of his Newcastle audience, "that Jefferson Davis and other leaders of the South have made an army; they are making, it appears, a navy; and they have made what is more than either,—they have made a nation.—We may anticipate with certainty the success of the Southern States so far as regards their separation from the North. I cannot but believe that that event is as certain as any event yet future and contingent can be."

It is little wonder that Minister Adams wrote in his diary next day: "If he be any exponent at all of the views of the cabinet, then is my term likely to be very short."[5]

But it was just at this point that differences were revealed in the cabinet; Sir George Lewis, the Secretary of State for War, going so far as to reply directly to Mr. Gladstone by announcing publicly that the time had not yet come for recognition of the Confederacy. The cabinet divergence proved to be so serious, indeed, that the meeting actually called for consideration of Napoleon's scheme was abandoned; the influence of Cobden and Bright being distinctly traceable in the matter, as also the effective diplomacy of the American Minister, of whom Lowell afterwards wrote: "None of our generals in the field, not Grant himself, did us better or more trying service than he in his forlorn outpost of London."[6] The divided mind of the British Govern-

[5] Charles Francis Adams, as cited, pp. 280, 287.
[6] Charles Francis Adams, as cited, p. 345.

ment had been well expressed in the initial remark of the premier to Mr. Adams, when he informed him that while the English wanted cotton, they did not like slavery.[7]

[7] For a careful study of this chapter in international relations, see A Crisis in Downing Street, by C. F. Adams; Proceedings Mass. Hist. Soc'y, May, 1914.

CHAPTER 59

THE BRITISH WORKING-MAN

English feeling on the question of slavery had been strongly intensified by the wide reading of "Uncle Tom's Cabin," especially among cotton mill operatives. This remarkable novel, the "best seller" of its day, had penetrated every corner of Europe, but was devoured most eagerly by the idle weavers and spinners of Lancashire, interested as they were in "the land of cotton" and the cotton war, which so vitally affected them. The melodrama of the book they accepted as sober realism; Uncle Tom, in his heroic rôle of philosopher and saint, being unquestioningly regarded as the unvarying type of his race, while Legree, the heavy villain, stood as a truthful undeviating symbol of the Southern planter. It is of course very much to the credit of these distressed victims of the Cotton Famine, however misled by sentimental and sensational fiction they may have been, that their emotions proved to be stronger than a cold and calculating self-interest, so that the very section of England that might most reasonably have been expected to send up a "ground swell" for the Cotton States, swung its sympathies over to the Union.

There was, also, a hard-headed principle of common sense commingled with the fervid British sympathy that now developed in behalf of the North among the working people and thoughtful middle classes. Perhaps the whole clear case is nowhere better stated than by Mr. John Watts in his book on "The Facts of the Cotton Famine:"[1]

"There were not wanting men," he says, "who saw, or thought they saw, a short way out of the difficulty, viz., by a recognition on the part of the English Government of the Southern confederacy in America. And meetings were called in various places to memorialize the Government to this effect. Such meetings were always balanced by counter meetings, at which it was shown that simple recognition would be waste of words; that it would not bring to our shores a single shipload of cotton, unless followed up by an armed force to break the blockade, which of course if adopted would be war; war in favor of the slave confederacy of the South, and against the free North and Northwest, whence comes a large proportion of our imported corn. In addition to interfering in the affairs of a nation 3,000 miles away, the cotton, if we succeeded in getting it, would be stained with blood and cursed with the support of slavery, and would also prevent our getting the food which we needed from the North equally as much as the cotton from the South."

The Emancipation Proclamation, treated contemptuously by the English governing classes when it came, moved the laboring people and middle classes most profoundly. Minister Adams writes that on January 2, 1863, he received a gentleman from Manchester, in the very heart of the Cotton Famine, then at its worst, who brought an address to President Lincoln from a meeting of workingmen held on the last day of the just closed year.[2]

[1] London, 1866; see especially Chapters viii and xii.

[2] Lincoln's reply to this address is well worth reading. In a

"It was quite a strong manifestation of good feeling," Adams says. "There can be little doubt that now is the time to strike the popular heart here; and the effect may be to checkmate the movement of the aristocracy." A little later he writes, after the addresses had begun to pour into the Legation "in a steady and ever-swelling stream:" "It is clear that the current is now setting strongly with us among the body of the people. This may be quite useful on the approach of the session of Parliament." [3]

Of the great mass meeting of January 29, Cobden wrote to Sumner as follows: "I know nothing in my political experience so striking, as a display of spontaneous public action, as that of the vast gathering at Exeter Hall, when, without one attraction in the form of a popular orator, the vast building, its

letter "To the Working-men of Manchester" dated Jan. 19, 1863, he said: "I know and deeply deplore the sufferings which the working-men at Manchester, and in all Europe, are called to endure in this crisis. It has been often and studiously represented that the attempt to overthrow this government, which was built upon the foundation of human rights, and to substitute for it one which should rest exclusively on the basis of human slavery, was likely to obtain the favor of Europe. Through the action of our disloyal citizens, the working-men of Europe have been subjected to severe trials, for the purpose of forcing their sanction to that attempt. Under the circumstances, I cannot but regard your decisive utterances upon the question as an instance of sublime Christian heroism which has not been surpassed in any age or in any country. It is indeed an energetic and reinspiring assurance of the inherent power of truth, and of the ultimate and universal triumph of justice, humanity, and freedom. I do not doubt that the sentiments you have expressed will be sustained by your great nation; and, on the other hand, I have no hesitation in assuring you that they will excite admiration, esteem, and the most reciprocal feelings of friendship among the American people. I hail this interchange of sentiment, therefore, as an augury that whatever else may happen, whatever misfortune may befall your country or my own, the peace and friendship which now exist between the two nations will be, as it shall be my desire to make them, perpetual."—Lincoln's Complete Works, as cited, ii, pp. 301–302.

[3] Adams, 299.

minor rooms and passages, and the streets adjoining, were crowded with an enthusiastic audience. That meeting has had a powerful effect on our newspapers and politicians. It has closed the mouths of those who have been advocating the side of the South. And I now write to assure you that any unfriendly act on the part of our Government—no matter which of our aristocratic parties is in power—towards your cause is not to be apprehended. If an attempt were made by the Government in any way to commit us to the South, a spirit would be instantly aroused which would drive that Government from power."[4]

So it was that the moral issue of slavery wrought a profound effect on the British attitude, and probably eventually determined it. Slavery, which the South had grown accustomed to regard as necessary to the successful cultivation of cotton, had become its Nemesis; not only at home in bringing on civil war, but also abroad in its influence on the result of that war when it had come. Of this fact no better evidence could be cited than the utterances of the London organ of the Confederacy, The *Index*, published during the war for the purpose of influencing European opinion. After learning of the effect wrought by Uncle Tom in Lancashire and elsewhere throughout England, and of the consequences of that effect then being manifested in Parliament, The *Index* said:

"It is the great peculiarity of England that the heart of the country is thoroughly religious. The plain issue, then, between the two nations, was therefore naturally not overlooked by those whose program in America was the law of conscience overriding the law of the land; and the prominence they

[4] Adams, 301.

gave to the slave question was especially directed to the religious public in England. And well has it answered their purpose. To this very hour the great mass of the people have no other terms to express the nature of the conflict. It is to no purpose that argument, fact, and experience have shown the utter indifference of the North to the welfare of the negro; the complete appreciation by the slaves themselves of the sham friendship offered them; and, still more, the diabolical preaching of the ministers of God's word, who rely on Sharp's rifles to carry out their doctrines. The emancipation of the negro from the slavery of Mrs. Beecher Stowe's heroes is the one idea of the millions of British who know no better, and do not care to know."

Bright and Cobden, indeed, proved themselves capable of keen insight and foresight by going so far as to say that the cotton crop of the South would be better off without slaves. In the June of 1863 Mr. Bright said: "I maintain that with a supply of cotton mainly derived from the Southern States, and mainly raised by slave labor, two things are indisputable: First, that the supply must always be insufficient, and, second, that it must always be insecure.—I maintain—and I believe my opinion will be supported by all those men who are most conversant with American affairs—that with slavery abolished, with freedom firmly established in the South, you would find in ten years to come a rapid increase in the growth of cotton, and not only would its growth be rapid, but its permanent increase would be secured.—There is no greater enemy to Lancashire, to its capital and to its labor, than the man who wishes the cotton agriculture of the Southern States to be continued under the condition of slave labor."

CHAPTER 60

NAPOLEON AND THE COTTON LOAN

NOTWITHSTANDING the British turn in favor of the cause of the North, Slidell and Louis Napoleon were able to give the American Minister one more critical engagement before retiring from the field in defeat. It is not discourteous to royalty to place the name of Slidell in precedence to that of Napoleon, in view of the fact that students of this dual relationship agree in regarding Slidell as a past master in the fine art of "wire pulling," so that the French emperor was little more than a marionette in his hands.

In January, 1863, Slidell took advantage of the acute stage which the French Cotton Famine had reached to persuade Napoleon to offer, on his own initiative and single handed, the services of his government to that of the United States as mediator with the Confederacy. Upon President Lincoln's courteous but firm rejection of this proposal, the Emperor proved lacking in courage to proceed further without additional support; [1] whereupon Slidell and Napoleon renewed their endeavor to secure the coöperation of England.

Before pushing this plan, however, Slidell assisted his London colleague, Mr. Mason, in negotiating the famous "Cotton Loan," through the French bank-

[1] Rhodes, iv, 348.

ing house of Erlanger et Compagnie.[2] This loan, which was for the sum of $15,000,000, received secret confirmation from the Confederate House of Representatives, and not until the advertisements of it appeared in foreign newspapers did the public, even in the South, know its details. The bonds were to run for twenty years, and bear 7 per cent interest; each bond being exchangeable at face value for New Orleans Middling cotton at the rate of sixpence the pound, at any time not later than six months after the ratification of a peace treaty between the North and the South. As Middling was then selling in Liverpool for twenty-two pence a pound, and the Confederate Government was known to be holding not less than 350,000 bales, the investment was regarded as perfectly sound, provided the blockade could be lifted. That foreign investors must have had faith in its lifting, and in the ultimate success of the Confederacy, is shown by the fact that within two days the bonds were reported as being three times over-subscribed in London alone, while the total subscriptions amounted to five times the face value of the loan. Although the bonds fluctuated with the news from the battle fields, they held the faith of foreign investors reasonably firm even until the fall of Charleston in 1865, as the English evidently believed that the cotton necessary for their redemption could be delivered even should the South suffer defeat; and, in fact, assumed that in this event their redemption would be undertaken by the United States Government itself. So late as the year 1883 there came a revival on the London market of dealing in the bonds of the Erlanger Cotton Loan.

Proceeds from the sale of these bonds consti-

[2] Schwab, as cited, p. 31 ff.

tuted the main source of the specie revenue of the Confederate Government, and enabled it to pay for the *Alabama* and other privateers secured during the first two years of the war.

CHAPTER 61

NAPOLEON, ROEBUCK, AND BRIGHT [1]

THE familiar incident of the privateer *Alabama* was of course a fruitful source of discord between the Westminster and Washington governments. Inasmuch as two formidable rams were also building in a British shipyard, and the inquisitiveness of the American Minister concerning their ownership was embarrassing to a cabinet which disliked slavery but wanted cotton, Mr. Slidell deftly arranged this matter of the rams by transferring their ownership to an obliging French firm before bringing his Napoleonic proposal to the open attention of Parliament. Furthermore, he succeeded in securing a cross-channel visit from two of the leading friends of the Southern cause then in the British Parliament, Messrs. Lindsay and Roebuck, who were duly entertained by the Emperor at the Tuileries, and authorized by him, so they afterwards asserted, to represent him to the House of Commons as being ripe and eager for the instant recognition of the Confederate States of America.

Unfortunately for Mr. Roebuck, who sustained a reputation for fluent and florid speech, he had on a previous public occasion described the French Emperor in somewhat ungentle terms; in fact, had denounced him as "a perjured despot." Therefore a trap was set for Roebuck when, on the thirtieth of

[1] Chief authority: Charles Francis Adams, as cited.

June, 1863, he moved in the House of Commons "to enter into negotiations with the great powers of Europe for the purpose of obtaining their coöperation in the recognition" of the Confederacy; and then proceeded to make himself Napoleon's mouthpiece by quoting the Emperor's language as follows:

"As soon as I learnt that that rumor was circulating in England (that I had changed my mind about recognizing the Confederacy), I gave instructions to my ambassador to deny the truth of it. Nay, more, I instructed him to say that my feeling was not, indeed, exactly the same as it was, because it was stronger than ever in favor of recognizing the South. I told him also to lay before the British Government my understanding and my wishes on this question, and to ask them again whether they would be willing to join me in that recognition."

The Emperor, according to Roebuck, continued:

"I give you full liberty to state to the English House of Commons this my wish. I have determined in all things to act with England, and, more particularly, I have determined to act with her as regards America."

Slidell's associates were able to report to the Confederacy at this time that there was at length a people's movement in England in favor of recognition, as well as a "people's champion," Roebuck. One of them had also "taken measures to placard every available space in the streets of London with representations of our newly adopted flag conjoined to the British national ensign—which I design simply as a 'demonstration' to impress the masses with the vitality of our cause."

Roebuck continued his speech in Parliament as follows:

"I have to-day had letters from Lancashire, which say that in thirteen of the great towns there have been large meetings in favor of the recognition of the South—that that has been carried by an immense majority of ten to one, and that there will be no end to the petitions sent up to this House for that measure."

The effect of this speech is described by Mr. Roebuck's own biographer as being what might be expected as the inevitable result of amateur diplomacy—leading the French Emperor to disavow, or to decline to be bound by, the version given of his conversation; while "the amazement and amusement, with which this mission to the 'perjured despot' of a few years ago was received by the general public, were expressed in very pregnant sarcasm by speakers like Mr. Bright," "who shook him as a terrier shakes a rat," says one who heard the debate.[2]

The American minister wrote in his diary next day:

"Mr. Roebuck succeeded in spoiling his case most completely as well as complicating the Emperor at Paris with the Ministry here and the Government at home."

Writing to Seward he said:

"The effect of Tuesday night's debate was very severe on Mr. Roebuck. His extraordinary attempts to influence the action of the House by the use of the authority of the Emperor of the French, as well as his presuming to make himself the medium of an appeal to Parliament against the conduct of the ministry, have had the consequences which might naturally be expected by any one acquainted with

[2] Trevelyan's Life of John Bright, as cited, p. 323.

the English character. Thus it happened that Mr. Roebuck, though addressing an assembly a great proportion of whom sympathized with him in his object, demolished his cause; whilst, on the other hand, Mr. Bright, even whilst running counter to the predisposition of most of his hearers, succeeded in extorting a general tribute of admiration of his eloquent and convincing reply."

On July 13 (1863) Roebuck withdrew his motion, without calling for a division. Within a few days news of Gettysburg and Vicksburg reached England, starting the cotton bonds on a rapid downward course, and greatly encouraging the friends of the Union, so that Bright wrote to Sumner:

"I need not tell you with what feelings of gratification and relief I have received the news of your recent successes. The debate on the foolish Roebuck proposition took place when there was much gloom over your prospects, and the friends of Secesh here were rejoicing in the belief that your last hour had come. How soon are the clouds cleared away; and how great is the despondency of those who have dishonored themselves by their hatred of your people and Government. The loan is down near 20 per cent. in a little more than a week and is now, I suspect, unsaleable, and people are rubbing their eyes, and wondering where the invincible South is gone to. Our Pro-slavery newspapers are desperately puzzled and the whole mass of opinion is in confusion."[3]

[3] Cited by Rhodes, iv, 376, note.

CHAPTER 62

THE FAILURE OF THE FAMINE

MEANWHILE, the two rams were nearing completion, one of them actually taking the water on the fourth of July, 1863. Minister Adams discreetly kept in his pocket communications from Secretary Seward on this subject, which, if conveyed to the British Government in their entirety, would have been practically equivalent to a declaration of war. He managed, however, to acquaint Earl Russell indirectly with the fact that his instructions were far more stringent than he had as yet been disposed to execute. On September 5 Earl Russell ordered that the vessels be prevented from leaving Liverpool, the very day on which Adams, unaware of the order, felt it needful to send the Earl his famous despatch containing the words: "It would be superfluous in me to point out to your lordship that this is war."[1]

A month later the Broad Arrow was placed upon the vessels; when this news reached the great audience which Henry Ward Beecher was addressing at Manchester, "the whole audience rose to its feet. Men cheered and waved their hats, while women waved their handkerchiefs and wept." The British Admiralty solved the problem of the ironclads by buying them.

Rhodes says that had they reached their destina-

[1] Rhodes, iv, 380.

tion they would undoubtedly have broken the blockade, and "the victories even of Gettysburg and Vicksburg might have been neutralized.—From some such damage Earl Russell, by his careful and decisive action, saved the North, and thereby prevented a war between the United States and Great Britain."[2] In a valuable note he quotes Captain Page, who had been selected to command these vessels, as saying in 1898: "My intention was to sail at once to Wilmington and to raise the blockade there and at Charleston. Having accomplished this, I intended to raise the blockade of the gulf ports and cut off all communications of the North by water with New Orleans. I had at the time perfect confidence in my ability to accomplish my purposes, and I now believe, in the light of what I have since learned, that if the rams had been permitted to leave England I would have been successful."[3]

In September Mr. Mason, after conferring with Slidell, informed Earl Russell that he would terminate his mission, and did so. Slidell coöperated with Louis Napoleon in constructing two iron-clads and four clipper corvettes in France, but these never reached their destination, Napoleon, as Rhodes says, having decided "to change his tune." After October, 1863, the danger of foreign intervention in the Civil War never recurred; England having proved to be the insurmountable obstacle to the recognition of the Confederacy by France and other European powers.[4] Jefferson Davis, in his Congressional message in December, expressed "dissatisfaction with the British Government," alluding specifically to their seizure of the iron-clads and their respect for the Federal blockade.

[2] iv, 385. [3] The same. [4] The same, 388.

In his "Rise and Fall of the Confederate Government,"[5] Mr. Davis explains the failure of the Cotton Famine, as a means of forcing European recognition, by the statement that the United States Government interfered with its efficacy, through fitting up military expeditions for the forcible seizure of cotton in Southern ports, which was afterwards doled out to England. He quotes a letter from Seward to Minister Adams, dated July 28, 1862, promising that the Federals would "speedily open all the channels of commerce, and free them from military embarrassments; and cotton, so much desired by all nations, will flow forth as freely as heretofore. We have ascertained that there are three and a half millions of bales yet remaining in the region where it was produced, though large quantities of it are yet unginned and otherwise unprepared for market. We have instructed the military authorities to favor, so far as they can consistently with the public safety, its preparation for and despatch to the markets where it is so much wanted."

Mr. Davis goes on to say that in pursuance of this policy "strong military and naval expeditions were fitted out to invade us and occupy the ports where cotton and other valuable products were usually shipped.—The ports of Beaufort, North Carolina, Port Royal, South Carolina, and New Orleans, Louisiana, were declared by proclamation of the President of the United States to be open for trade under the new system. Licenses were granted to foreign vessels by United States consuls and to coasting vessels by the Treasury Department, and the blockade was relaxed so far as related to those ports, except as 'to persons, property, and information con-

[5] As cited, vol. ii, ch. xxxvi.

traband of war.' Collectors were appointed at the above-mentioned ports, and a circular was addressed to the foreign ministers at Washington announcing the reopening of communication with conquered Southern localities."

But the report of the Boston Board of Trade for 1863 pays Mr. Davis's government the tribute of a confession that it had largely outwitted these plans of the Federals for accommodating Europe with cotton. It says: "The Confederates have guarded this article with unusual vigilance, burning and destroying all likely to fall into our hands, knowing that the 'Cotton Famine' of Europe was their most active agent in bringing about a recognition of their confederacy."[6] The exportation to Great Britain was considerably increased, however, rising from 72,000 bales in 1862 to 132,000 in the following year and 198,000 in 1864.

On both sides of the war there was great glee when, by burning, this commodity could be kept from conversion into an asset of the enemy's war-chest. Planters of the precious sea-island fiber did not falter in applying the torch to the entire year's crop when Port Royal was taken by the Federals, the Charleston *Courier* commenting as follows: "At eleven o'clock last night the heavens towards the southwest were brilliantly illuminated with the patriotic flames ascending from burning cotton. As the spectators witnessed it they involuntarily burst forth with cheer after cheer, and each heart was warmed as with a new pulse." Again: "We learn with gratification that the patriotic planters on the seaboard are hourly applying the torch to their cotton." And still later: "The 'fires of patriotism'

[6] Cited in Hammond's Cotton Industry, p. 263.

continue; thirteen cotton houses have been burnt on Port Royal Island, one on Paris, and one on St. Helena, since the Yankee occupation."[7]

On the other side, Grant in his Memoirs gives this graphic account of an incident connected with his occupation of Jackson: "Sherman and I went together into a manufactory which had not ceased work on account of the battle nor for the entrance of Yankee troops. Our presence did not seem to attract the attention of either the manager or the operatives, most of whom were girls. We looked on for a while to see the tent cloth which they were making roll out of the looms, with 'C. S. A.' woven in each bolt. There was an immense amount of cotton in bales, stacked outside. Finally I told Sherman I thought they had done work enough. The operatives were told they could leave and take with them what cloth they could carry. In a few minutes cotton and factory were in a blaze."[8]

[7] Cited by Rhodes, iii, 551, 552, note.

[8] U. S. Grant, Personal Memoirs: New York, 1885, 1886; vol. i, p. 507.

CHAPTER 63

ECONOMICS AND FATALISM

To an unprejudiced observer it seems clear that the South failed to make the best use of its cotton resources as a basis of revenue and finance. Too much reliance was placed on the efficacy of the Cotton Famine on the other side of the water, and not enough attention was paid to economic efficiency at home. As Dr. Curry says in his Civil History of the Confederate States,[1] how to deal with cotton and make it most available as an auxiliary to the Southern cause did not secure a concurrence of judgment or consistent and effective action. To the present writer it seems that the best plan suggested was the one urged on the Confederacy by Senator Hammond of South Carolina, to prohibit the private export of cotton, purchase it with bonds of the new government, and hold it abroad and at home as a basis of credit. As the sequel showed, it might have added a value amounting to two billion dollars in gold to the resources of the Confederacy.[2] But the incantatory phrase to which Senator Hammond himself had given such wide currency wrought its benumbing witchery even on the minds of the leaders of the Southern government, so that they depended on the magic scepter of "King Cotton" alone to

[1] Cited in Library of Southern Literature, iii, 1135.

[2] See Sketch of James Henry Hammond, by Major Harry Hammond: n. d.

take care of his realm, and even to turn the blockade of the enemy into a panoply of defense and deliverance.

Considerations of this character are pertinent at the close of this section, as an offset to the almost fatalistic impression that the student sometimes receives while tracing the skeins of the cotton influence through the woof of American history. A contemporary French writer has said, concerning war, that "economic phenomena are the substructure of history. This means that history advances through the antagonism of peoples moved by the nature of their conflicting needs, and thus economic fatalities sometimes dominate the will of man as the blind divinities of antiquity were said to do."[3]

There is much to lend color to this view in the study of the influence of cotton in American history. At times it seems to weave its way relentlessly almost as though the soul of Arachne had actually found lodgment in its boll. But the truth is, of course, that the wills of men yielded supinely to the sway of this portentous economic force, instead of setting themselves resolutely to dominate it and control it for wisdom and righteousness. There are scores of turning-points in its history where, if wisdom had taken the skeins from the hands of prejudice and passion, a righteous and peaceful pattern might have been the result. A sad illustration of the opposite course is found in the substitution of the madness of Douglas politics for the calm sanity of the policies of Webster. The writer rejects the implied philosophy of Maurice Lair, just quoted, and

[3] Maurice Lair in *Revue Bleue;* cited by *Literary Digest:* New York, Aug. 8, 1914. For further discussion of Fatalism and Economics, see Seligman, as cited, Part II, ch. i.

will let another economist answer him, most admirably:

"To this philosophy the civilist opposes another: that in man there is that which sets him apart from the plants and the animals, which gives him control of and responsibility for his social acts; which makes him the master of his social destiny if he but will it; that by virtue of the forces of his mind he may go forward to the completer conquest, not merely of nature, but of himself, and thereby, and by that alone, redeem human association from the evils that now burden it."[4]

[4] Norman Angell: The Foundations of International Polity: London, 1914; p. xlviii.

BOOK VI

THE OLD SOUTH AND THE NEW

CHAPTER 64

COTTON AND THE OLD SOUTH

A LETTER from Eli Whitney to his friend Robert Fulton contained the following passage:

"My invention was new and distinct from every other; it stood alone. It was not interwoven with anything before known;—and I have always believed, that I should have had no difficulty in causing my rights to be respected, if it had been less valuable, and been used only by a small portion of the community."[1]

The eagerness of Southern planters to grow upland cotton, after it could be ginned, almost passes belief. Five months after he had obtained his patent Whitney wrote: "We shall not be able to get machines made as fast as we shall want them. We have now Eight Hundred Thousand weight of cotton on hand and the next crop will begin to come in very soon. It will require Machines enough to clean 5 or 6 thousand wt. of clean cotton pr Day to satisfy the demand for next Year.—And I expect the crop will be double another year."[2] Ten years after the gin was invented he wrote: "The cotton cleaned annually with that machine sells for at least five Million of Dollars."[3]

This astonishing leap in cotton production of

[1] Howe's Memoirs, as cited, pp. 130–131.
[2] Whitney's Correspondence, as cited, p. 101.
[3] The same, p. 122.

course arose from the fact that Whitney's gin made it possible exactly at the moment when the great series of English inventions, rounding to completion in the power-loom of Cartwright, had created an insatiable demand. As Baines said, "The spinning machinery in England gave birth to the cotton cultivation in America; and the increase of the latter is now in turn extending the application of the former. In the vast machine of commerce, the spindles of Manchester are as necessarily tied to the plow and hoe of the Mississippi, as to their own bobbins.—Thus do mechanical improvements in England, and agricultural improvements in America, act and re-act upon each other: thus do distant nations become mutually dependent, and contribute to each other's wealth."[4]

Coöperating with this commercial coincidence occurred a large increase in Yankee ship-building. Massachusetts and Maine, for example, by exceeding, just prior to Whitney's invention, the heaviest tonnage of colonial times, enabled Tench Coxe to discredit effectually Lord Sheffield's confident prophecy that American shipping would come to an end after the colonies left the crown. By the year of Whitney's death, 1825, the domestic exports of the United States showed a value of over $66,000,000; and of this amount more than $36,000,000 arose from raw cotton shipped by the South to England.

Robert Fulton, a friend of both Whitney and Cartwright, by applying the steam-engine of Watt to override the immense ocean barrier dividing the gin from the home of the power-loom, manifolded a thousand times over the carrying power of the ships; while Samuel Slater, the British spinner, by setting

[4] Baines, 317.

up from memory at Pawtucket a successful factory just three years before Whitney invented his gin, initiated in New England a demand for Southern cotton second only to that of the old England from which he had fled. It is little wonder that the South devoted itself thenceforward with undivided attention to the production of that precious commodity for which two continents clamored, and which the South alone could supply.

Certainly the life of the South from this time forward revolved around the cotton plant. Early in the spring the negroes with their multitudinous mules begin the plowing of straight, long, deep furrows in the fragrant mellow soil,—the deeper the better, since cotton has a tap-root which, if properly invited, will sink four feet in searching for fresh food and moisture. Fertilizer, consisting of manure and malodorous guano, or, in later times, expensive phosphates, is laid in the center of the "beds" thrown up by the furrows; and the time of actual planting awaited. When the first song of the "turtle dove" is heard, and the starry blooms of the dogwood light up the edge of the forest, and the frosts are thought to be over, came, in the old days, flocks of black women with hoes, scooping out the beds at rough intervals, followed by other women dropping careless handfuls of seed. The tender green plants, thrusting their way upward shortly, were thinned out, one stalk to a foot. When two or three weeks above the surface, more plowing was needful, to break the new crust of the soil, and kill weeds. Then, every three weeks thereafter, until the steaming "dog days" of August, the patient plow would break the crust again and again, so that on the larger plantations the plows never ceased, but returned continually from the last furrows of far-stretching acres to break the first furrows of another three weeks' task. Hoeing, meanwhile, kept the women busy with the grass and weeds. In early August the crop was "laid by," and required no more work till picking time.

Meanwhile, under proper conditions this incessant labor would transform the fields into flower gardens.[5] By June the beautiful blossoms are blushing; bell-shaped and softly brilliant, here and there, with the magic trick of changing their colors, as a maid her clothes. Shimmering in the morning in a creamy white or pale straw dress, and closing its silky petals in the evening, the flower on the second day of its fragile life shifts to a wild-rose color, deepening by evening to magenta or carnation: all this, for three brief but brilliant days, on graceful stems knee-high, rich in glossy dark green foliage; so that the aspect of a spacious level field, with fresh blossoms budding into cream or cloth of gold, while elder sisters smile in pink and red amidst the trembling verdure, is of a splendid variegated beauty that lends to the Southern landscape half its charm. It is in this summer season that the Southern children sing:

> First day white, next day red,
> Third day from my birth I'm dead;
> Though I am of short duration,
> Yet withal I clothe the nation.

From mid-August until winter, however, and especially in that "season of mellow fruitfulness," October, the cotton shrub becomes a thing of won-

[5] Belonging to the family *Malvaceæ*, cotton is kin to the hollyhock, to which its blossoms show a refined resemblance.

der; adding to its garniture of bloom the bursting pods of snowy fleece that dominate the coloring of the fields into the semblance of a vegetable snow-storm. Then, on the old plantation, swarmed forth the turbaned mammies and the wenches, shining pickaninnies and black babes in arms, with bags and huge baskets and mirth, and nimble fingers as it were predestined to the cotton pod, to live in the sunshine amid the fleecy snow, and pile up white fluffy mounds at the furrow ends, chanting melodious minor chords of song as old as Africa, the women trooping home again at night-fall with poised overflowing baskets on their heads, to feasts of corn-pone and cracklin' and molasses in the blaze of a light'ood fire, within sound of the thrumming of the banjo.

Cotton was and is the Southern "money crop." From autumn to autumn the banker and merchant "carry" the South on their ledgers, and scant is the interchange of coin; but when the "first bale of cotton" rolls into town behind a jangling team of trotting mules, their grinning driver cracking out resounding triumph with his whip, money makes its anniversary appearance, accounts are settled, and the whole shining South "feels flush." The gin houses drive a roaring business, the air is heavy in them and the light is thick with downy lint, and their atmosphere pungent with the oily odor of crushed woolly seeds. Steam or hydraulic presses, with irresistible power, then pack towering heaps of seedless fleece into coarse casings of flimsy jute wrapping, metal-bound. These bales, weighing roughly to the tale of five hundred pounds, pass the appraisement of the broker, swarm the platforms of the railway warehouses and overflow to the hospitable ground; then are laden laboriously into freight cars, and, after being squeezed to the irreducible minimum of size by some giant compress, are hauled to the corners of the earth.

Of the distinctive civilization of the old Southern cotton life no words could be more pertinent than Grady's.[6]

"That was a peculiar society," he said. "Almost feudal in its splendor, it was almost patriarchal in its simplicity. Leisure and wealth gave it exquisite culture. Its wives and mothers, exempt from drudgery and almost from care, gave to their sons, through patient and constant training, something of their own grace and gentleness and to their homes beauty and light. Its people, homogeneous by necessity, held straight and simple faith, and were religious to a marked degree along the old lines of Christian belief. This same homogeneity bred a hospitality that was as kinsmen to kinsmen, and that wasted at the threshold of every home what the more frugal people of the North conserved and invested in public charities.—Money counted least in making the social status, and constantly ambitious and brilliant youngsters from no estate married into the families of planter princes. Meanwhile the one character utterly condemned and ostracized was the man who was mean to his slaves. Even the coward was pitied and might have been liked. For the cruel master there was no toleration.

—"In its engaging grace—in the chivalry that tempered even Quixotism with dignity—in the piety that saved master and slave alike—in the charity that boasted not—in the honor held above estate—

[6] "The New South," in the New York *Ledger*, 1889.

in the hospitality that neither condescended nor cringed—in frankness and heartiness and wholesome comradeship—in the reverence paid to womanhood and the inviolable respect in which woman's name was held—the civilization of the old slave *régime* in the South has not been surpassed, and perhaps will not be equaled, among men."

During the season between the two cotton crops, "Southern hospitality" touches its climax. With leisure and money at command, the "big house" of the old plantation threw wide its welcoming doors to troops of guests, the men folk rode to hounds across the fields, or stalked the deer amid the swamps, or hunted the wild duck and turkey and whistling coveys of quail (called "pa'tridges"), while the women spread the damask in the evening, and laid out the family silver to grace a savory feast that has no counterpart in all the world: fried chicken and corn pone and yams, 'possum, and the esoteric dainties of the freshly slaughtered pig, heaps of snowy, steaming, home-grown rice, slices of delicate peanut-fed ham, teased with the contrasting exquisite flavors of quince and crab-apple jellies, watermelon "preserves," "cookies" and tarts and spiced brandy peaches!

Nor was the slave debarred from the pleasures of this halcyon season. The writer knows not how better to cap this attempt to impart some faint aroma of the social fragrance of the old-time South than by citing this versified description of the pastimes of the slave, written long before the war by a Carolina scholar and statesman, William John Grayson. Against the somber background of slave life, dark enough, in truth, as it was, but in the books depicted with monotonous sameness to the exclusion of every penciling of light, it is well to set this colorful medallion, truthful and charming:

When autumn's parting days grow cold and brief,
Light hoar frosts sparkle on the fallen leaf,
The breezeless pines, at rest, no longer sigh,
And pearl-like clouds stand shining in the sky;
When to the homestead flocks and herds incline,
Sonorous conchs recall the rambling swine,
And from the field, the low descending sun
Sends home the Slave, his fleecy harvest done,
In field and wood he hunts the frequent hare;
The wild hog chases to the forest lair;
Entraps the gobbler; with persuasive smoke
Beguiles the 'possum from the hollow oak;
On the tall pine tree's topmost bough espies
The crafty coon—a more important prize—
Detects the dodger's peering eyes that glow
With fire reflected from the blaze below,
Hews down the branchless trunk with practised hand,
And drives the climber from his nodding stand;
Downward, at last, he springs with crashing sound,
Where Jet and Pincher seize him on the ground,
Yields to the hunter the contested spoil,
And pays, with feast and fur, the evening toil.

When calm skies glitter with the starry light,
The boatman tries the fortune of the night,
Launches the light canoe; the torch's beam
Gleams like a gliding meteor on the stream;
Along the shore the flick'ring firelight steals,
Shines through the wave, and all its wealth reveals.
The spotted trout its mottled side displays,
Swift shoals of mullet flash beneath the blaze;
He marks their rippling course; through cold and wet,
Lashes the sparkling tide with dext'rous net;

With poised harpoon the bass or drum assails,
And strikes the barb through silv'ry tinted scales.—

Not toil alone, the fortune of the slave!
He shares the sport and spoils of wood and wave.[7]

[7] Library of Southern Literature, v, 2022–2023; slightly transposed.

NOTE.—Readers interested in technical information should know that the baling process mentioned on pages 305–306 produces at the gins a bale 28 x 56 x 42 inches in size, weighing approximately 500 lbs., including 20 lbs. bagging and steel straps, thus having a density of about 14 lbs. per cubic foot. "In this condition the cotton is bought by cotton buyers for export or for delivery to American mills, the seller delivering the same to a railroad or compress point, where the cotton is sorted according to grade (see note on p. 374), compressed and marked, the size being reduced to 28 x 56 x 18 inches, giving a density of from 28 to 30 lbs. per cubic foot." Two excellent articles on the marketing and financing of cotton may be found in the Annals of the American Academy of Political and Social Science for Sept., 1911, by A. R. Marsh and J. J. Arnold, experts in these branches of the business.

CHAPTER 65

THE NEW SOUTH: COTTON AND POLITICS

Ben Hill of Georgia quite aptly and accurately expressed the political attitude of the average intelligent man of the new South when he exclaimed: "There was a South of slavery and secession—that South is dead. There is a South of union and freedom—that South, thank God, is living, breathing, growing every hour."

From the roots of the cotton plant grew the Upas tree of slavery. It took the pruning hook of war to cut it down, and this war paralyzed the roots of the cotton industry itself, so that at the end of the struggle only one bale of cotton was being raised where fifteen were grown at its beginning, while other cotton growing countries had meanwhile energetically endeavored to destroy the American monopoly of European markets; yet so great was the prolific power of this plant in its occidental setting that it took the Southern planter, without slave labor, only thirteen years to win back his supremacy.[1] In spite of the defiant valedictory of Senator

[1] *Bulletin No. 33*, as cited, p. 14.—"What had been the weakness of the South—its dependence on a single crop—now proved its chief strength in the moment of need. Stricken to a point of desperate poverty by the war, its salvation lay in the fact that at once an eager market was clamoring for its cotton. In the twelve months following the close of the war the exports of cotton, though less than half the quantity of the years immediately preceding the war, reached the unprecedented money value of over $200,000,000. High prices continued for seven or eight years, and counterbalanced the lower production, which did not reach the *ante-bellum* level till

Hammond, the North had dared to make war on cotton, and cotton for a while was conquered. But only for a while. That little persistent white rose of the South smiled up in the face of the soldier gardener throughout the dark days of Reconstruction, darker than those of the war, and even lured back the liberated slave to do it homage. The soldier farmer, his wits sharpened on the whetstone of war, fed new nourishment to his white rose garden, his former slave assisting in the labor, and the garden spread in gracious acreage, with the result that whereas in 1830 the American crop for the first time reached a production of a million bales, and never once during slavery attained a higher production than five and a half million bales, yet within twenty years after the beginning of the war that highest point had been exceeded by two million, and the crop for 1914 nearly trebled it.

As President Alderman of the University of Virginia has said, "Slave labor is now gone and the legitimate sovereignty of cotton is an assured fact. Three-fourths of this great crop, which must be relied on to clothe civilization, and in the exploitation of which, two billions of capital are used, is raised in the South. It is a stupendous God-made monopoly."[2]

This speech was delivered in 1908. If the present writer may be permitted to change the figures to correspond with the facts of 1916, President Alderman would continue as follows:

1871. The South had money to buy the goods it so sorely needed, and the North had a ready market for its surplus."—H. C. Emery on "Economic Development of the U. S.," in Cambridge Modern History, as cited, vii, p. 697.

[2] "The Growing South," in Library of Southern Literature, xiv, 6213.

To-day, the South has invested, in 777 mills, with their 9,200,000 spindles, $225,000,000, as against $21,000,000 twenty-five years ago. The fields of the South furnish the raw material for three-fourths of the mills of all the world with their 110,000,000 spindles. The South now consumes 2,300,000 bales, which is about the amount consumed by the rest of the country and is a four-fold increase over its consumption in 1890. If the time should ever come when we can spin and weave all of our present crop, we would need 7,770 mills to do it, and the world at large would need an annual crop of thirty million bales. This three-fold increase of the crop can be brought about by increasing, by means of improved agriculture, the productivity of the land, and by reclamation of land along the Mississippi Valley. If this increase could be accomplished; if the labor could be found to handle it; if the markets for it could be secured in such volume that the price could remain near to its present standard; and, if our capacity to spin and weave our share of the increase could be maintained, the Southern States of America would become the richest portion of the earth. The present value of the cotton crop, raw material and manufactured product, is about $1,250,000,000. Trebled in value, it would amount to three or four billions annually. It is easy to lose one's judgment in this mounting mass of values, but one thing seems very clear: The opportunity to develop the potentialities of cotton, in field and in mill, to train and handle the labor involved in the development, which would cover the whole field of the poor white, the immigrant and the negro, to evolve the financial genius to move and market this world staple, makes of the Southern States a field for industrial talent and industrial leadership unsurpassed in the world.

President Alderman points out the enormous development in Southern cotton manufacture, to which attention will be called in the closing section, on "Cotton and World Trade." For the present it is pertinent to indicate briefly the effect produced by this development on political and social conditions.

Just as in the early days of Southern manufacture, when Calhoun was proponent of protection, so now, those sections of the South where manufacture is regaining its importance are veering toward protection. Among the many epigrams of American politics, it would be difficult to surpass in terse homely truthfulness the saying of General Hancock, "The tariff is a local issue." Just as Daniel Webster swung away from free trade when the interests of New England demanded a tariff, so now, Louisiana with its sugar industry, Alabama with its steel mills, and the cotton factory towns throughout the entire South testify to those "emergent and exigent interests" which Webster attributed to the South and fully justified (see page 215).

The same principle appears in the attitude of the Southern States to the Shipping Bill so strongly advocated by President Wilson, himself a Southerner and a former exponent of States-rights. Such a measure involves, of course, concentration of additional power in the hands of the central government; but the South, its cotton trade badly crippled by the Great War, felt driven by the force of contemporary circumstances to support in 1914 a policy in behalf of that same cotton industry which had led it in previous epochs to attack the "insidious encroachments" of Washington on the "sacred domain of States-rights."

Perhaps the most extreme illustration of the influence of economics on politics that has thus far been afforded in America by the Great War is the effort made by the South in 1914 to secure governmental "valorization" of cotton in a manner strikingly analogous to the Brazilian method for governmental control of the coffee crop, which, only three years previously, was denounced as extortionate monopoly. As Professor Alvin Johnson of Cornell has said,[3] the Brazilian method of control of the coffee market consists, in the first place, in the warehousing of the existing supply, and the limitation of shipments from the government warehouses to such amounts as will not depress prices unduly. In the second place, shipments on private account are checked by a heavy export duty. By its control of conditions under which coffee is accepted at the warehouses, the State is able to keep production within bounds.—Four-fifths of the coffee of the world comes from Brazil; not far from three-fourths of the cotton comes from the United States.—The huge coffee crop of 1906–1907 (twenty million bags, as compared with an average crop of twelve millions) forced upon the attention of the Brazilian mercantile community and the state government, the inadequacy of a *laissez-faire* policy in the matter of this chief staple. The present European war, with its attendant disorganization of markets consuming one-third of the world's cotton supply, is producing a similar effect upon American opinion. This opinion centralizes in the South.

The growth of mill towns in the South, involving as they do the transition of population from iso-

[3] In the *New Republic*, Nov. 7, 1914.

lated rural life to the solidarity of urban communities, has perceptibly affected politics. Trusting in the leadership of cotton mill managers, and at other times maneuvered by astute and unscrupulous politicians to their own hurt, the mill operatives are beginning to furnish solid masses of votes in a manner that makes them a power. Suddenly torn away as they now are from custom, uprooted from the traditional and unthinking vote-casting of partizanship "back home" in the rural districts, and transplanted into a new economic environment favorable to the explosive force of new ideas as well as to the ferment of political discussion, these mill folk introduce into the "solid South" the thin edge of a wedge that may rift it. Already there are cases of a solid mill population voting the Republican ticket, and of mill managers that are quoted as saying that their operatives are "all Republican without knowing it." Unquestionably an important impetus in the wave of laws for liquor restraint that has recently swept over the South was supplied by far-sighted mill management, anxious to enlist temperance in the interest of efficiency, and inducing operatives to vote for it. Unquestionable also is the more or less ominous fact that a class consciousness is slowly evolving in the mill people, which must profoundly affect the political South of the future. The native clannishness of Southerners, and especially of "mountain whites," intensified as it is now by self-interest, is provided with a closely knit and compact community life, entirely isolated from contact with the general community, that affords a tilled hot-bed for the growth of class consciousness, as though all the elements had been carefully arranged for that purpose.

CHAPTER 66

THE NEW SOUTH: SOCIAL CHANGES

NOWHERE has the persistent social contrast between the North and the South been portrayed more vividly or with franker open-mindedness than by a veteran of the Confederate army in a book entitled, "The Brothers' War."[1] Cross the Ohio, he says, and you have entered another country: behind you, a land of corn pone, biscuits, three hot meals a day, and houses tended shiftlessly by negro servants; before you, a land of bakers' bread, with hardly more than one warm meal a day, and the houses kept as "neat as a pin" by the mothers and daughters of the family. Behind you, a crude and feeble rural school system, no government by town meeting, scant direct legislation, great public activity by the county and hardly any on the part of its subdivisions; before you, a common school system energetically improving, government by town meeting instead of representatives, and buoyant energy of the township in public affairs. Southerners are quick to return a blow for insulting words, and are prone to the use of deadly weapons; while Northerners are generally as averse from personal violence as were the Greeks and Romans. "The battle cry of the Confederates was a wild cheering—a fox-hunt yell, as we called it; that of the Union soldiers was huzza! huzza! huzza! From the beginning to the end, even at Franklin and Bentonville, and at

[1] By John C. Reed: Boston, 1906; p. 60.

Farmville, just two days before I was surrendered at Appomattox, the Confederates always, if possible, took the offensive; the Union soldiers were like the sturdy Englishmen, whose tactics from Hastings to Waterloo have generally been defensive."

The differences of which such contrasts are symptomatic derive largely from the fact that the South, in consequence chiefly of slavery, which debarred immigration, has remained singularly homogeneous, old-fashioned and unchangeable, while the North, stirred by a constant influx of new blood as well as by the stimulus of a diversified economic activity, may lack charm, but certainly possesses efficiency.

The South is beginning to change, however, not only politically, but socially—profoundly and rapidly so. These changes are largely connected with the extensive introduction of manufacture, and chiefly cotton manufacture. All three white classes of the old-time South are involved: the "first families," wealthy planters and former slave-holders; the "poor whites," or small tenants, despised by the ante-bellum negro and widely misapprehended today; and the great middle class who have always existed in the South in spite of an evident determination on the part of many writers to ignore them.

From each of these classes large numbers are "going into business;" keen young scions of "de quality" vying in manufacturing enterprise with the sons of their fathers' overseers, while from the middle class as well as the ranks of "poor whites" the people are flocking to the mills and forsaking country homes for the city. What Holland Thompson says of North Carolina [2] is true, to a greater or less

[2] From the Cotton Field to the Cotton Mill; a Study of the Industrial Transition in North Carolina: New York, 1906; p. 8.

degree, of the South as a whole. "Communities which had altered little since the days of Cornwallis are feeling the modern industrial spirit. 'Business' is being exalted to a position heretofore unknown. A type of shrewd, far-sighted business man is being developed. The 'Southern Yankees' devote themselves exclusively to their work and need ask no favors in any contest of commercial strategy. Social lines are shifting. Families which have decidedly influenced the spirit of the community become less important, unless they take part in the new movement. There are signs of class distinctions based upon wealth and business success. The whole attitude of mind has changed more during the last fifteen years than in the fifty preceding."

A discussion of the amazing development of cotton manufacture largely responsible for this change is reserved for the last section of this book. Meanwhile it may not come amiss to attempt a portrait of the Southern leader as he is to-day: cotton mill president or manager, banker or attorney or editor —the man who, more than any other, is making "the new South" and being made by it.

It would be folly to question his Americanism; to himself it never occurs that this could be open to question. His loyalty to the flag and the Union, being quietly unconscious of itself, is an ingrained habit of thought. Perhaps his sires fought in the Revolution, so that all of his earlier family traditions are interwoven with Union patriotism; while the Civil War he is likely to regard as a final arbitrament of issues inherent in the Federal Constitution, issues as between States-rights and a centripetal sovereignty, which had to be determined in some way, and happened to be determined by a war; a war which he looks back upon as terrible, but in connection with which he would never think of apologizing for the part his own people took in it. He thinks they were every whit as honest and as patriotic as the Unionists. Being rather better educated in constitutional law than men of his kind in the North are apt to be, and gifted in oral expression, he is quite ready to demonstrate the Confederate point of view in an argument; but he will tell you frankly that the theory would never have worked out in practise, and will certainly rejoice with you in the passing of African slavery. He thinks that Lincoln was a very great man, and that Lee was very great also. Stonewall Jackson he admires, but is not so enthusiastic over Davis. He is generally ready to give the great Union soldiers their due, although he is likely to think, with Grady, that General Sherman was sometimes "rather careless with fire."

He takes a broad outlook on the world to-day, knowing his New York as a matter of course, and probably reading a New York newspaper daily; but his interest is also keen in Liverpool and London, Bremen and Havre, and in the prospects for increased cotton trade with the Orient. He is likely to have more imagination than his corresponding type above the border, and to possess, quite unconsciously, an ingratiating social charm that manifests itself sometimes in a generosity bordering on extravagance. Rather than seem mean—a cardinal sin in his decalogue—he may occasionally spend more than his income. Very polite to the ladies, he gives up his seat in a crowded car without question, and shows great deference to his wife, although it is perhaps to be doubted whether he exercises any greater alacrity than his Northerly neighbor in getting up on wintry mornings to start the fire.

He is a hard worker, and takes pride in his work; but is able to forget it more easily than the average American business man, tossing it lightly from his shoulders when enjoying a "day off," and letting the world go hang in a spirit of boyishness that always seems ready for summons. Self-confident and easy, he lacks to a relative degree what Owen Wister calls "the nervousness of democracy."

Writing of George Washington's simplicity, this brilliant author has expressed a pungent criticism of which Americans ought to take notice. "Our fathers," he said, "had more of it than we of to-day, and it would be well for us if we could regain it. The Englishman of to-day is superior to us in it; he has in general, no matter what his station [and this applies also to the typical Southerner], a quiet way of doing and of being, of letting himself alone, that we in general lack. We cannot seem to let ourselves alone; we must talk when there is nothing to say; we must joke—especially we must joke—when there is no need for it, and when nobody asks to be entertained. This is the nervousness of democracy; we are uncertain if the other man thinks we are 'as good' as he is; therefore we must prove that we are, at first sight, by some sort of performance. Such doubt never occurs to the established man, to the man whose case is proven; he is not thinking about what we think of him. So the Indian, so the frontiersman, does not live in this restlessness. Nor did Washington; and therefore he moved always in simplicity, that balanced and wholesome ease of the spirit, which when it comes among those who must be showing off from moment to moment, shines like a quiet star upon fireworks."[3]

And yet there is a certain "techiness" about your typical Southerner that he were very much better without. "Honor" is too much to the surface, with him, his skin is too thin, there are needless chips on his shoulders. You can usually stir him up easily, especially if you talk about race questions. As a matter of fact, he treats the negro not only fairly, but kindly; he is almost certain to have one negro friend who proudly claims him as a sort of feudal defender in time of trouble, and whom he would go to great lengths to help out of it. But "race equality" is meaningless to him unless it implies intermarriage, which of course is the final test of racial equality; and so when you touch on that topic, however remotely, he is likely to show irritation. Inclined to impatience with what he deems Northern presumptuousness, based, as he thinks, on crass ignorance, he resents patronage or condescension or even well-meaning apology for his "Southland" as he would a pestiferous plague. Yet nobody could hate more intensely than he does such books as "The Clansman," or such political diseases as Bleaseism. Acutely aware of the problems of the South, including the race problem, child labor, and illiteracy, what he is likely to call "Yankee meddling" irritates him profoundly, and he believes that the South will solve its own problems in time, and the less "meddling" the sooner will she solve them. Tender and reverent toward religion, albeit reserved to the point of shyness about it, he withal cherishes a fine sort of idealism that thus far, in spite of his new ab-

[3] The Seven Ages of Washington: New York, 1907.

sorption in business, and a really surprising efficiency in it, has saved him from exalting money into an end in itself, and enabled him to treat it as "means."—Altogether, a fine type of man, lovable for some of his faults, and likely to outgrow the others. When he goes to live in New York or other large cities he almost always "makes good." But he should stay where he is. The South needs him.

CHAPTER 67

THE NEW SOUTH: SOCIAL PROBLEMS

THE race problem is, of course, the most deplorable relic of slavery. Some one has said that the Southern people are inside this fog, and cannot see out, while the Northerners, outside of it, cannot see in. A better understanding, however, is coming about with the facilitation of travel, which is profoundly educative, and with the emergence of race problems in other parts of the country, leading both sides to substitute intelligent sympathy for stupid recrimination. To men like the late Booker T. Washington among negroes and William D. Weatherford among Southern white men the leaders of both races may look with bright hopes of the future. The Southern Sociological Congress, organized of white and black members "to study and improve social, civic, and economic conditions in the South"; "to enlist the entire South in a crusade of social health and righteousness" on a platform of "Brotherhood," has already held several annual meetings. Inaugurated by Governor Ben W. Hooper of Tennessee, founded by Mrs. Anna Russell Cole of Nashville, supported from the start by all Southern governors, except one who has since been repudiated by his people, this Congress investigates such questions as public health, courts and prisons, child welfare, organized charities, race problems, and "the Church and social service," in a spirit of tolerant open-minded sympathy. At the close of a volume of proceedings the following statement is made for this Congress:

"No one who has attended the sessions of this sectional conference could fail to realize that there is a growing and deepening interest on the part of Southern white men in the nine million negroes who live by our sides in the South.—The meeting was characterized by sanity, scientific investigation, a spirit of coöperation, and an intense desire for helpfulness to all. A great many of the leading universities in the South were represented by their professors or presidents, and it was evident from the very outset that the best thinkers of both races had come together with the determination to study, without prejudice, this greatest problem of the entire South."[1]

Just as it was cotton that brought the negro to the South and enslaved him, so it is this plant now that chiefly employs and improves him as he labors with liberated hands. Constituting thirty per cent of Southern population at large, he makes up forty per cent of all persons engaged in Southern farming. In every State south of the Mason and Dixon line he forms a dwindling element of general population, but in all of these States except Louisiana he is an increasing factor in the farming population. Not only so, but a steady drift of negroes is proceeding from the cities to the country, and it is in cotton farming that the negro chiefly succeeds. Nearly one-fourth of all the black farmers in the South own the lands they cultivate—amounting in value to

[1] Readers who may be interested in this, the most important of all movements for solution of the Southern race problem, may obtain information by addressing J. E. McCulloch, General Secretary, Southern Sociological Congress, Nashville, Tenn.

$500,000,000, for in less than fifty years the negro has acquired nearly 20,000,000 acres of land. The Russian serfs, after fifty years of freedom, have not made greater headway. They have not done so well, indeed, in their conquest of illiteracy.[2]

Illiteracy is no doubt the heaviest incubus, except the race problem itself, loaded on the South by negro slavery. It is not confined to the negroes. The support of the system of slavery was so exacting on the time and energy and spirit of the masters as to retard the establishment of an adequate system of schools; pointedly illustrating the acute remark of a British economist, "We are apt to think of one as bond, and the other as free; but both are bond."[3] The "white trash" of the South, neglected by the ante-bellum ruling classes and despised by the slave as "po' buckra," are only now beginning to escape from the shackles of ignorance. But the Southern States are showing an amazing interest in education, their public school systems probably proceeding at a more rapid rate of improvement in recent years than in any other part of the nation. Between 1900 and 1910 the percentage of illiteracy in the South as a whole fell from 23.3 per cent. to 15.6 per cent., while the census report calls attention to the decline in the proportion of illiterates among the negroes of the South,—from nearly one-half down to one-third,—as "particularly conspicuous." During the seven year period between 1907 and 1914, the number of high schools in South Carolina grew from ninety-five, with 235 teachers, to 175, with 560 teach-

[2] W. M. Hunley, The Economic Status of the Negro, in The Human Way: Nashville, 1913; p. 27.

[3] For an interesting amplification of this principle, see Norman Angell: The Foundations of International Polity: London, 1914; page 13.

ers; and this is a fair representation of what is happening throughout the whole South.

There can be no doubt that the labor of children in the cotton mills, bad as it is, is nevertheless an influential agency in reducing the illiteracy of "poor whites." From personal observation covering an extended period in cotton mill towns of the South, as well as in the "backwoods," the present writer believes that the condition of youthful operatives in these mills makes on the whole more for their advancement than did the environment from which they have frequently removed. This is not to say that conditions are by any means ideal; far from it. But just as the hook-worm disease is disappearing by virtue of the substitution of measurable sanitation for none at all, so the schooling now provided by mill management for adolescent operatives is far better than backwoods illiteracy; while the welfare work carried on by such "soldiers of the common good" as D. E. Camak at Spartanburg and J. A. Baldwin at Charlotte, in cordial coöperation with the mill owners, sets an example to the country and the world.[4]

Mrs. J. Borden Harriman said, at the sixth annual meeting of the National Child Labor Committee: "Those familiar with the history of cotton manufacturing in New England tell us that the first impetus toward uplifting the social status of the working people of that section was given by the cotton factory. If such has been the case in New England, more especially has it been so in the South.—In every mill village of any importance in either North or South Carolina or Virginia I found some sort of

[4] See the *World's Work* for July and August, 1914: New York.

welfare work for both elders and children. I cannot believe that anywhere is there a finer spirit or stronger wish to uplift the weaker classes than among some Southern mill owners.''[5]

Critics of child labor in Southern cotton mills should remember not only such facts as those above cited, but also certain differences in economic environment that invalidate New England conditions as a proper analogy for unqualified application to the South. New England manufacture, long established and therefore proportionately expert, has reached a stage of development in which the finer grades of goods are produced on a scale as yet unattained in most of the young mills in the South (see page 342). This not only means a higher wage scale in New England in return for the skilled labor necessary to the production of finer goods, but it means, conversely, that children may be employed in Southern mills at simple tasks for which no equivalent employment exists in New England. Crompton's "mule," for example, now evolved into highly complex machinery, is used almost exclusively for the spinning of the higher grades of yarn. As it is

[5] Annals of the American Academy of Political and Social Science; Supplement: Philadelphia, March, 1910.—"Some of the finest and most generous sentiments against child labor was expressed to me by leaders in the South, and among mill-owners and managers themselves there are many examples of desire to promote the welfare of the cotton-mill child and his parent. I think the chance of a modern Dickens to exploit cotton-mill fiction is fading. The native Southern mill-owner, like the native Southern railway-owner before him, has developed brutality in less degree than some of his Northern prototypes. Some of the largest mill-owners whose names I heard again and again in the South are at heart staunch friends of strict child-labor legislation.—From what I learned, I think the evils of child-labor are likely soon to disappear, and with a minimum of friction and antagonism, if some of the Northern cotton capitalists who are becoming interested in the Southern mills keep their hands off."—F. M. Davenport, staff correspondence in the New York *Outlook*, Feb. 23, 1916; p. 428.

physically impossible for children to operate mules, no demand for child labor arises from their extensive use in New England. In the South, however, the "mule" is almost unknown; the indefinitely simpler "ring frames" being adequate to the production of the coarser cheap yarns, which children can easily spin on these frames.

Much of the Southern child labor, moreover, is light and intermittent. "Doffers," or boys who look after the bobbins, work from twenty to forty-five minutes in each hour, spending their spare time in one another's company within the mill, or even playing outside in the yard. The younger girls, who serve as thread-menders, often have long periods of rest, although compelled to watch carefully for possible breaks.

On the whole, Mr. Holland Thompson[6] is right in asserting that the child labor of Southern cotton mills is far less detrimental than that of glass factories or coal mines, and preferable either to newsboy labor or even to that of a cash boy or cash girl in a busy department store, where ventilation is usually decidedly inferior to the air in a cotton mill.

As to the wage scale, it should be remembered, further, that the cost of living is lower in the South than in New England. But when all is said, it still remains true that the strain of long hours of confinement to the care of exacting and noisy machinery drains the precious vitality of Southern children, especially when account has been taken of the poorly chosen and badly cooked food with which untutored parents provide them. As Mrs. Borden Harriman herself said, no one of any humanity, especially no

[6] As cited, p. 228.

mother, can see a little child at work in a mill, with all that this may mean, without a feeling of horror and indignation. No circumstances make child labor right. It is a phase in the evolution of the Southern cotton industry which is properly doomed to disappear. Meanwhile, there is immediate hope for such measures of alleviation as the raising of the minimum age for employment from twelve years, now universal throughout the South, to fourteen; the enactment of an eight-hour law, which is vitally necessary; and, perhaps, for the transfer of schooling facilities from mill management to a system conducted by the State. It would be a further distinct advantage could the mill villages be broken up, and the operatives encouraged to possess their own homes, dispersed in the general community.[7]

John Stuart Mill's indictment of machinery still challenges debate, while the hint of hopeful prophecy with which he follows it seems far from fulfilment. "It is questionable," he says, "if all the mechanical inventions yet made have lightened the day's toil of any human being. They have enabled a greater population to live the same life of drudgery and imprisonment, and an increased number to make fortunes. But they have not yet begun to effect those great changes in human destiny which it is in their nature and in their futurity to accomplish."[8] The eighteenth century riots in England against the inventions of Kay and Hargreaves and their companions in genius were doubtless not based on intelligent reasoning, but they at least expressed a true prophetic instinct.

7 S. J. Derrick, "The Cotton Mill Population of the South," in *Newberry* (S. C.) *College Bulletin:* February, 1915, p. 35 ff.
8 Cited by Norman Angell.

Enough has surely been said to show the enormous influence, political, financial, and social, which cotton still wields in the South; changed in form from that which obtained before the Civil War, but equally powerful; an influence that achieves its most picturesque and convincing illustration, perhaps, when, on the mills closing down in hard times, the operatives may occasionally be seen moving, with their meager belongings, back to the farms, so as to cultivate once more the plant of which the temporarily inflated price has simultaneously made its manufacture unprofitable, and its production alluringly remunerative. Thus, at such times, a fluctuating market actually exerts a literal back-and-forth pull on a part of the Southern population; prices having driven the small farmers into the mill towns in the first place, so as to better their condition, and high prices luring them back for a season; for "there is always the land to which they may return if beaten." But nearly all of them drift back to the mill towns again, for the sake of better housing, better food, better clothing, and, above all, better social facilities than can be found in the deadly isolation of the backwoods.

In other words, most of these people who feel the pull of the mill yield to it rather from choice than from the compulsion of absolute necessity. One of them, dowered with a touch of philosophy, put their feeling into the clever phrase, "It's not doing well that makes people contented, it's doing better!"[9]

When more intelligent agricultural methods come to prevail and rural life is redeemed from its loneliness, they may find a fuller contentment on the

[9] Holland Thompson, as cited, p. 210.

farm. Improvement of rural conditions should be the chief aim of all Southern statesmanship.[10]

[10] The writer lacks the experience and knowledge necessary to trace the powerful but highly intricate and complicated influence of cotton manufacture on social conditions in New England.

An important national Child Labor bill has just passed both houses of Congress as this book goes to press. It remains to be seen whether the courts will declare it unconstitutional, as was the case with the Lever bill attempting to regulate "futures."

BOOK VII

COTTON AND WORLD TRADE

NOTE ON THE WORLD'S COTTON MARKETS

The cotton markets which by force of economic circumstances have risen to the place of great world-markets are New York and New Orleans, in the United States; Liverpool, in England; Bremen, in Germany; Havre, in France; Alexandria, in Egypt; and Bombay, in India. But among these seven markets there are differences in the degree to which their economic and commercial functions are developed, so that in only five can it be said that every kind of operation required in the cotton business is continuously carried on—Bremen merchants being obliged by German governmental action to rely mainly upon Liverpool and New York to transact an essential part of their business, while Bombay, besides being deficient in commercial methods, deals in a kind of cotton which, though of general value, is of a peculiar quality and much less desirable for spinners than cotton of other growths. Of the five remaining markets, two, Havre and Alexandria, have limitations which remove them from the class of very first importance. The business of Havre, though fully developed in all its forms, is chiefly confined to serving the needs of France, which is comparatively low in the list of cotton-consuming countries. In Alexandria, all operations are confined to cotton of Egyptian growth, which is produced in comparatively small amounts and consequently affects only to a moderate extent the general problem of the supply of cotton and the demand for it. Thus we are brought to the conclusion that even among the major cotton markets of the world there are only three of the very highest class, New York and New Orleans, in the United States, and Liverpool, in England. The entire cotton trade looks to them for guidance day by day.—Condensed from A. R. Marsh, as cited.

CHAPTER 68

"THE MONEY CROP"

An enthusiastic and unusually well informed professor of agriculture in North Carolina said to his audience:

"You get up in the morning from a bed, clothed in cotton. You step out on a cotton rug. You let in the light by raising a cotton window-shade. You wash with soap made partly from cottonseed oil products. You dry your face on a cotton towel. You array yourself chiefly in cotton clothing. The 'silk' in which your wife dresses is probably mercerized cotton. At the breakfast table you do not get away from King Cotton; cottolene has probably taken the place of lard in the biscuit you eat. The beef and the mutton were probably fattened on cottonseed meal and hulls. Your 'imported olive oil' is more likely from a Texas cotton farm than from an Italian villa. Your 'butter' is probably a product of Southern cottonseed. The coal that burns in the fire may have been mined by the light of a cotton-oil lamp. The sheep from which your woolen clothing came were probably fed on cottonseed. The tonic you take may contain an extract of cotton root-bark. The tobacco you smoke not unlikely grew under a cotton cover and is put up in a cotton bag. Your morning daily may be printed on cotton waste paper—and even in that skirmish it tells about, the contending forces were clothed in khaki duck, slept under cotton tents, cotton was an essential in the high explosives that were used, and when at last war had done its worst, surgery itself called cotton into requisition to aid the injured and dying."[1]

The professor's words would have fitted almost as well had he been addressing an audience in Europe or Australia or Japan, so inextricably has this "vegetable wool" from the Orient interwoven itself with the civilization of the globe; and yet a century and a quarter ago its influence had but just broken out of India into England, and meant nothing whatever to America. In 1783 the value of raw cotton exports from the United States was nil, in 1883 it was nearly $250,000,000, and in 1913, or thirty years later, it was more than double what it had been in 1883. A report of the United States Department of Commerce has already been cited to illustrate its present relative value as an export (see page 3). This may be supplemented by an exhibit of the exports for 1911.[2] The total raw cotton exports for that year exceeded by $53,000,000 the next four largest groups of exports, namely: wheat and wheat flour; cattle, meat, and dairy products; iron and steel manufactures; and copper manufactures—these four great groups aggregating $556,789,750, while the raw cotton exported within the same period amounted to $610,475,301, to say nothing of nearly $29,000,000 worth of exports in cotton manufactures. The American crop amounts roughly to one billion dollars, of which about 40 per cent is consumed at home.

[1] Adapted from the introduction to Cotton; C. W. Burkett and C. H. Poe: New York, 1906.

[2] See Appendix F: 2d for comparative table.

Not only has cotton grown within a century and a quarter from a share of only 4.4 per cent in the chief raiment supplies of known markets, to 73.13 per cent,[3] but nearly three-fourths of the crop of the world is grown in the United States, which produced only ⅖ of 1 per cent when Whitney invented the gin. India now follows with 11.3 per cent, Egypt with 6.5 per cent, Russia with 5.4 per cent; then China, Russia and Brazil, and "miscellaneous." Measured by value instead of by volume, the United States leads with 70 per cent, India comes next with 12 per cent, while Egypt, because of superiority of product, yields 10 per cent in values as against only 6.5 per cent in volume, the remaining 8 per cent being distributed in the order above mentioned. Set down in dollars, the world trade in cotton is accounted as follows:

United States	$1,015,625,000
British India	170,000,000
Egypt	155,000,000
Miscellaneous	112,500,000
	$1,453,125,000[4]

While readers may have been puzzled to account for the overweening influence exercised by the cotton plant in United States history, the extraordinarily rapid rise of the now incomparable dominance of the American share in this monopolistic world crop explains a good deal, especially if it be remembered that production is practically confined to a relatively small Southern section.

Let us look into this interesting matter a little

[3] See page 5.

[4] Computed by John Wormald, Esq., of Manchester; the *Sprinkler Bulletin:* Manchester, June, 1913; p. 702. But see p. 339, n.

further. Speaking by and large, cotton may fairly be described as *the only natural monopoly of a world-wide necessity;* and it is this fact which explains its peculiar importance in the interdependence of trade. The prime necessities of man are, of course, shelter, food, and raiment. His luxuries are manifold, but his actual necessities are limited to these prime three. Now, while there is obviously not even an approach to monopoly in any one kind of food-stuff or building material, yet when raiment is considered, cotton is found so far to surpass the other textile fabrics, such as silk, linen, and wool, in respect of easily obtained quantity, in cheapness, and in general convenience, as to set it beyond the bounds of comparison; monopolizing approximately three-quarters of the world's raiment supply, and so leaving only one quarter to be divided among all of its outstripped rivals.

Just as cotton holds a practical monopoly of the world's clothing supply, so a small group of South-eastern States in North America possess at present a virtual monopoly of the cotton crop; nearly three-fourths of the world's entire supply being produced in the famous "Cotton Belt" of the United States, comprising the Carolinas, Georgia, Alabama, Mississippi, Louisiana, Arkansas, Texas, and Oklahoma, with parts of Virginia, Tennessee, and Florida: a territory of 700,000 square miles. Cotton is a sun plant. Ideal conditions for its growth require, in exactly proper combination, the elements of bountiful sunshine; a deep, mellow, rich soil; a warm, steamy atmosphere, with plenteous moisture until the bolls are well developed; but a dryer soil and atmosphere while the fiber is being ripened and harvested. These conditions confine it to a latitude extending about thirty-six degrees in both directions from the Equator, and to altitudes of not more than a thousand feet. Outside of the "Cotton Belt," this peculiar combination of conditions has not yet been developed on any large scale except with the aid of irrigation. It is little wonder that short-sighted Southern planters cultivate their natural monopoly to the exclusion even of food-stuffs necessary to self support, enticed as they are by this "money crop," so that, when the price falls, as in war, they feel the sudden pinch of poverty, and commit the economic fallacy at all times of paying the producer's and "middleman's" profits on supplies requisite to their own maintenance, instead of producing all of these themselves.

NOTE.—To avoid misapprehension, it should be remembered that the figures shown on page 337 represent only the known trade in cotton, and not the absolute total. Mr. A. R. Marsh says: "Nobody knows exactly how much cotton the world grows, for there are still great portions of the earth, where cotton is known to be raised on a vast scale, which are either incompletely or not at all covered by statistical information. India, e.g., produces every year a crop about whose magnitude exact information is limited to the portion that reaches the ports. There are some reasons for thinking that China is the greatest producer of cotton of all countries." The Indian and Chinese staples are, however, greatly inferior to those produced in America.

CHAPTER 69

SOUTHERN MANUFACTURE

SLOW to realize that the production of cotton and a plentiful supply of both coal and water power puts into their hands a two-fold source of prosperity, the Southern people, once awake to their manufacturing opportunities, have improved them with amazing rapidity. As noted in a previous chapter, they surpassed the New Englanders in general manufacturing enterprise a century ago; but when cotton agriculture developed with such sudden munificence they turned their attention wholly to planting, and let manufacture slip through their fingers. It seems a far-reaching pity that they did so. Had they established cotton factories side by side with their fields, the diversification of economic interests would in all probability have proved to be a source of great benefit to the South, quickening the shrewd native enterprise, inducing white immigration, serving as a check upon slavery and also on intensified sectionalism, and possibly even averting the Civil War.

Bygones, however, are bygones. Now, being wiser through observation and experience, the Southerners do build factories in the midst of their fields, and conserve the larger profits of their fortune. President Alderman [1] tells what has happened, most succinctly:

"Five hundred million pounds of cotton is an

[1] Library of Southern Literature, as cited.

average South Carolina crop. Thirty years ago, Massachusetts bought this crop at seven cents a pound, leaving $35,000,000 in South Carolina pockets. Massachusetts then converted it into cloth at twenty cents a pound, and turned into her own pockets $100,000,000. South Carolina now does her own converting into cloth, and keeps the $100,000,000 change."

The race with New England, fairly beginning about 1880, when the Southern planter had regained his feet after the shock of the war,[2] was won in twenty-five years. In 1880 the South consumed only 188,748 bales, while New England took 1,129,498. By 1890 the South had passed the half-million mark, while New England took a million and a half. In 1900 the South kept a million and a half, while New England took nearly two million. In 1905, the South consumed 2,140,151 bales, while New England lagged behind with 1,753,282. From that time on the South has maintained a steady lead, the figures in bales for home consumption in 1914 being 3,023,415, as against 2,251,041 for New England.[3]

In fact, the South now outdistances all other States combined in the consumption of cotton; the last twenty years showing an increase of nearly three hundred per cent in the South, with less than seventy per cent in the rest of the country, which consumed 2,861,318 bales in 1914. As an optimistic young journalist says, nothing can prevail against a cotton mill with the cotton field at one door and the music of the turbine water-wheel singing at the other.

But the South has still far to go in the quality of

[2] It was not until 1900, however, that the whole South regained its per capita wealth of 1860.

[3] See Appendix F: 2e for comparative table.

the manufactured product. In 1902 an enterprising Carolina manufacturer issued a unique volume[4] that picturesquely illustrates the possible value of technical training if applied to the North Carolina cotton crop, which was then about half a million bales. On every alternate page is pasted a sample of actual piece-goods, beginning with the cheap qualities commonly made in North Carolina, such as duck, drill, and sheeting; then following in an ascending scale with the finer products of New England mills, such as gingham, lawn and poplin; and concluding with the exquisite products of German and Swiss mills, represented by Persian lawn and embroidery. Facing these samples Mr. Tompkins has printed a simple computation, showing in each case the increment accruing to the raw crop value from conversion into ascending grades of cloth. Even the first and cheapest sample (of duck) adds $20,000,000 to the annual wealth of a single State, while the conversion of 500,000 bales into fancy gingham would add over $500,000,000. But the domestic manufacture of the finer goods now "made in Germany" only, would add nearly a thousand million, while Swiss embroidery would mean five thousand million, or more than enough to buy all the cotton and woolen mills in the world!

The compiler of this interesting volume says: "To manufacture the entire crop into embroidery would be as undesirable as to turn it all into duck. These extreme figures are given to show the wide range of possibilities in the business.—All of the samples shown are made of cotton; but some of the finest were not made of the ordinary cotton of our

[4] D. A. Tompkins, Cotton Values in Textile Fabrics: Charlotte, 1902.

commerce, and therefore it may be contended that the claim for such princely values in our cotton is beyond the mark. But the goods were made of a kind of cotton. The cotton was grown under certain conditions. If these conditions were well understood, and the production of cotton carried on with sufficient skill, these fine grades of cotton could be raised over large areas now devoted to the ordinary kind. Therefore the argument resolves itself into a question of proper education and thrift, to turn a possible cotton crop into thousands of times the money now realized on it by the people who produce it."

In 1913 North Carolina consumed almost all of its cotton crop of 946,000 bales, and thereby greatly augmented its wealth. It is conceivable that the States of the "Cotton Belt" may eventually approximate a position similar to that now occupied by Massachusetts and Rhode Island, in which agricultural products represent less than one-twentieth of the values created by manufactures, which are largely of cotton. And many thoughtful students of this subject believe that the example of North Carolina must be followed by the United States as a whole if the immense opportunities afforded through cotton production are to be intelligently appropriated.

CHAPTER 70

ARE AMERICANS EFFICIENT?

THERE are critics who say roundly that American technical skill is entitled to but little credit for the national wealth accruing from the cotton crop. Even in the handling of raw material, these critics declare, the United States is stigmatized by the most unscientific and indeed slovenly methods of any cotton producing country in the world; the ill ginned and worse packed bales, shamefully mangled by bad methods of sampling,[1] contrasting sharply with the neatly packeted products of Egyptian and Indian ginneries as they all lie heaped together on the docks of Hamburg and Liverpool. Sir Charles Macara observes: "If American cotton were properly packed and compressed it would occupy much less space than at present, and the reduced cost of freight and carriage, together with the preventing of immense waste caused by the present slovenly packing, would mean an enormous annual saving estimated to amount to millions of pounds sterling."[2]

To state the sum of all such criticisms, Americans have simply presumed on the bounties of nature, and, seemingly secure in control of a great natural monopoly, have evinced not only a contemptuous indifference to the ordinary amenities of trade in handling the raw material, but an amazing lack of

[1] J. A. Todd, The World's Cotton Crops: London, 1915; pp. 123–128.

[2] Leading the World; Lancashire's Cotton Industry: London, 1913; p. 6.

farsightedness in the matter of manufacture and the consequent commerce in goods. A shrewd nation of money getters, it has been said, they nevertheless permit Europe so far to surpass them in the dextrous manipulation of their natural monopoly as to sell them back two dollars' worth of cotton goods for every dollar's worth they ship abroad. For example, the tables of the thirteenth census show that in 1907 the United States exported 27½ million dollars' worth of cotton manufactures, while importing more than sixty millions. In 1908 the figures were as 20½ to 54 millions; in 1909, $27,631,899 to $51,949,866.[3] This commercial ineptitude, the critics aver, becomes still more impressive when it is noted that in respect of mere volume, the American exports of manufactured goods far exceeded the imports; in the year last mentioned, for example, the United States exported 367,631,542 square yards of cotton cloths, and imported only 68,376,608 square yards.[4]

In other words, as we are told, the United States exports to all parts of the world huge volumes of very cheap and crude cotton products, for which it receives only enough to cancel about half of its European bill for highly finished cotton products, although these latter are in bulk less than one-fifth the bulk of corresponding American exports; and yet Europe has been at the immense disadvantage of hauling five-eighths of its raw supply from American shores, and then hauling the manufactured product back to America again—*we* paying ocean charges both ways!

[3] Report of 13th Census, vol. x, p. 62.
[4] Report of 13th Census, vol. x, p. 62.

Is this the annual tribute paid by nervous "hustle" to patient training, the price paid by complacent inefficiency to technical skill? One writer has said, picturesquely: "There is no logical reason why it should continue to be possible and profitable for a little, half-frozen country on the roof of Europe to reach out to America, purchase hundreds of thousands of bales of cotton, and, after carrying them across the Atlantic, ship them back to the United States in finished form and in quantities amounting in value to fifteen million dollars in a year.—Switzerland, which grows no cotton, whose mountains yield no coal for its factories, a country that has not an inch of seacoast or a plank afloat, sends to us, in the ships of other nations, more finished cotton goods than we export to all the countries of Continental Europe combined."[5]

But there are economists who dissent from this violent indictment of American efficiency. Instead of agreeing with Whelpley that "the seller of staples and raw materials is the least intelligent and prosperous of the world's traders,"[6] they say that "the staple branches alone seem to offer good opportunities for the characteristic industrial qualities of the American inventor and business man."[7] Three factors, they contend, must be carefully weighed for the determination of American economic efficiency in the cotton trade: the national facility in the invention and operation of automatic machinery, especially the automatic loom; the distinctive American genius for industrial organization and management of both

[5] D. J. Sully, in the *Cosmopolitan:* New York; Feb., Mar., 1909.

[6] J. D. Whelpley, The Trade of the World: New York, 1913; p. 50.

[7] F. W. Taussig, Some Aspects of the Tariff Question: Cambridge, 1915; p. 295.

men and goods in the mass; and a plentiful supply of cheap unskilled labor, for spinning, supplied in the North by an incessant stream of European immigration [8] and in the South by the great movement of "hands" from the field to the factory, as already described.

The Northrop automatic loom has been brought to such a high pitch of perfection that a single weaver, formerly able to attend to six or eight ordinary looms, can now look after twenty, twenty-four, or even thirty of these highly automatic machines.[9] While the operation of this machinery brings the weaver high wages, the output is a crude low-priced product, in immense quantities, in which the American manufacturer can compete successfully with his European rivals in their own territory, because of the "comparative advantage" [10] derived from this combination of prolific machinery, well-paid labor, and effective supervision; his yarn being meanwhile supplied by a constant influx of cheap labor which, albeit unskilled, can manage the "ring-frames" so extensively used in America instead of the complicated "mule" almost universally prevalent in Europe, and demanding skilled labor.[11] "Goods of the

[8] Andrew Carnegie began life in America at the age of ten as a cotton mill operative at a wage of $1.40 a week.

[9] Taussig, as just cited, p. 276.

[10] Taussig, as cited, chs. iii, xvii, xviii. ("Briefly stated, the doctrine is that a country tends under conditions of freedom to devote its labor and capital to those industries in which they work to greatest effect. It will be found unprofitable to turn to industries in which, though labor and capital may be employed with effect, they are applied with less effect than in the more advantageous industries. The principle is simple enough, nor is it applicable solely to international trade.—The lawyer finds it advantageous to turn over to his clerk that work which he could do as well as the clerk, or even better, confining himself to the tasks in the profession for which he has by training or inborn gift still greater capacity."—p. 30.)

[11] "Ring spinners are always women and children, who can be

most expensive sort fail to be made within the United States because labor is applied to them with less machinery, less of labor-saving devices, less effective organization,—in sum, with less *advantage* than to the cheap and medium grades.''[12]

It is certainly not fair to indict American efficiency solely on the ground of foreign trade, without taking into account the manufacture for domestic consumption. The appended table, prepared by Copeland,[13] shows not only a notable increase in spindleage, consumption, and value of product,—five-fold or more in each instance,—but, what is far more to the point for the present purpose, only a sluggish increase of imports, thus indicating a constantly augmented ability to supply the home market, while the export figures mentioned at the be-

U. S. Cotton Manufactures Since the Civil War

Year	No. of Establishments	No. of Spindles (millions)	Cotton Consumption (in million lbs.)	Persons Employed (thousands)	Value of Products (million dollars)	Imports (million dollars)
1860	1,091	5.2	422.7	122	115.7	38.2
1870	956	7.1	398.3	135	177.5	23.4
1880	756	10.7	750.3	175	192.1	29.9
1890	905	14.2	1,118.0	219	268.0	29.9
1900	973	19.0	1,814.0	298	332.8	41.3
1910	1,208	27.4	2,332.2	371	616.5	66.5

easily trained and easily replaced."—Taussig, as just cited, pp. 270–271, 272. Of the 56,000,000 spindles in the United Kingdom, about 46,000,000 are mule spindles; of the 30,000,000 spindles in the U. S., only about 5,000,000 are mule spindles.

[12] Taussig, p. 362. Emery says of the American: "He possesses neither the laborious patience of the hand-labourer nor the æsthetic sense of the true artisan; but his practical sense finds full scope in the production of large quantities of uniform commodities by quick machine methods."—As cited, p. 700.

[13] The Cotton Manufacturing Industry of the U. S.: Cambridge, 1912; p. 17.

ginning of this chapter dwindle to insignificance in the total mass of American cotton manufacture.

Foreign trade, as may be seen, has had but little to do with the development of cotton manufacture in America, which has looked chiefly to the supply of the home market. "A field favorable for the talents of the Yankee, a great population ready to purchase staple goods by the million, a labor supply adapted for the utilization of quasi-automatic machines,—here we have the explanation of the progress made in the industry."[14]

In spite of this progress, however, the United States ranks second among the cotton manufacturing nations, the disparity between American and British spindles still being enormous—30,579,000 for the United States, and 55,576,108 in Great Britain, out of a world's total of 142,000,000.[15] Seventy-five per cent of the British product is for export, as against only five per cent in America. There is obviously a vast opportunity for increased manufacture in the United States in connection with the development of oceanic trade, in those classes of goods in which America confessedly possesses "comparative advantage." The present writer further believes that it is feasible and highly desirable, through the introduction of technical education among the mill operatives, to acquire gradually a facility in the manufacture of those finer fabrics which now have to be brought from abroad.

[14] Taussig, Some Aspects, as cited, p. 294.

[15] Sir Charles Macara, as cited, pp. 8, 9. See Appendix F: 3b. It is estimated that about £120,000,000 is now invested in the British cotton industry, and that the annual value of its output is about £130,000,000. The exports of cotton cloths for the year ending Aug. 31, 1912, amounted to £91,098,023, and of yarns, £16,052,876. To the value of the cloths exported must be added 18 or 20 per cent for home consumption. The quantities for 1912 were: Cloths, 6,843,259,600 yards; yarn, 243,188,700 pounds.

CHAPTER 71

SEA SHUTTLES

THE importance of cotton as a factor in international trade is constantly increasing, and shows no signs of abatement. A score of years ago, when the world's cotton crop was about twelve and a half million bales (of five hundred pounds each), Mr. Edward Atkinson estimated that in the far future, should the consumption for the entire world come to equal that of the leading nations at present, a crop of 42,000,000 bales might perhaps be demanded;[1] but already one-half of Mr. Atkinson's possible ultimate demand is supplied, and still the world clamors for more.[2]

China offers a striking case in point. When the witty Mr. Wu Ting Fang visited North Carolina in 1901 he facetiously remarked that if every one of his countrymen could be induced to add but one inch to the length of his shirt, it would require at least two million bales of cotton to meet the increased demand.[3] The Chinese have arisen as if in response

[1] Cited in *Manufacturers Record:* Baltimore, March 27, 1913; p. 20.

[2] At the International Congress of Master Cotton Spinners' and Manufacturers' Associations held at Brussels in 1910, it was estimated that cotton now supplies nine-tenths of the clothing of the world's inhabitants; that these inhabitants number 1,500,000,000; that of these, only 500,000,000 are completely clothed, while 750,000,000 are but partially clothed, and 250,000,000 are not clothed at all. As Sir Charles Macara then remarked, these figures indicate the vastness of the industry and the possibilities of its further development.

[3] The Southern Manufacturers' Club Banquet to His Excellency, Wu Ting Fang: Charlotte, 1901.

to this challenge, and demanded more clothes!—so that the consumption of the mills of China has exactly doubled since the year in which Mr. Wu spoke. In 1891 the first Chinese mill was erected. There are now more than thirty, representing an investment of $15,000,000, and consuming 400,000 bales annually, in addition to an immense homespun industry, dating from very ancient times.

Other parts of the Far East have also greatly increased their consumption of cotton, since the year of Mr. Wu's speech. Japan, for example, has more than quadrupled its raw imports and almost doubled its spindles, finding its chief market in China. In 1901 Japan took only 45,870 bales from the United States, but in 1914 (in spite of the war) took 353,440. India, however, supplies Japan with more than half of the raw material, and the value of Indian cotton imported into Japan during 1912 showed an increase of $25,000,000 over that of the year preceding.[4] The opening of the Panama Canal brings Shanghai and Yokohama into as close relations with the Gulf ports as Liverpool itself, leading a recent English writer to the opinion that Japan will soon become the Lancashire of the Far East, being able to choose her supplies from the two leading markets of the world, America and India.[5]

In India itself, the original home of the cotton plant, a powerful movement has developed for domestic manufacture, similar to that of the Southern States in America versus New England,—so that Lancashire may not much longer expect to import

[4] India produced in 1914 the largest crop ever grown in that country. See Appendix F: 3a.

[5] Dr. John Bates Clark tells the writer that he expects the eastern littoral of Asia to become the greatest cotton manufacturing center in the world.

raw material from India and send it back to Bombay and Calcutta in piece-goods at a notable profit. At the beginning of the present century India had become the largest single market for English manufactured cotton goods, taking yearly almost $100,000,000 worth; but with an enthusiasm equaling that of the American colonists in the eighteenth century (see page 119), the Hindus are once more becoming a nation of spinners and weavers, with the result that an impetus must inevitably and increasingly be given to the amount of per capita consumption.

Mr. Saint Nihal Singh writes: "The all-conquering character of this enthusiasm is best illustrated by the fact that many Indians to-day are preferring to wear comparatively coarse cloth made in their own land, and are even willing to pay more for it than they would be charged for finer fabric made in Lancashire. This sentiment, known as 'Swadeshi'—literally 'Own Country,' meaning the patronage of home products—is actually building a substitute for a high-tariff wall to protect the native mill industry—a rampart invisible to the eye, but none the less effective.—An idea of the gigantic strides that the Indian cotton-mill industry has taken can be formed by studying the figures for the last generation. In 1880–81 there were 55 cotton-mills, containing 1,434,364 spindles and 12,739 looms, and giving employment to 46,530 men. Twenty years later the number of spindles and looms had more than trebled. During the next decade progress was made at a still more prodigious pace, and in 1909–10 the number of mills had grown to be 216, with 5,773,824 spindles, 74,585 looms, giving employment to 215,419 persons, and producing 593,206,855 pounds of yarn and 215,360,904 pounds of cloth.

During 1911–12 the Indian mills consumed 6,000,000 hundredweight out of the 14,000,000 hundredweight India had produced during that year."[6]

The development of the Far East, however, stupendous as it is beginning to be, affords only a partial explanation of the continually increasing demand for the cotton fiber. The doctrine of Sartor Resartus, that "society is founded upon cloth," and that advancing civilization is largely a matter of more clothes, gets striking illustration from the per capita consumption of cotton within the United States itself during the last forty years, as exhibited in the following table:

1870	*1880*	*1890*	*1900*	*1910*
9.46 lbs.	14.74 lbs.	15.96 lbs.	22.57 lbs.	29.53 lbs.

Mr. Theodore Price, considering these figures, points out that an increase of only one pound per capita in the world's consumption means an increased demand for more than four million bales of the fiber, and concludes that "the specter which, for the next decade, must haunt the cotton trade, is not the possibility of a surplus, but rather the probability of a deficient supply, such as wrought disaster among American manufacturers in 1910.[7]

Mr. Price's conclusion, which would fairly seem open to question, is certainly not weakened by the fact that American exports of cotton are increasing at a far greater rate than the total volume of exports, rapid as the total rate is. Between 1900 and 1912 the total exports mounted from $1,394,000,000 (in round numbers) to $2,204,000,000, while raw cot-

[6] In the *London Magazine; see Literary Digest:* New York, May 24, 1913; p. 1170.

[7] Written before the Great War broke out: *Cotton and Finance:* New York, March 9, 1912.

ton rose from $241,832,000 to $565,849,000. In other words, while the total exports failed of doubling during that period by $584,000,000, the cotton exports doubled and had $82,000,000 to spare.

The matter may also be illustrated by reference to the comparative increase of exports in Northern ports such as New York, on the one hand, and Southern ports such as New Orleans and Galveston on the other; cotton in the latter case constituting five-sevenths of the volume of exports, as against the immense miscellaneous export trade of the North. Within thirty years great changes have been recorded. Instead of Atlantic ports handling 78 per cent of the American export trade and the Gulf ports 14 per cent, the latter now handle 22 per cent and the former only 58 per cent. Within the last decade, indeed, Gulf exports increased 64 per cent and those through Atlantic ports only 20 per cent; and it is to be remembered that the Gulf ports had not yet felt the stimulus of the Panama Canal when these figures were published, so that this marked relative increase is, apparently, attributable solely to the influence of cotton on international trade.[8]

One of the romances of modern history,[9] it has been said, is the story of the discovery and development of the manifold uses of cottonseed. For at least five thousand years cotton has been cultivated and its fiber manufactured into clothing, yet the seed which the downy lint enfolds was, except for purposes of reproduction, treated practically as so much waste until about thirty years ago. Not until 1890

[8] *Saturday Evening Post*, cited in *Cotton and Finance:* New York, Oct. 26, 1912; p. 339.

[9] Todd, as cited, p. 354.

was it regarded as of sufficient importance to be included in the government reports, but in that year it was shown that the Southern planters had just sold 1,789,895 tons of it, for the sum of $16,000,000.[10] The writer well remembers his excitement and alarm when, as a boy on a Southern farm (about 1885), the pet cow having broken into an out-house, he discovered her greedily devouring the cottonseed piled up on the floor for the next planting. The seed was then thought to be not only useless for cattle, but actually poisonous, whereas it is now recognized as one of the best cattle feeds on the market; so that some enterprising students of Southern agriculture, such as Dr. V. P. Clayton of Charleston, have believed that to supplement sheep grazing with this native provender would put the South well forward in wool as well as in cotton production—the sheep, in addition to their high value for both wool and mutton, furnishing a valuable fertilizer.[11]

The clearly demonstrated uses of cottonseed are already so multifarious and important as to occasion an insistent world-wide demand. From the "cottolene" or "crisco" at breakfast time to the "olive oil" at dinner, from the "felt" of the early slipper or from the dainty soap and cosmetics of the ladies' dressing table to the fleece-lined night-wear, from the

[10] A. Carnegie, Triumphant Democracy: New York, 1893; p. 264.

[11] Dr. Clayton told the writer that he knew a South Carolina farmer who has been feeding cottonseed to sheep for over 40 years, with remarkable success, during the four or five months when they are not turned out to grass—the despised Bermuda grass affording excellent pasturage. Clayton believed that the value of the seed as a fertilizer would be reduced by only about 10 per cent if fed to the sheep and subsequently husbanded, and that in connection with this fertilizing value the profit in mutton and wool would double the present value of cottonseed when sold at the mill. See also Burkett and Poe, ch. xxxii, and Bulletin No. 33, as cited, pp. 385–421.

carpet or linoleum to the roofing and its varnish, from the wadding in the mattress to the putty in the window panes, from the photographic film in your "kodak" or the phonographic roll in your "dictaphone" to the nitro-cellulose in French or German guns—man lives not by bread alone, but he lives and trades and slays with the new-found cottonseed, as may be learned from the diagram about to follow. Thirty years ago it was regarded almost as a nuisance, which cost money to get rid of unless it could be used as manure, and sometimes as fuel.[12] Ten years ago it was a stock illustration of the utilization of by-products. To-day it is an industry in itself, with a "turnover" worth probably (the world over) $250,000,000 a year, and its finished products are the raw material of a hundred trades, from cattle-rearing to soap-making.[13] Todd cites it as an especially striking illustration of the world-wide commerce generated by the cotton plant, for there is certainly no race of people in the world, he thinks, who, even if they do not wear cotton clothes, fail to use soap or candles made from cottonseed oil, or to consume it in some one of its many edible forms. The accompanying diagram is self-explanatory.

Back and forth across the oceans the great steam shuttles ply, forever capitalizing the genius of Watt and Fulton and Whitney, as they weave "the warp and the woof of the world's civilization." Out from the ports of Galveston and New Orleans, Savannah and Charleston, Los Angeles and San Francisco,

[12] "In many places in the old days cotton gins were purposely built on streams in order that the water might carry away the great accumulations of supposedly worthless seeds and in some States laws were passed requiring ginners to clear away the seed, the rotting piles otherwise becoming offensive to the neighbors!"—Burkett and Poe, pp. 275–276.

[13] Todd, p. 354.

PRODUCTS AND USES OF COTTON SEED*

- **COTTON SEED.**
  - LINTERS
    - Batting.
    - Wadding.
    - Stuffing material for
      - Pads.
      - Cushions.
      - Comforts.
      - Horse collars.
      - Mattresses.
      - Upholstery.
    - Absorbent cotton.
    - Mixing with shoddy.
    - Mixing with wool in hat making.
    - Mixing with lamb's wool for fleece-lined underwear.
    - Felt.
    - Low-grade yarns
      - Lamp and candle wicks.
      - Twine.
      - Rope.
      - Carpets.
    - Cellulose
      - Writing paper.†
      - Guncotton, nitro cellulose, or pyrocellulose.
        - Smokeless powder.
        - Pyroxylin
          - Varnishes
            - Coating for metals.
            - Artificial leather.
            - Waterproofing
          - Plastics
            - Celluloid.
            - Collodion.
            - Varnishes.
            - Artificial silk.
            - Photographic films.
  - HULLS
    - Feed.
    - Fertilizer.
    - Fuel.†
    - Packing.
    - Household utensils.
    - Bran—Cattle feed.
    - Fiber
      - Stuffing for horse collars.
      - Basis for explosives.
      - Cellulose—Used same as under Linters.
      - Paper stock—Pressed paper products.
  - MEATS
    - CAKE AND MEAL
      - Fertilizer.
      - Dyestuffs.
      - Feed for
        - Cattle.
        - Poultry.†
        - Horses and mules.
        - Swine.†
        - Sheep.
      - Flour †
        - Bread.
        - Cake.
        - Cracker.
    - CRUDE OIL
      - Refined oil.
        - Prime summer yellow oil.
          - Cosmetics.
          - Bleached or deodorized oil.
            - Animal compound lard.
            - Cooking oil.
            - Salad oil.
          - Hydrogenated oil.
            - Lard substitutes.
            - Synthetic stearin—Vegetable-compound lard.
          - Cold pressed oil.
            - Winter oil
              - Salad oil
              - Setting olives.
              - Packing sardines.
              - Winter white oil.
            - Stearin—Oleomargarin.
          - Emulsion for medical purposes.
          - Substitute for sweet oil.
          - Deodorized oil.
        - Off-grade summer yellow oil.
          - Soap.
          - Miners' oil.
          - Hydrogenated oil—Synthetic stearin—Soap.
      - Putty.
      - Foots
        - Washing powder.
        - Acidulated foots or black grease.
        - Soap.
          - Glycerin—Nitroglycerin.
          - Fat acids
            - Candle pitch.
            - Distilled fat acids.
              - Stearic acid—Candles.
              - Washing powder.
              - Soap.
              - Stearin pitch or cotton-oil pitch.
                - Roofing tar.
                  - Composition roofing.
                - Linoleums.
                - Insulating materials.
                - Oilcloth.
                - Waterproofing.
                - Cheap-paint base.
                - Cotton rubber.
                - Artificial leather.
                  - Upholstering.
                  - Bookbinding.
              - Oleic acid
                - Soap.
                - Washing powder.
                - Fulling ware.

---

* From Bulletin No. 131, U. S. Dept. of Commerce: Washington, 1915.

† Possible uses to which small quantities only are devoted.

laden down to the water line with the world's raiment riches, these steamers sail in the summer and autumn of normal peaceful years;—the largest group to the United Kingdom, supplying the great mills of Lancashire and other factory towns with three and a half million bales annually; another fleet to the river ports of Hamburg and Bremen, beyond the German Ocean, bearing provender for the hungry factories of Chemnitz and Mülhausen, about two and a half million bales every year; another fleet to Russia, with a hundred thousand bales, a larger one to France, with more than a million; still other fleets to Austria, with a hundred thousand bales, to Italy, with half a million, to Switzerland and Belgium, Portugal and Holland, Denmark and Norway, to South America, to Japan and to China—wherever men have learned or are learning the use of machinery, these cotton shuttles ply with their burdens. Back across the oceans flows a thin white stream of paper, pledging the world's credit in payment; back even flows a steady stream of gold, five hundred million dollars every autumn, when the crop has been moved—thus easing the tension of credit in the South, paying debts and filling the vaults of the savings banks, brightening a million homes of planters and "factors" and bankers, and establishing a national balance of trade.

Then, when in manifold far-scattered foreign factories this fleece has been unpacked and carded and spun and woven and bleached and printed and again packeted, it starts once more on globe-girdling journeys. "From the factories of Europe and Japan countless ships carry increasing cargoes of cotton fabrics to every civilized port. Goods woven of this staple constitute a vast proportion of the merchandise hauled by train across all continents, and where modern methods of transportation pause, primitive and picturesque carriers take up the burden of the world's cotton output and trudge with these goods to eager customers along the most remote frontiers. Cotton cloth paves the way for Christianity in the jungles of the Dark Continent; to the savages of the Congo cotton cloth is more precious than ivory or gold. Under the midnight sun arctic dogs drag sleds laden with cotton goods. The condor and the eagle look down wonderingly upon pack-trains carrying the product of European cotton-mills across the Andes. The yak goes burdened with cotton goods into Tibet. Godowns along Chinese streams are stored with cotton goods awaiting shipment, and to the upper reaches of the Yang-tse and Hoang-ho the native Chinese trader on his junk carries cotton cloths and garments to interior tribes. Burros laden with cotton goods from England and Germany pick their way across the mountains of Mexico. The elephants of India and the camels of the Levant and Egypt carry cotton goods." [15] Thus the lands are bound together in a world-encircling web. As Professor Todd says, there is nothing that can happen, from a revolution in China to a bad monsoon in India, the cutting of a canal or the building of a railway, which is not certain to affect cotton in many ways.[16]

15 D. J. Sully in the *Cosmopolitan:* New York, March, 1909.
16 J. A. Todd, The World's Cotton Crops: London, 1915; p. 365.

CHAPTER 72

WHEN WAR BREAKS

The lines of the telegraph are scarcely more quickly responsive than the skeins of this web when the "mailed fist" strikes. Instantly upon the declaration of war the cotton market drops, like a semi-tropical thermometer suddenly stricken with abnormal frosts, and brokers, like fruit-growers, tumble into bankruptcy. Wheat, on the other hand, rises; to fall back towards normal a little later, while the cotton market slowly climbs up again, although it continues to fluctuate.

The explanation of the first swift movement in prices is simple, and may be given in the parable of the humorous negro who was quizzed by a stranger because his body, while sleek and fat, was draped in rags:

"Ma back will stan' fo' credit, Boss, but ma stomach call' fo' cash!"

The first thought of the world, when its delicate commercial net-work is suddenly torn like a spider's web by the rough hand of war, is for food; a little later it realizes that it must also be clothed. Even the shortage resulting from suspension of mills must sooner or later be rectified, so that, while the world-wide ramification of an annual cotton supply may be rudely disturbed and very seriously retarded, it must ultimately go forward again. Meanwhile, distress afflicts every member of the "economic entity" (see page 4), whether on plantation or in the stock exchange or at the factory.

The commercial interdependence of nations was illustrated in a manner never to be forgot when the Great War of 1914 broke out. Austria declared war against Servia on Tuesday, July 28. Within three days the cotton trade throughout the world was in a state of collapse. The first thing that brought the trouble home to those not directly interested in the trade was the sudden closing on Friday, July 31, of the Cotton Exchanges, particularly in Liverpool, New York, and New Orleans. The striking point to be noted here is the fact that this was before the actual declaration of war between any of the Great Powers. When the declaration of war between England and Germany actually occurred on Tuesday, August 4, shipping practically came to a standstill, and, for a time, all export trade ceased.[1] The effect in the United States was cataclysmic. An American statistician, Roger W. Babson, shortly afterwards showed that in spite of the most bountiful crops in the history of the country,[2] and the largest amount of money in circulation that statistics had ever recorded, bank clearings dropped to a dangerous ebb, stocks and bonds were selling at abnormally low prices, the largest number of unemployed men were roaming the streets since the panic

[1] Todd, as cited, pp. 370–373.

[2] The values of the principal farm crops this year were: Corn, $1,702,599,000; wheat, $878,680,000; hay, $779,068,000; cotton, $519,616,000; oats, $499,431,000; potatoes, $198,609,000; barley, $105,903,000; tobacco, $101,411,000. The United States occupies only about one-sixteenth of the globe and has only about one-fifteenth of its population, yet it produces 73 per cent of the world's cotton, 68 per cent of the world's corn, 63 per cent of the world's petroleum, 65 per cent of its copper, 42 per cent of its iron ore, 40 per cent of its coal, 35 per cent of its tobacco, 30 per cent of its lead, silver and live stock, and 20 per cent of its gold, wheat, and timber.

of 1907, mills were shutting down, and, in fact, "most of the twelve million people of this country dependent upon export trade are suffering from the world's failure to recognize the brotherhood of man." Not even in the Civil War were American stock exchanges compelled to close for a single hour; but the shattering of international relationships caused by the Great War locked their doors for months. "With the differences in the climate and resources of the nations of the world, we must recognize that our prosperity is interlocked. Neither this country nor any other that is now neutral can enjoy to the fullest the blessings of peace until all the nations are bound together in some form of alliance, based, not upon a Declaration of Independence, but on a Declaration of Interdependence."[3]

Even in times of peace, the annual cotton crop is so huge that apparently insignificant fluctuations, perhaps caused by some slight disturbance in a remote far-away skein of this sensitive world-web, may upset the economic equilibrium of all civilized lands. A rise or fall of only one cent a pound represents a difference in assets of $100,000,000. The difference in the American crops for 1900 and 1912 was $540,000,000, a sum which exceeds the average value of the world's annual output of gold and silver combined for the same twelve years. If we shift the ground of illustration to Egypt, we find, according to the Financial Adviser to the Khedive, that the value of the Egyptian cotton crop rose steadily from $80,000,000 in 1901 to $122,500,000 in 1906; in 1907 and 1908 it leaped to $150,000,000, fell to $120,000,000 in 1909, jumped again to $180,000,000 in 1911, and stood once more at $150,000,000 in 1912. As Mr.

[3] Editorial article in the Los Angeles *Times*, Jan. 10, 1915.

John Wormald of Manchester says, "These figures represent enormous differences in balance, and fully demonstrate that cotton has a vitally important bearing on the incidence of international finance."[4]

The reader is now in position to judge of the effect on American finance produced by the outbreak of the Great War of Europe in respect of cotton alone, as indicated by the following startling contrast in raw cotton exports for the years 1913 and 1914, during the month of August:[5]

	1913		*1914*
To the United Kingdom.	77,488	bales	6,370
To Germany	72,928	"	52
To France	52,933	"	5
All other countries	53,823	"	14,783
Total	257,172		21,210

September, however, is a heavier export month than August. In 1913 the United Kingdom took 376,426 bales, but in 1914 only 50,980; while Germany and France got absolutely none in 1914, as against 290,805 bales and 131,950 bales respectively in 1913. October is a still heavier month. Great Britain had by this time in 1914 reorganized her shipping arrangements so as to take 232,065 bales, or somewhat less than half as many as in the year before, while France succeeded in landing 22,302 bales, and Germany still got none as against 465,525 bales in the October of 1913. In November Germany managed to secure a hundred bales, and in the last month of the year took 47,076 bales, making a total of 48,128 bales for the first five months of the war as against

[4] The *Sprinkler Bulletin:* Manchester, June, 1913; pp. 702–703.
[5] Department of Commerce Reports.

1,673,049 bales for the same period of the year preceding. Great Britain, however, brought her December, 1914, purchases up to an excess of a hundred thousand bales over the same month in the previous year, and had almost exactly reëstablished a balance for the five months' period, while at the same time resorting to the most strenuous measures to prevent further shipments to Germany. The result of this commercial phase of the war for the first half of the year 1915 (as compared with 1914) may be tabulated as follows:

		United Kingdom	*Germany*
January	1914	437,231	308,116
	1915	585,534	99,913
February	1914	328,794	212,599
	1915	2,414,619	88,508
March	1914	264,999	219,948
	1915	440,490	6,112
April	1914	147,298	118,198
	1915	378,828	*None*
May	1914	140,618	132,123
	1915	359,675	*None*
June	1914	121,726	80,639
	1915	118,890	*None*

While Germany, in spite of these figures, was able for a while to obtain some cotton by way of Scandinavia, that channel was subsequently closed; and a competent German trade expert gave it as his opinion that during June, 1915, "not a gramme of cotton had found its way into Germany." A government order was therefore issued July 1, to take effect August 1, which was equivalent, according to the German trade journal for the clothing industry, to "the total stoppage of the German cotton industry, except in so far as it is engaged in the production of military supplies or of certain specialties."[6]

As this book goes through the press the following figures are available for the year ending July 31, 1916, as compared with the preceding year:

Country to which exported	Year ending July 31 1916	1915
United Kingdom	2,852,306	3,771,646
Germany	None	242,661
France	918,272	682,630
Italy	788,905	1,109,541
All other countries	1,644,705	2,738,085
Total Bales	6,204,188	8,544,563

The importance that England attaches to the control of cotton supplies during war time is shown by the lengths to which the Government seemed willing to go in support of a "mid-ocean blockade." That such figures as those just tabulated necessarily have an important bearing on the course and outcome of war must be obvious to the most casual observer.

The fact is, cotton has now come to be in itself an essential to warfare, to a degree that few people suspect. Apart from the clothing needs of civilians, the standing armies and navies of the world consume annually, even in times of peace, between 175,000 and 200,000 bales in fatigue uniforms alone. Their demand is of course greatly augmented by the wear and tear of active campaigns, the "life" of the average field uniform being only three months. Wool has been largely displaced by its vegetable rival, even in overcoats; the service overcoats of private soldiers in the cold countries of Northern

[6] W. J. Ashley on "Germany and Cotton," in the *Atlantic Monthly:* Boston, January, 1916, pp. 119–120.

Europe being now made of cotton duck lined with fleece. In 1904, when Japan and Russia were fighting, manufacturers found the demand for duck the one buoyant feature of a trade temporarily paralyzed by the wild speculation of the notorious "Sully year." Duck is needed not only for clothing, but for tents and tarpaulins, in enormous quantities.[7]

Gun-cotton has, during recent years, been developed into far the most important form of propulsive ammunition; consisting simply in nitrated cellulose, cellulose itself subsisting, in an almost pure form, under the guise of cotton wool, which, when nitrated, becomes susceptible of enormous explosive effectiveness if detonated by fulminate of mercury. While cellulose, the chief constituent of wood, is of course the common property of many substances, other forms of it have hitherto been found unsuited to the proper manufacture of gun-cotton for use in the heavier artillery, cotton itself being regarded as the basic requisite.[8]. Sir William Ramsay, the British chemist, in an effort to spur his tardy government to declare cotton contraband of war, wrote for the *English Review* of May, 1915, a clear and vigorous exposi-

[7] C. T. Revere, "War's Effect on Cotton Prices," in *Cotton and Finance:* New York, Nov. 2, 1912; p. 48.

[8] The ingenuity of chemists, even before the war, had succeeded in producing a nitro-cellulose out of wood-pulp, though it had never actually been used in heavy guns. But as a propellent it is weaker; and this means that its use would necessitate new firing chambers and new sighting in all existing guns. Rifles might possibly be altered with field appliances; heavier guns would have to go to a workshop. There are rumors that propellents are now being made in Germany from wood pulp; and it is even said that the Krupps have begun to make suitable guns. But conceive of the difficulty of shifting from one propellent to another in the midst of war, and the complications resulting from the simultaneous use of non-interchangeable ammunition.—W. J. Ashley, as cited, p. 117.

tion of the uses of cotton on the firing line.[9] He computed, for example, that for rifle ammunition alone the German army consumes an average of fifty-one tons a day, or 18,600 tons a year, while their machine guns require at least an equal amount, and the lighter ordnance more than three times as much—making an annual total consumption by this one army of not less than a hundred thousand tons, or 400,000 bales, American weight, for ammunition purposes only. Considering all classes of ordnance, it is computed that on the average a bale of cotton is consumed to every 150 shots, and that every company of 300 soldiers carries three bales of cotton in the shape of cartridges.[10] As for the navy, it is said that a twelve-inch gun consumes three hundred pounds of ammunition, or about half a bale of the cotton from which this is made, with every discharge; so that a battle-ship, firing at its greatest capacity, might use five thousand to six thousand pounds of powder, or from ten to twelve bales of cotton, every minute during an action!

While it thus becomes apparent that active warfare creates a specific and peculiar demand for cotton unknown in times of peace, when waste or rejected lint is sufficient to satisfy the needs of military practise and of the sporting world for powder, it is nevertheless perfectly obvious that the total general effect of war is to disturb cotton values, inflicting distress on the planter; whose chief danger, however, it should be distinctly remembered, arises not so much from war itself as from the augmented demand almost certain to occur with its sudden ces-

[9] On Aug. 20, 1915, the British Government by an order-in-council added raw cotton, cotton linters, cotton waste and cotton yarns to the list of absolute contraband.

[10] American Year Book: New York, 1916; p. 512.

sation, an effect due to the accelerated resumption of foreign manufacture for the replenishment of long depleted supplies, and thus luring the unwary planter once more to a delirium of over-production and to the sacrifice of his unromantic life-boats of food-crops on the Lorelei rock of this "money crop."

Early in the course of the Great War (1914) the United States Government adopted wise and energetic methods for relief of the nation-wide stringency caused by the sudden check to this money crop, which was precisely ready for movement, and more especially for relief of Southern farmers whose whole year's living was at stake. Prices had dropped, immediately after the outbreak of hostilities, to the lowest ebb ever touched since railway and telegraph lines have provided broad markets for the most generally used single commodity in all the world. The Government promptly utilized its banking system to afford measurable relief, by accepting notes on warehoused cotton at 75 per cent of their face value, on the basis of eight cents a pound; a procedure which could hardly have been justified except for the fact, pointed out at a conference called by the Secretary of the Treasury, that cotton does not deteriorate when properly warehoused, being as good twenty years after it is picked as when it is first gathered, so that "it can therefore be carried over until the restoration of normal business conditions enables the world's consumption to absorb it."

Aided by these measures, and also, to a less degree, by the "Buy a bale" popular movement, planters exercised such wise deliberation in marketing the crop that prices soon rallied and steadied a little, while by the month of February, 1915, the

American factory consumption of cotton had returned to normal proportions. A year later, the Hon. John Sharp Williams of Mississippi said in the Senate:

"Cotton is worth 12.38 cents a pound spot in the Memphis market. If peace came to-morrow, cotton would not be worth over ten cents a pound. Whatever else this war has done, it has not lowered the price of cotton. For the first four or six months of the war, the war did lower the price because it dislocated the entire financial and trade exchange systems. But at present what is becoming of the cotton crop?

"Why, Great Britain, France, and Italy and their dependencies in normal times take 73 per cent of our entire cotton exports, and 73 per cent is going to them now. More than that is going to them, for the neutral countries are not only getting their share, but a little bit more, so that it is about 83 per cent that is not interfered with."[11]

The Great War has probably brought permanent good to the South. The warehouses erected to meet the emergency have a storage capacity sufficient to house the largest crop, allowing for the natural export movement of cotton during the period of harvesting.[12] These will be retained and improved, so that planters may have permanent weatherproof means for holding back their product from the market when prices are temporarily deflated by speculators. Not only so, but the farmers seem for the first time to have grasped firmly, as a result of the lessons taught by the War, the importance of diversification. "Never again," says a hopeful writer,

[11] New York *Times*, Jan. 21, 1916; p. 2.
[12] *Bulletin No. 131*, Dept. of Commerce: Washington, 1915; p. 72.

"will the South put all its eggs into one basket." A visit by the present writer at the close of 1915, after an absence of seven years, produced on his mind an irresistible impression of greatly improved conditions. As a matter of fact, the people of the South had produced during that year more wealth than in any other year of their history, and from diversified crops: "less cotton, but more money for it than ever before; hay, corn, oats, hogs, piled high on the credit side of the ledger." [13]

If indeed the South has truly learned its lesson, the ill wind will have blown it great good.

[13] F. M. Davenport on "The Southern Renaissance," in the *Outlook:* New York, Feb. 23, 1916; p. 428.

CHAPTER 73

BRITISH PROSPECTS IN EGYPT

Great Britain, with rueful recollection of the Cotton Famine that resulted from the American Civil War and endangered her paramount industry, has made many efforts to develop cotton areas in her huge colonial possessions throughout the world. Perhaps the most impressive tribute ever paid to the American Cotton Belt is that contained in the report of a British commission which once investigated the cotton-growing possibilities of East Africa. "All efforts to raise cotton successfully elsewhere than in the Southern part of the United States have failed," the report confesses. "This is the home of the cotton plant, and if it will grow and fruit elsewhere to the extent that the staple have a substantial commercial value, the fact is yet to be demonstrated. It was experimented with under different suns during and after the American Civil War, and all the experiments failed. Providence has given the Southern farmer a monopoly of the indispensable cotton crop, and he need not take fright when the price soars and there are heard threats of turning Africa, Egypt or other countries into cotton fields and making them furnish the world's supply." [1]

In 1902, however, the British Cotton Growing Association was formed, with the strong-hearted pur-

[1] Cited by Burkett and Poe, p. 34.

pose of "establishing and extending the growth of cotton in the British Empire," so as to relieve Lancashire from its dangerous dependence on the United States for raw material.[2] Undismayed by the negative reports of obsolete government commissions, this Association set about the actual cultivation of cotton in India, Uganda and Nyassaland, West Africa, the Anglo-Egyptian Sudan, and in the West Indies,—with the result that it now has a capital of $2,500,000, and $1,500,000 invested in the practical cultivation of new fields, some of which are very promising.

Production in Uganda, for example, has increased from 500 bales in 1906 to 29,000 bales in 1912, with the prospect of 40,000 bales for the crop next due. "The quality is rather better than Texas and fetches from ½ *d.* to 1½ *d.* per pound over Middling American." It is claimed that Lagos cotton is to-day the most regular and even in quality of any cotton produced in any part of the world. Nyassaland, entered by the Association so recently as 1910, gave two years later a crop of 6,800 bales, worth from 1 *d.* to 2½ *d.* over Middling American. Altogether, the Association has developed new fields so as to produce 360,640 bales, with a value of almost $26,000,000, during the twelve years of its labors.

Naturally, the Association is deeply interested in Egypt, not only because the rich Valley of the Nile has recently become a British possession, but because chiefly of the extraordinary value of the far-famed

[2] The King said in his speech at the opening of Parliament in 1904: "The insufficiency of the raw material upon which the cotton industry of this country depends has inspired me with great concern. I trust that the efforts which are being made in the various parts of my Empire to increase the area under cultivation may be attended with a large measure of success."—Todd, p. 161.

Egyptian cotton, which, next to the sea-island variety, is probably the finest in the world. Napoleon Bonaparte's great "Description de l'Egypte" shows that at the time of his invasion two different species of cotton were grown there. One of these was a short-staple Asiatic variety, of former commercial value, which has now disappeared; the other, a tree-cotton of Upper Egypt, probably identical with that of which Professor Alpino had furnished the first botanical record, about the close of the sixteenth century, when it was used as an ornamental shrub. At the suggestion of M. Jumel, a Franco-Swiss engineer, this plant was taken from a garden in Cairo, under a system of state control favored by Mohammed Ali, founder of the Khedivate, and propagated with such success (from the year 1820) that it soon displaced the short-staple Asiatic type, as the brown, strong lint, readily ginned from the almost naked seed, quickly made its reputation with the spinners, and this type of lint has been typical of the Egyptian product ever since.[3] It is especially adapted for thread, fine yarns, fine underwear and hosiery, and for goods requiring smooth finish and high luster. It can also be used for the manufacture of sewing thread and other articles which need to be exceptionally strong, and for which long-fiber cotton is required. It takes dyes unusually well, the Mit Afifi variety, indeed, giving the écru shade to such goods as lace curtains and "balbriggan" without dyeing. Its superior market value has already been noted (see page 337).

Of all the experiments and investigations conducted by the British Cotton Growing Association,

[3] W. L. Balls, as cited; pp. 1–3.

those for the purpose of developing additional cotton areas in Egypt afford the richest promise. The Gezira Plain, in the Anglo-Egyptian Sudan, contains about 4,500 square miles, consisting of a Delta formed between the two Niles ages ago by the deposit of rich alluvial soil from the Blue Nile. The whole cultivable land of Egypt is only 12,000 square miles; therefore this one plain in the Sudan is one-third as large as the whole of Egypt for agricultural purposes. Its complete irrigation would cost about three million pounds sterling, there being sufficient water in the Blue Nile, at the season required, to permit of the cultivation of a million acres without hurting Egyptian interests.[4]

In 1912 a deputation from the Cotton Growing Association, after visiting the Sudan, reported on the Gezira Plain as "one of the finest cotton propositions in the world"; saying that there seemed to be no reason why in the next few years there should not be raised annually 50,000 bales or more of really high-class Egyptian cotton, with the prospect of the production increasing to 250,000 bales within ten to fifteen years, and with further possibilities later on of a production of a million bales or more.

To sum up: At the International Congress of Tropical Agriculture, which the writer attended in London in June, 1914, the chairman of the council of the British Cotton Growing Association asserted that this Association had "definitely proved that the British Empire can produce the cotton which Lancashire requires. The quantity is, of course, at present small in comparison with Lancashire's total con-

[4] Sir. Wm. Mather, Egypt and the Anglo-Egyptian Sudan: Southampton, 1910; p. 36.

sumption, but the rate of progress we have achieved is infinitely greater than was the case in the early days of cotton growing in the United States of America.''[5]

[5] J. Arthur Hutton, The Work of the British Cotton Growing Association: London, 1914; p. 35.

NOTE ON STAPLES AND GRADES.—The "staple" of American cotton, omitting the limited special variety of sea-island cotton, with a fibre of great length and strength, varies in length from about ⅝ inch to about 1½ inches. Every increase in the length of the fibre results in an increase in the value. This is particularly true when the fibre has a length of 1 1/16 inches or more. From that point every addition of 1/16 inch to the fibre adds cumulatively to the price. The trade name for the shorter stapled cottons is "upland"—from ⅝ inch to 1 inch in length. The somewhat longer stapled cottons (from 1 inch to 1 3/16 inches) are known as "Gulf" and "Texas" cottons. The long stapled cottons (from 1 3/16 to 1½ inches), grown in the Mississippi Delta, are known as "rivers" or "benders," because raised on the rich alluvial land in the bends of the rivers.—No matter what the length of staple may be, its value varies in respect to color (white, tinged, and stained) and the aomunt of dry leaf, dust, and other extraneous matter. As this matter must be taken out of the cotton before it is spun, and is a pure loss to the spinner, the relative amount of it in any particular cotton further affects the value. Consequently all cotton has to be separated into "grades." That grade which seems originally to have been thought to represent a fair average of quality is known as "middling." The scale of the additions to or subtractions from the value of "middling," to arrive at the value of the other grades, is known as the scale of "differences."—Marsh, as cited.

CHAPTER 74

CALIFORNIA AND OTHER RIVALS OF THE SOUTH

So choice is Egyptian cotton that in some of the progressive Southern mills in America only this imported fiber is handled, although the surrounding fields may be white with the short-staple variety. sea-island cotton is grown wholly on the South Atlantic seaboard, yet during the last ten years American importations of Egyptian lint have exceeded its total production, averaging 140,000 bales annually. Recognizing the peculiar value of Egyptian cotton, the United States Department of Agriculture has experimented with it in Arizona and Southern California. Five hundred acres were planted, with profitable results, in 1912, and several thousand acres in 1913, yielding, with proper attention, a bale to the acre. Southern California has not only demonstrated, on a very broad scale, the possibility of successful competition with the Cotton Belt —by means of irrigation—in short-staple cotton, but can also successfully produce the Egyptian variety on a commercial basis.

The Imperial Valley of Southern California affords an interesting analogy to the Delta of the Nile. Having held in former ages the northern arm of the Gulf of California, it is now a huge dry basin, below sea level, with an area of a million and a half acres, into which the Colorado River has for thousands of years been pouring sediment until now the rich alluvial soil has a known depth of more than a thousand feet. With the beginning of the present century, private enterprise undertook the irrigation of this vast sunken garden, but in 1905–'06 the river broke through its bounds, forming the Salton Sea, and threatening irreparable destruction. Through the coöperation of President Roosevelt and Mr. Edward H. Harriman the river was dramatically forced back into its old bed, with infinite labor, and then by a strange "act of God" two channels were carved through the yielding soil in such a manner as to produce just the right drainage system needed to redeem the soil from "sourness" and make irrigation effective.[1] In an urgent message to Congress Mr. Roosevelt predicted land values of $1,500 per acre should reclamation succeed. Much of this land is now actually yielding a net return of ten per cent on a value of $5,000 per acre, 375,000 acres having water, and almost the entire valley being susceptible of irrigation.

A few acres planted in cotton in 1908 produced such effective results that in the following year three hundred bales were ginned in the Valley. Since that time the production in bales has increased as follows: 1910, 5,986; 1911, 9,790; 1912, 8,215; 1913, 22,838; 1914, 49,835.[2]

There are now about fifty thousand acres under cultivation, and a bale to the acre is usually produced, just as the Government had predicted; on February 9, 1915, the Department of Agriculture reported that both long- and short-staple cottons in California were yielding 500 pounds to the acre.

[1] A pleasant story of the development of the Imperial Valley is told by Mr. Harold Bell Wright in The Winning of Barbara Worth.

[2] *Bulletin*, U. S. Dept. of Commerce, Cotton Production, June 16, 1915; p. 5.

The State making the next best showing was Missouri, where "long" runs 325 and "short" 295 per acre, while the yield in Louisiana was only 150 pounds per acre for long-staple and 162 for short.[3] The value of the California crop for 1913 was $1,-530,000; that of 1914 would have been worth, under normal conditions, $5,500,000. The bulletin of the Department of Agriculture for the preceding year rated the general condition of cotton crops in several of the cotton areas as follows: Oklahoma, 42 per cent, Texas, 63 per cent, South Carolina, 70 per cent, Georgia, 72 per cent, Virginia, 75 per cent, Florida, 78 per cent, and the Imperial Valley, 100 per cent, or perfect.

Among the features that render this "American Nile" land so favorable to cotton growing may be mentioned its uniformly warm and sunny climate; the almost complete absence of rain, and a consequent stainlessness of product; the certainty of sufficient water at just the right time, and no other; the soil-enriching deposits of the Colorado River, making the expensive use of artificial fertilizers unnecessary; favorable labor conditions, with excellent transportation facilities; and an apparent immunity from the boll weevil.

While Egyptian cotton can be and is successfully cultivated in the Imperial Valley,[4] it is not so popular as the new "Durango" variety,[5] and for an interesting reason. The burr of the Egyptian boll curls

[3] Los Angeles *Times*, Feb. 9, 1915.

[4] "During the season of 1913–14 a considerable quantity of the Yuma variety of Egyptian cotton was shipped to Liverpool, and it is believed that the results were very satisfactory, not only to the owners of the cotton, but to the spinners who bought it."—Todd, p. 235.

[5] So called from the name of the Mexican State from which the seed were obtained.

backward at picking time, so as to remove proper protection from the fiber, which often strings out or is blown away, making the picking tedious, expensive, and comparatively unsatisfactory; while the Durango burr, like the Upland, holds the fiber compactly in place, yet opens sufficiently for easy picking.

Durango staple is a quarter-inch longer than Upland, giving it a greater value of three cents to the pound, although costing little more to produce. Five thousand bales of the 1913 crop were Durango, selling at $85 a bale as against $62.50 for Upland. But that Upland is successfully grown in the Valley appears from the fact that the Land and Irrigation Exposition held at Madison Square Garden, New York, in 1911, awarded to this locality its "Grand Sweepstakes Prize" for the best short-staple cotton grown in the United States in 1911, foreshadowing the grand prize for cotton growing awarded to the Imperial Valley by the Panama-Pacific Exposition at San Francisco in 1915.[6]

[6] Southern California cotton was easily the feature of the California State section in the Palace of Agriculture at the Panama-Pacific International Exposition. Designed merely to call attention to the most significant of the later developments of agriculture in California, the cotton display not only led in interest in the Golden State's own exhibits, but constituted one of the sensations of the Exposition itself. To the utter amazement of all, Southern California cotton was awarded the grand prize for the best display of cotton and its by-products over the oldest cotton growing sections in the country.—The handling of the display was a good example of the exhibitor's art at its best. Flanked on either side by bales of snowy cotton and by manufactured cotton goods, stood an old-time spinning wheel that from morning till night turned lint into cotton thread. Mrs. Ella Swickard, who learned as a girl in Texas to fashion the insubstantial lint into strong even thread, was the manipulator of the antique machine. Her deftness was the marvel of the visitors, most of whom had never seen a spinning wheel in use. While she took the cotton from the bolls and drew it out into thread on the wheel she lectured to the crowd. The cotton spun was sent to various California schools to be woven.—The highest

The earliest bale of cotton ever ginned in the United States was grown near Calexico, the "cotton capital" of the Imperial Valley, and ginned on June 17, 1914, three days earlier than the previous record, held by Brownsville, Texas. What makes this record the more interesting is the fact that this cotton was grown as the third crop on the same stalks. Moreover, seed taken from this record cotton and planted on its native acre produced a second bale, which was ginned on October 15 of the same year.[7] The climate of the Imperial Valley is such that plants usually live through the winter. If these are cut down in March to within six inches of the ground, and the water is turned on, the next crop "volunteers" from the stumps of the old, and is ready for picking in September. While a volunteer crop yields less than an original planting, it has the double advantage of early maturity and extremely low cost.

The extent of the cotton industry in the Imperial Valley has called for the installation of twenty-two modern gins, three cottonseed oil mills, and two compresses.

Not only Southern California, but parts of New Mexico and Arizona are now forcing admission to the hitherto exclusive "Cotton Belt" with the magical key of irrigation. Daniel Webster chose a singularly infelicitous illustration for his argument in 1850 against the Wilmot Proviso (see page 219). Arizona produced 2,299 bales in 1913, and 7,142 bales

grades of cotton were included in the exhibit. The by-products shown indicated the remarkable uses to which cotton and its seed may be put. A striking feature of the display was a single cotton plant bearing 250 well-formed bolls, the largest number on record.—P. H. Magill, Jr., in the Los Angeles *Times*.

[7] Twenty-fifth Annual Report of the California Development Board: San Francisco, 1915; p. 44.

in 1914. Todd thinks that irrigation may become the ruling method of cotton growing.[8]

South America, when it begins that development which will surely be a challenging economic opportunity of the twentieth century, may be confidently expected to contest the monopoly of the Cotton Belt. The late Edward Atkinson in 1889 described the high pampas of the Paraguay and Parana rivers as sufficiently elevated to be free from tropical conditions, endowed with a soil of wonderful fertility, and capable of unlimited crops of cotton and wheat—one section of the earth's surface where, in his judgment, there can be competition with our Cotton States.[9] Professor Todd believes that there are perhaps greater possibilities of cotton growing in the Argentine Republic than in any other country in the world,[10] while Mexico is not to be despised,[11]—and, to take a long jump, the site of the original Garden of Eden, in Mesopotamia, affords potentialities almost unlimited![12] Russia also is making rapid

[8] Pp. vii and 11.

[9] While the cotton crop of Peru amounts to only 142,000 bales (1913–14), it is noteworthy both because of its ancient history and on account of its excellent quality (see p. 116). Peru grows a special variety of cotton, called "gossypium Peruvianum," a tree-like variety, reaching 9 to 15 feet in height; its life is six years, when the crop begins to fall off. This variety can better endure the want of water than the Egyptian cotton; in fact, on good land it requires only one watering to insure a good crop. The crop begins to appear in 18 months, increasing in yield until the sixth year. The fiber is long and frequently exceeds 35 millimeters, but it is rough and known in the English market as "full rough Peruvian." When carded it looks greatly like wool, and is often used by manufacturers as a mixture in the manufacture of woolen goods. The Egyptian or soft cotton is also grown along the entire coast of Peru, but its life is only two years.—Resources of Peru: San Francisco, n. d. For Edward Atkinson on Cotton, see e. g., The Industrial Progress of the Nation: New York, 1889, ch. i.

[10] Todd, p. 218.

[11] Todd, p. 131.

[12] Todd, p. 81.

strides forward, as shown by its production in bales for ten years, as follows:[13]

1904–05	554,000	1909–10	785,000
1905–06	585,000	1910–11	981,000
1906–07	655,000	1911–12	939,000
1907–08	620,000	1912–13	917,352
1908–09	846,000	1913–14	1,004,328

The writer, for many years a believer in the ability of the Cotton Belt to retain monopolistic control of cotton production, has come to the conclusion, after a study of the subject in several different parts of the world, that his former opinion was wrong. He believes, however, that the South has no serious cause for alarm, but plenty of reason for caution. It seems very likely that cotton will, on the whole, become and remain high in price, owing to a constantly increasing demand. If the statement be true, or anywise nearly true, that only one acre out of seventeen in the Cotton Belt is as yet under cotton cultivation, then the South for an indefinite period can extend its acreage, while foreign areas are still in the stage of experiment.

But it is far more important to encourage intensive cultivation. While the average yield of cotton in the Southeastern United States is only about 190 pounds of lint to the acre, yet on many large tracts, carefully cultivated, a yield of from 500 to 800 pounds is not infrequently obtained.[14] Dr. Dabney says that the cotton crop should be doubled on the same acreage by the use of good seed and careful methods of tillage and fertilization. Furthermore, impoverishment of the soil should certainly be avoided, as may

[13] Todd, p. 397 (U. S. Dept. of Commerce figures).

[14] C. W. Dabney, "Relations of Agriculture to Other Sciences," in Congress of Arts and Sciences: Boston, 1906; p. 724.

be done through rotation of crops, which would operate further in the direction of sound economics by giving the planter independence in the matter of food-stuffs and provender; and the ravages of the boll weevil should be checked by intelligent methods, including the enforcement of strict laws for the protection of birds—the quail particularly being an inveterate enemy of this destructive and apparently indestructible pest. There is no reason, if due intelligence and industry be used, why the optimism of the present American Ambassador to England should not be confirmed, and "the cotton grower in the old Slave States become the most prosperous tiller of the earth"—justifying the eloquence of Grady, who once exclaimed:

"Cotton—what a royal plant it is! Not the fleeces that Jason sought can rival the richness of this plant, as it unfurls its banners in our fields. It is gold from the instant it puts forth its tiny shoot. The world waits in attendance on its growth; the shower that falls whispering on its leaves is heard around the earth; the sun that shines on it is tempered by the prayers of all the people; the frost that chills it and the dew that descends from the stars are noted, and the trespass of a little worm upon its green leaf is more to England than the advance of the Russian army on her Asian outposts.[15] Its fiber is current in every bank and when, loosing its fleeces to the sun, it floats a sunny banner that glorifies the fields of the humble farmer, that man is marshaled under a flag that will compel the allegiance of the world and wring a subsidy from every nation on earth." [16]

[15] Written in 1887.

[16] H. W. Grady, Writings and Speeches: New York, 1890; p. 107, and Burkett and Poe, p. 3.

CHAPTER 75

EVOLUTION AND HUMAN WELFARE

INCOMPLETE, and with only meager suggestions, here and there, where independent volumes would be warranted, has been this sketch of the course of our narrative from prehistoric times to the present. Beginning with perplexing myth and ancient legend, but planting our feet on firm historic ground in ancient India, we followed the course of empire ever westward, through Renaissance and revolution and civil war, the power of cotton evolving with the evolution of the power of man, only to reach our conclusion at a moment when the subject engaging our attention holds an unusual share of world-wide interest by virtue of its complex entanglement in the maddest human havoc that has ever cursed the earth,—a havoc made deadly beyond the wildest dreams of ancient hate through those very powers of civilization that spell the highest gifts of man.

It is a fact by no means encouraging to the lover of his kind that while the housing of well-to-do men and their clothing are scarcely on a higher level now than they were in ancient Egypt long before the earliest date in cotton history,[1] the war-club of that time has become the 42-centimeter gun, the puny bow is now a seven-league catapult, and Pharaoh's

[1] Of course the comforts of life are far more widely distributed; men of average means now share them with the well-to-do; this, rather than an absolute advance in housing and clothing, would seem to denote the chief material advantage of the modern world over the ancient.

chariots have evolved into battleships and Zeppelins. The art of weaving produces no more beautiful raiment than those Tyrian hues wrought by Arachne on her primitive Mæonian loom, nothing more fine and delicate than those "webs of the woven wind" conjured from the heart of the cotton boll by the Hindu with his handful of reeds,—and yet our innocent fleece has been transmuted in the crucible of war to a veritable magic of condensed power for the mutilation and destruction of human life and property.

A brilliant dramatist, impressed with this discouraging discrepancy, imagines Satan as thus taunting man:

"Have you walked up and down the earth lately? I have; and I have examined Man's wonderful inventions. And I tell you that in the arts of life man invents nothing; but in the arts of death he outdoes Nature herself, and produces by chemistry and machinery all the slaughter of plague, pestilence and famine. The peasant I tempt to-day eats and drinks what was eaten and drunk by the peasants of ten thousand years ago; and the house he lives in has not altered as much in a thousand centuries as the fashion of a lady's bonnet in a score of weeks. But when he goes out to slay, he carries a marvel of mechanism that lets loose at the touch of his finger all the hidden molecular energies, and leaves the javelin, the arrow, the blowpipe of his fathers far behind. In the arts of peace man is a bungler. I have seen his cotton factories and the like, with machinery that a greedy dog could have invented if it had wanted money instead of food. I know his clumsy typewriters and bungling locomotives and tedious bicycles: they are toys compared to the

Maxim gun, the submarine torpedo boat. There is nothing in Man's industrial machinery but his greed and sloth: his heart is in his weapons. This marvelous force of Life of which you boast is a force of Death: Man measures his strength by his destructiveness."[2]

There is poetry in this dramatic monologue, and also poetic license; but that there is some truth in it, who can deny? A sober biologist, writing on the topic, "War, Science and Civilization," matches this sardonic eloquence of Bernard Shaw's devil with the measured statement that dominant ethical theory seems to be essentially what it was when human history was supposed to have begun with Adam and Eve, or Romulus and Remus, "or other full-fledged mythical personages," while if the history of leading nations during the last half-century be viewed in the light of the course and nature of scientific discovery, "the supposition seems justified that civilization is well on the road to self-destruction through its power of creating and using mechanical appliances for thus disposing of itself."[3]

Professor Ritter confirms the opinion, already expressed in Chapter 21, that the widespread acceptance of the jungle law of struggle and survival as the single, permanent, and inevitable condition of social progress accounts largely for those hideous anomalies whereof he writes. The abuse of this doctrine, he believes, has done "incalculable harm, not only to biology, but to sociology and to human welfare generally. The doctrine that all human progress is accomplished by somebody's beating some-

[2] Bernard Shaw, Man and Superman: New York, 1913; pp. 106–107.

[3] W. E. Ritter, War, Science and Civilization: Boston, 1915; p. 20.

body else, usually to the death, has had such vogue during the last few decades, particularly in business and politics, that it sometimes seems hopeless to get people to see how far it comes from agreeing with all the relevant facts."[4]

As pointed out in Chapter 21, the law of struggle and survival, which was brought to light against the gloomy background of conditions occasioned by the Industrial Revolution in England, suggests at most not more than half of the secret processes at work in the laboratories of Nature. A green field on a summer's day reveals to the searching eye not only overcrowding and strife, but, quite as clearly and certainly, organization and sacrifice. The *vegetative* process of mere expansive growth, by which the plant as an individual presses upward and outward ambitiously, and at hazard to itself and its neighbors, is continually controlled and modified by that *floral* process which appropriates the strength of the individual toward the function of family reproduction, —a flower being essentially a sort of "protean birth-robe" for seed.[5] Biologists assure us that the further we carry our studies of plant anatomy, the more we shall find of this subordination of the merely vegetative or nutritive process to the reproductive, so that the "self-interest" in which the utilitarian economists found the all-sufficient spring of action, and which naturalists too long and too uncritically adopted from these, turns out to be enlightened by family interest, species interest, however "subconscious," so to speak; and the ideal of evolution is thus seen to be no mere "gladiator's show," as was

[4] The same, p. 75.

[5] P. Geddes and J. Arthur Thomson, Evolution: London, n. d.; pp. 95, 241, 243.

formerly thought, but rather a coöperative commonwealth; diversified through differentiation and checked by competition, it is true—natural selection furnishing the brake, however, rather than the steam or the rails for the journey of life, or, as in St. George Mivart's figure of speech, not guiding the ramifications of the tree of life, but applying the pruning-knife.

Cotton itself, our beautiful and beneficent "Gossypium," is an exquisite example of the check on mere vegetative expansion—as typified in grass—by subordination to the claims of the family. First the delicate flowers, cream-colored and pink and then crimson, proclaim and prepare the way for the great procreative ceremonial to which the life of the plant is dedicated. Then appears a tightly closed casket holding its precious embryos. When these seed-children have been nurtured toward maturity, the casket, opening to the sunlight, and rocking in the breezes, becomes a veritable cradle, lined with that downy fleece which forms our cherished article of commerce, but which has no other object in the economy of botany than the care of the family seed, to which the entire vegetative process is subordinated.

The whole phenomenon of organization, coöperation, or "integration," as it is comprehensively called, holds quite as important a place in the evolution of plants and animals as differentiation, which arises from natural selection. Indeed, the animal kingdom is higher than the plant kingdom, not only because the individual animal is more differentiated, but because it is more highly integrated than any individual plant. And yet, as Professor Ritter remarks, thought about evolution has been cast so exclusively in molds of antagonism, and combat to the death, that the constitutive and coördinative aspects of the process have had little chance of recognition. Men have taken whatever measures they deemed necessary to overcome their competitors, justifying their conduct by appealing to the phrase, "the fittest survive." At this moment militarists are loudly invoking "the struggle for existence" and "natural selection" in justification of war, while the truth is, as emphasized by Kropotkin in his book on "Mutual Aid as a Factor of Evolution," that organic evolution is just as fundamentally an organizing, an integrating, process, as it is a differentiating process.[6]

Coming now to more familiar and less technical ground,—Nature affords abundant and impressive community examples, among insects and animals, of the benefits of coöperation. Ants are even more remarkable than bees. The formicary is a labyrinthine set of catacombs, some chambers being utilized as storehouses, others as nurseries, and still others as stables for "pets," such as crickets, or for the ants' "cattle," such as Aphides, which are shut up for safety during winter, and turned out to pasturage in the spring and summer. Here we come upon the challenging fact that not only do single species coöperate in commonwealths for the general welfare, but various species, utterly unlike, form international unions, as it were, for the common good. Indeed—not to tarry longer with our wealth of illustrative material—perhaps the fundamental fact of all nature, and the most important, is found in the interminable linkages, the universal interrelations, which constitute a vast web of life, the threads of one life getting caught up and intertwined with those

[6] Ritter, p. 42.

of another, and so on indefinitely or infinitely, so that in literal truth no creature lives or dies to itself, and

> "Thou canst not stir a flower
> Without troubling a star."

Darwin was not unmindful of this. Of the phrase, "the struggle for existence," he expressly said: "I use this term in a large and metaphorical sense, including dependence of one being on another, and including not only the life of the individual, but success in leaving progeny."[7] The social and political greed of men has led to the abortive seizure of the half-truth that suited their purposes, with the result that great economic forces, such as the cotton industry, have been made to contribute to social misery and to political disaster instead of the further binding together of mankind into a great coöperative commonwealth. It is high time that we forsake the dominant ethical theories of the Cro-magnon cave man of a score of thousand years ago, and learn from our mother Nature the clear and simple truth, that *modern human evolution rests necessarily and fundamentally on integration among many nations.*

The evolution of man's inventive genius has hastened the formulation and application of this law. Steel rails now bind continents into a network of rapid mobilization, so that the wide barriers of space which formerly shut off the Alaskans from the Panamanians have been transformed into areas of cosmopolitan intercourse, while the incessantly moving steamships that ply in the oceans are but so many ladles serving the "melting pot" which has come to be a synonym for America. Even East and West,

[7] Cited by Geddes and Thomson, p. 167.

which since the time of Alexander have marched back to back from the Himalayas until now they stand confronting each other across the Pacific, are intermingling in such numbers that already people are beginning to question the truth of the poetic phrase, coined only yesterday, and intended to express an axiom,—"Never the twain shall meet." Transportation, it may be noted in passing, has dissipated one term of the old Malthusian problem, pressure of population, by distributing populations from points of high to spots of lower pressure, as well as by bringing food supplies from unpeopled plains to dense cities,[8] while scientific agriculture threatens to explode the other,—an inevitable failure of the necessary means of subsistence,—so that scientists are now willing to stimulate in us "a mighty faith that there is practically no limit to Nature's capacity for yielding to man all those things which, from sources outside himself, he truly needs."[9] In a word, the streams of ethnic evolution, for millenniums differential and divergent, are now become convergent and integrational, while man's inventive genius promises capacity for supply of all his needs, if he will but busy himself in the coöperative industries of peace.

Coincidentally with this physical convergence, as we have seen all through the course of this volume, the same facilities of transportation, supplemented to an important degree by such advanced implements of communication as world-wide girdles of electrified cables, and now by the wireless ether itself—these clever devices, perfected largely at the behest of military rivalry, have brought the markets of the world into intimate correlation, so that the economic

[8] McGregor's Evolution of Industry, as cited, pp. 70, 78.
[9] Ritter, p. 99.

interests of men are so closely interwoven that a citizen of California is compelled to affix tax-stamps to domestic telegrams because Germany and Japan are fighting.

Never was the economic destructiveness of warfare so clearly demonstrated, or its ghastly futility so powerfully proved, as by the Great War of 1914. War has become an anachronism. And yet, by virtue of the closely woven web of delicately adjusted cosmopolitan interrelations that we have from time to time through this book been considering, never has the peril of incessant and overwhelming wars been so great, when,—as we have seen to our stupefied wonder,—the pulling of a single pistol trigger in Bosnia may inflame millions of men, of every color and condition, and in every quarter of the civilized globe, to a mad frenzy of butchery and pillage. Obviously, if our race is not to perish at the hands of its militant Frankenstein, it must rise to an intelligence high enough to learn a simple secret from Nature, and discover that only through coöperation in social and political affairs, as in every other circle of universal life—*only by a broad internationalism can human society avoid destruction.* The printer Franklin once gave to the factional American colonies a cartoon of a rattlesnake cut into thirteen pieces and labeled with the pungent motto, "Join or die." His advice is just as pertinent now, internationally, as it was in the eighteenth century to the American colonies.

The present writer believes strongly in "preparedness." The fact that the law of struggle has been over-emphasized is no reason for wheeling about and under-emphasizing it. The world being what it is, a nation is not likely to "survive" that does not keep itself "fit." "National service" must become our national law. Professor Oliver has condensed a whole volume into the sentence—"A democracy which asserts the right of manhood suffrage, while denying the duty of manhood service, is living in a fool's paradise."[10] Internationalism itself, in any except a false and maudlin sense, implies a coöperative bond among a group of virile independent nations, each adding to the whole its gift of self-reliant strength for common welfare. If America is to exist as a nation among nations, it must be prepared to struggle for survival. But, as Mr. Norman Angell has so clearly and so cogently explained,[11] force-preparation, while absolutely indispensable, is only half preparation: there must be an athletic thought-preparedness as to how this force is to be used, there must be an intelligent formulation of international policies, there must be understanding clear as day with the other members of the world-group, so that force may become less aggressive, thought more authoritative, and intelligent coöperation finally take the place of a murderous and ultimately suicidal competition. With the bloody lesson of the European War staining the firmament for all the world to read, it would seem that if man cannot learn the truth now, his case is hopeless and his doom is sealed. Mutual suspicion and misunderstanding and stupid economic strife brought on the war, while it is equally true that an intelligent taking counsel together and a mutually regardful economic coöperation could have established, very literally, a *modus vivendi,* whereas our

[10] F. S. Oliver, Ordeal by Battle: London, 1915; p. 400. (One of the most thoughtful and valuable discussions provoked by the European War).

[11] The Dangers of Half-Preparedness: New York, 1916.

present much-boasted "efficiency" results only in a highly effective *modus moriendi.*

Cotton itself has already entangled us in a costly civil strife, and there are signs of its contributing, in the immediate future, to the further complication of our already perplexed foreign relationships. The struggle for the "mastery of the Pacific," for example, involves cotton as a prime consideration. Shall we permit this economic web to enmesh us again, like stupid and greedy flies, or shall we not rather grasp and weave it to a pattern of intelligence and far-reaching welfare? If Japan is to become the Lancashire of the Orient or if the whole Eastern littoral of Asia is to become the world's most plentiful workshop in the cheaper grades of cotton manufacture,[12] as economists confidently prophesy, these results will be due to great geographical, climatic, and sociological causes that are absolutely beyond our control in the long run, although the ultimate event may be artificially hindered and retarded. A struggle to hinder and retard would only secure temporary profit at the cost of eventual loss and a probable war, whereas an intelligent mutual study of the problem in all its phases would undoubtedly discover some feasible plan of economic coöperation, besides contributing to that "better understanding" which is the best known antidote to war. If Japan and China have distinctive advantages with respect to cheap manufacture, America has a practical monopoly of production, as well as virtually unlimited possibilities in the development of certain grades of manufacture to which the Oriental genius is ill-adapted. There should be a frank recognition of

[12] See page 351.

respective advantages, and such a substitution of intelligence for stupidity that "the struggle for the mastery of the Pacific" should give way to a partnership in the freedom of its seas. Certainly Japan should not turn to India for its cotton supplies because of a justified suspicion and increasing dislike of Caucasian methods of intercourse, and for the gradually forming purpose of welding an empire of unnumbered brown men into a force that shall struggle with white men. "That way madness lies." Let history enlighten economics with the torch of the past, so that history may hereafter yield an interpretation of intelligence. Crass individualism must make room for the sanity of coöperative service. The law of differentiation must be made whole and wholesome by its junction with the law of unitation if man is to live and thrive.

The economic interpretation of history, a nascent science, will have justified its birthright should it succeed, by the addition of a single note to Nature's "thousand voices," in piercing the heedless ear of man with the law which, elsewhere universally prevalent, must govern his social theory. It is the poets, after all, who see most deeply into life. Henry Timrod, the poet of the cotton boll, drew from its "cloven sheath" a vision of

> That mighty commerce which, confined
> To the mean channels of no selfish mart,
> Goes out to every shore
> Of this broad earth, and throngs the sea with ships
> That bear no thunders; hushes hungry lips
> In alien lands;
> Joins with a delicate web remotest strands; . . .
> And haply, as the years increase,
> Shall, working with its humbler reach

With that large wisdom which the ages teach,
Revive the half-dead dream of universal peace![13] . . .

[13] Henry Timrod, "The Cotton Boll" (written about 1859) in Poems: Boston, 1899, p. 10. Adapted.

APPENDIXES

A. Cotton and the Balance of Trade
B. The Fable of Arachne and Minerva
C. The Rev. John Dyer and "The Fleece"
D. Tom Moore on Cotton and Corn
E. Notes for Webster's Speech of 1850
F. Illustrative Statistics
G. Authorities

APPENDIX A

COTTON AND THE BALANCE OF TRADE

(See page 4, note 4)

By means of the following table and calculations, Mr. Theodore Price attempts an arithmetical demonstration of the claim that cotton maintains a balance of trade in favor of the United States in its annual dealings with Europe.

UNITED STATES EXPORTS AND IMPORTS [1]

Fiscal year ending June 30.	Merchandise Imported.	Merchandise Exported.	Balance in favor U. S.	Net value gold and silver. Imported.	Net value gold and silver. Exported.		Total net balance in favor U. S.
1914	$1,893,925,657	$2,364,579,148	$470,653,491		$70,138,289		$540,791,780
1913	1,813,008,234	2,465,884,149	652,875,915		38,914,392		691,790,307
1912	1,653,264,934	2,204,322,409	551,057,475		26,232,294		577,289,769
1911	1,527,226,105	2,049,320,199	522,094,094	$32,284,651			489,809,443
1910	1,556,947,430	1,744,984,720	188,037,290		85,292,977		273,330,367
Total	$8,444,372,360	$10,829,090,625	$2,384,718,265		$188,293,301	Net	$2,573,011,666
Average	1,688,874,472	2,165,818,125	476,943,653		37,658,660		514,602,333
Total value raw cotton exported							$2,759,447,880
Average value raw cotton exported							551,889,576

[1] During the fiscal year ending June 30, 1911, total exports included the following classes of materials, the value of which was in excess of $50,000,000: Cotton (including manufactured cotton goods valued at $28,844,627), $639,319,928; wheat and wheat flour, $142,407,631; cattle, meat, and dairy products, $132,926,979; iron and steel—manufactures of, $106,559,621; copper—manufactures of, $144,895,519; oils, $144,708,447; tobacco and manufactures of, $60,445,440; wood manufactures—timber and lumber, $66,953,878; coal, $59,921,013. Total, $1,498,138,456.

The foregoing figures will make clear the following important facts not generally understood:

1. That during the past five years a total foreign trade of over nineteen billions of dollars has been "cleared" by the shipment back and forth of only $220,577,952 worth of gold and silver; which means that hardly more than one per cent of the balances arising from this enormous commerce have been settled in cash or bullion.

2. That during the same five years the trade balance in favor of the United States (including gold and silver) aggregates..... $2,573,011,666
and that during the same period the total value of raw cotton exported was.......... 2,759,447,880

3. That for the past five years the average *annual* balance of trade in favor of the United Staes (including gold and silver) has been 514,602,333
and that the average value of the raw cotton exported has been 551,889,576

The sequence of these statements will make it plain that our annual payments in merchandise, gold, and silver to foreign countries exceed their payments to us in kind by $514,602,333
and that since the value of our cotton exports exceeds this sum it is accurate to say that "our debts are paid in cotton."

These who have studied the subject closely estimate that this annual balance in our favor of, say $500,000,000
is applied to the liquidation of the following debits:

Interest at five per cent in a principal of $4,000,000,000, being the normal value of American stocks, bonds, and other evidences of American debt held abroad $200,000,000

Spent in Europe annually by Americans resident or traveling abroad 100,000,000

Remitted out of their earnings

by Europeans resident in America	100,000,000	
Insurance and freights	100,000,000	$500,000,000

These figures are of course conjectural, but it is evident that, if any of the items are underestimated, American indebtedness abroad unpaid must be increased by the amount of such underestimate, for our *payments* cannot exceed the net balance of trade in our favor, known and ascertained to be about $500,000,000 a year.

—Theodore H. Price in the *Outlook:* New York, Sep. 9, 1914.

APPENDIX B

THE FABLE OF ARACHNE AND MINERVA[1]

(See page 44)

ONE of the most engaging passages in Ovid's "Metamorphoses" describes the fabled tilt between Pallas and Arachne. The Mæonian maiden wrought one day at her loom with such superhuman skill that the nymphs and naiads who were watching swore that Minerva herself must have taught her. Arachne, flushed with pride, not only denied this, but contemptuously offered to engage in a weaving contest with the goddess of weaving herself.

> "Let her come"—she cried—"and try
> With me her skill,—and, if she conquer, mine
> Be then what doom she will!" and Pallas came.
> —The looms were set,—the webs
> Were hung: beneath their fingers, nimbly plied,
> The subtle fabrics grew, and warp and woof,
> Transverse, with shuttle and with slay compact
> Were pressed in order fair. And either girt
> Her mantle close, and eager wrought; the toil
> Itself was pleasure to the skilful hands
> That knew so well their task.

The graceful poetry of Ovid portrays the successive tapestries wrought in this mythical contest. One antique fable and then another sprang from the nimble fingers of Arachne and grew beneath the deft hands of the goddess; until at length Pallas, suddenly jealous of her rival's handiwork, "fierce tore the web;" and then "upon her brows the maid she struck, twelve times."

[1] The Metamorphoses of Publius Ovidius Naso, translated by Henry King: Edinburgh, 1871; bk. vi, 1.

—The high-souled Maid
Such insult not endured, and round her neck
Indignant twined the suicidal noose,
And so had died. But, as she hung, some ruth
Stirred in Minerva's breast:—the pendent form
She raised, and "Live!" she said—"but hang thou still
Forever, wretch! and through all future time
Even to thy latest race bequeath thy doom!"
And, as she parted, sprinkled her with juice
Of aconite. With venom of that drug
Infected dropped her tresses,—nose and ear
Were lost;—her form, to smallest bulk compressed,
A head minutest crowned; to slenderest legs,
Jointed on either side, her fingers changed:
Her body but a bag, whence still she draws
Her filmy threads, and, with her ancient art,
Weaves the fine meshes of her spider's web.

Such is the hoary myth of the origin of the spider, deftest of weavers, whose family are called the Arachnida in tribute to the beautiful early poetry of our race.

APPENDIX C

THE REV. JOHN DYER AND "THE FLEECE"

(See page 60)

AN English clergyman and a poet of considerable taste and ability, Dyer's attention was attracted, like that of the later clergyman, Cartwright, to the fascinating subject of the loom; so that in 1757 he published in London his versified eulogium of "The Fleece." This was just at the commencement of the Industrial Revolution, when delicate and strange cotton fabrics from India were beginning to unsettle the complacent British industry in wool; and Dyer, like Daniel Defoe, writes as a partizan of the woolsack. Extremely quaint, in these days, seems his jealous poetic fling at flax and silk, but more especially at the upstart rival from the Ganges:

Our happy swains
Behold arising, in their fatt'ning flocks,
A double wealth; more rich than Belgium's boast,
Who tends the culture of the flaxen reed;
Or the Cathayan's, whose ignobler care
Nurses the silkworm; or of India's sons,
Who plant the cotton-grove by Ganges' stream.
Nor do their toils and products furnish more,
Than gauds and dresses, of fantastic web,
To the luxurious: but our kinder toils
Give cloathing to necessity; keep warm
Th' unhappy wand'rer, on the mountain wild
Benighted, while the tempest beats around.
No, ye soft sons of Ganges, and of Ind,
Ye feebly delicate, life little needs
Your fem'nine toys, nor asks your nerveless arm
To cast the strong-flung shuttle, or the spear.

Dyer lived late enough to witness and describe the operation of the very first in the series of wonderful inventions that were destined to revolutionize England—the spinning-frames of Wyatt and Paul—although his enthusiasm arose from their efficiency in the manufacture of wool. If we imagine ourselves to be passing with the poet through one of the earliest of British factories,—

—We next are shown
A circular machine, of new design,
In conic shape: it draws and spins a thread
Without the tedious toil of needless hands.
A wheel, invisible, beneath the floor,
To ev'ry member of th' harmonious frame
Gives necessary motion. One, intent,
O'erlooks the work: the carded wool, he says,
Is smoothly lapp'd around those cylinders,
Which, gently turning, yield it to yon cirque
Of upright spindles, which, with rapid whirl,
Spin out, in long extent, an even twine.

APPENDIX D

TOM MOORE ON COTTON AND CORN[1]

(See page 91)

THIS whimsical poem by Thomas Moore, written in anticipation of the repeal of the Corn Laws, indicates the influence of cotton in the English politics of the period:

Said Cotton to Corn, t'other day,
  As they met, and exchanged a salute—
(Squire Corn in his cabriolet,
  Poor Cotton, half famish'd, on foot)

"Great squire, if it isn't uncivil
  To hint at starvation before you,
Look down on a hungry poor devil,
  And give him some bread, I implore you!"

Quoth Corn then, in answer to Cotton,
  Perceiving he meant to make *free*,—
"Low fellow, you've surely forgotten
  The distance between you and me!

"To expect that we, peers of high birth,
  Should waste our illustrious acres
For no other purpose on earth
  Than to fatten curst calico-makers!—

"That bishops to bobbins should bend,—
  Should stoop from their bench's sublimity
Great dealers in *lawn*, to befriend
  Your contemptible dealers in dimity!

"No—vile manufacturer! ne'er harbor
  A hope to be fed at our boards;
Base offspring of Arkwright, the barber,
  What claim canst *thou* have upon lords?

[1] T. Moore, Poetical Works: Philadelphia. 1856.

"No—thanks to the taxes and debt,
And the triumph of paper o'er guineas,
Our race of Lord Jemmys, as yet,
May defy your whole rabble of Jennys!"

So saying, whip, crack, and away
Went Corn in his cab through the throng,
So madly, I heard them all say
Squire Corn would be *down*, before long.

APPENDIX E

NOTES FOR WEBSTER'S SPEECH OF MARCH 7, 1850[1]

(See page 215)

Causes which have so suddenly produced this state of things—
War declared May '46—
Armies over run Mexico—& seized her Capitol—
Navy seized her ports—
—Feb. 48. Treaty—& cession of her Provinces—
—9000 miles of coast on Pacific.
—Revolution in California, mean while, July 1846
—Col Fremont
Soon as war known, U. S. flag hoisted—
Great numbers rushed to Mexico, in '46. '47—
In Jan. 48 Mormons discov^{d}. gold—
Same winter, or Sp'g, Sutters & Marshall's discoveries.
In May '48—digging commenced.
—Success incredible. Larkins Letters, June 1. & 28
Col Masons Rep^{t} Aug. 17. 48
On the peace, a new rush—
1000 large vessels—70,000 passengers
Amt. of gold remitted—& amt. merchandize
vid Aspinwall—6 Steamers—4 or 5 small ones
—Trade & revenue. 15 millions of Gold to
Congress passed no law U. S. & England
2 or 3 to Oregon—
—a great deal used at home
California called a Convention—Formed a Free Constitution.—
chosen Senators and members
of Congress
& now asks for admission.

[1] From the original manuscript, in Mr. Webster's handwriting, in the New Hampshire Historical Society.

—Her Constitution excludes Slavery—
—War waged for Territory—expected to be Slave Territory—
Events have decided the matter otherwise & hence the present controversy, & the present excitement.[2]

Slavery

The North regards it as a great moral & political evil, &, in its nature, founded in wrong.
Slavery has existed from the earliest times.
Oriental, Jewish, Greek. Roman. Feudal Servitude
There is no positive injunction ag[t] it, in the old Testamt or the new.
The theocracy of the Jews tolerated it
—The religion of the Gospel deals little with political relations of men.
—The teachings of Jesus Christ are addressed to the hearts & consciences of individual men.
—They seek to purify the soul, & to regulate the life
But it cannot be doubted that the principle of Slavery is opposed, in the abstract to the meek spirit of the Gospel. It is founded in the power of the strongest.
It is conquest, a permanent conquest of man over man.
It is against the law of nature.
It is like unjust war, or any other form of oppression or subjegation
These are the sentiments of the North.

It is probable many in the South are hardly prepared to deny these truths in the abstract
—But, in general, they are accustomed to it; born & bred where it exists, & taught to consider it as no wrong.
And they are honest, & conscientious, in this.
No doubt, there are thousands of men, deeply religious, & whose consciences are as tender as those of any other Christians, see no way for them but to treat their slaves with kindness & humanity

[2] All of the foregoing notes are on one leaf, endorsed on the back by Mr. Webster, "History of Events that have produced the present state of things."

They are far from thinking, that in all cases manumission would be useful to the Slaves themselves—

The Methodist Church equally conscientious in both branches.

I have read their proceedings, & lamented the result.

When religious excitement takes place, men run to extremes—

Algebra

Absolutists. Fault finders with the sun.

Impatient waiters on Providence

They do not enough heed St. Paul.

=Mr. Butler—War-horse!

=They think they can draw light from angry clouds—

—*They want candor, & charity*

And not willing to leave things with him, who sees the end from the beginning.

How Slavery was considered, in 1789; & reason of changes

In 1789, when Constitution adopted, everybody regarded Slavery as a great evil.

The sentiment stronger in the South, or oftener expressed, because the South had more of it.

It is called now, an "Institution," a "good," a "blessing," a "Religious, moral, & social blessing"—

Then it was denominated a "blight," a "blast," a "mildew," "a curse"—

Mr. Campbell's speech.—see his extracts

The Ordinance of 1787—all the South agreed to it

Contemporaneous with the Constitution

I honor the liberality of Va—

80 millions of Dollars

The true is that in Aug. 87. v. Association of 1774

1. Provision was made for limiting the importation of slaves, & it was believed that Slavery would gradually die out. Mr. Madison & others thought the time allowed too long.
2. That the Prohibition should be laid on all the Territory—Mr. Madison's reason for omitting the word.

3. Slavery as it existed in the States, should not be interfered with—

In the first Congress, this was all reaffirmed, as I have stated Before—

☞ The whole Country unanimous, in all this.

But now: *What has caused the change?*

In the North a stronger religious feeling, & a horror at seeing

Slavery increase—

In the South, *Cotton*—

In 1790–91, &c—Cotton hardly exported—vid Tables

—Sudden growth of this created eagerness for acquisition of Slave Territory—

Cession of Georgia——1802
Louisiana— 1803
Florida— 1804.

And Finally *Texas*

This, the great Consummation.

And now my Gen[l] proposition:

"There is not a foot of land, in any State or Territory of the U. S. the character of which as to free soil or slave soil by some Law—

1st as to Texas. read the clause of the 2. Resolution—read it

Now, what is to be said ag[t] this?

Nothing can be stronger

Mr. Bell's first Resolution adds noth'g to it—and, looking to the difficulties of getting any prospective Resolution thro' the House, I think it best to adhere to *practical* measures & make no resolutions for the future—

—I am obliged to Mr. Clay—& Mr. Bell—

But, referring to the difficulties of the case, I prefer to follow the Presidents recommendation.

But now Texas was brought in by Northern & New England votes—in both—

But for these votes, she must have staid out.

New England could have kept her out—but N. E. thought her—
Con: N. H. & Maine. And New York.—
Mr. Dix—& Mr. Niles.—voted for Texas, *& then turned Free Soilers*—
If they were here now, could they apply Wilmot?
It would be a violation of law & faith—
They helped to bring in every foot of Slave Territory this side the Rio Grande—&
Then turned Free Soilers—
Then set up the symbol—the empty symbol of the *Wilmot Proviso.*
—as a Gentleman careless of his stables. &c—
This matter is now absolutely settled by Law
So much for Texas   My Previous Votes—
Vid next sheet—page 2[a]

(Here there is a four page sheet in another hand, as follows:)

Speech at Niblo's Garden. 1837
" On Admission of Texas. 1845.
" Three Million Bill Mar. 1st 1847.
" Springfield—Sept. 27—1847.
" In Senate—Mar. 23. 1848.
" Oregon Bill Aug. 12. 1848.

Now as for California & New Mexico

This is all Free Country by the Ordinance of Nature. There is no slave there, in our sense of that word, & never can be—
It is an Asiatic formation, & Slavery—
Immense Mountains, & deep vallies—
Especially New Mexico
—Mountains with white tops—parched *vallies—no culture but by Irrigation*

Wilmot, here, would be perfectly without effect.

[a] The notes from the lines "How Slavery was considered in 1789 & reason of changes," down to this point, are on one sheet, endorsed by Mr. Webster: "No. 3. How Slavery was considered in 89—& Acquisition of Texas."

Inquire of the California Senators—& members—
—Inquire of any Body—
It is a point of honor with the South—
I do not wish to show force, merely would this point of honor
I follow the example of Mr. Polk, in Oregon
My proposition then is proved
1. As to Texas
2. As to California & New Mexico—
Then what is the value of Wilmot—
I wish to be distinct—
I shall not vote for Wilmot, in New Mexico—
Nor in Texas.
As to Texas, I will not violate faith, & repeal the Law of Congress—
As to New Mexico & California—
I will not reaffirm an Ordinance of Nature or attempt to reenact the Will of God.[4]

[4] The notes from the line "*Now as for California and New Mexico,*" to this point are on one sheet, endorsed on the back, in Mr. Webster's handwriting, "No. 5. California & New Mexico."

All of the above notes, including footnotes, are copied from Webster's Writings and Speeches: Boston, 1903; vol. x, Appendix.

APPENDIX F

ILLUSTRATIVE STATISTICS

1. England

a. *A Century of Growth*

THE RELATION OF INVENTIONS TO COTTON IMPORTS AND EXPORTS [1]

(See page 88)

Volume of Cotton Imported	Value of Cottons Exported	Inventions
1730 1,545,472 lbs.	£13,524	1730 Wyatt's Roller-Spinning (pat. 1738)
1741 1,645,031 lbs.	£20,709	1738 Kay's Fly-Shuttle
1764 3,870,392 lbs.	£200,354	1764 Hargreaves's Spinning-jenny, for weft only (pat. 1770)
1766 4,767,589 lbs. (estimated)	£220,759	1768 Arkwright's Spinning-Frame, for warp (pat. 1769)
1780 6,766,613 lbs. (estimated)	£355,060	1779 Crompton's Mule—finer and more even yarn
1785 18,400,384 lbs.	£864,710	1785 Cartwright's Power-Loom; Watt & Boulton's Steam Engine used
1793 19,040,929 lbs.	£1,733,807	1793 *Eli Whitney's Cotton Gin*
1813 50,966,000 lbs.	£17,655,378 (estimated)	1813 Horrock's Dressing Machine
1830 261,200,000 lbs.	£41,050,969	1830 The "Throstle"—used almost exclusively in England for spinning warp
1832 287,800,000 lbs.	£43,786,255	1832 Robert's self-acting Mule perfected

[1] Tables based on Baines and Hobson, as cited.

b. *The Growth of Population* [2]

1751–1821

(See page 90)

Increases of Population in each 10 years

Maximum for any decade prior to 1751	3%
1751–1761	6%
1761–1771	6%
1771–1781	6%
1781–1791	9%
1791–1801	11%
1801–1811	14%
1811–1821 (Greatest recorded)	18%

c. *The Change of Occupation* [3]

1811–1821, in every 10,000:

(See page 90)

Agriculture
934
decrease

Manufacture
272
increase

Professions, etc.
600
increase

For present condition of Manufacture in England, see "The World's Cotton Spindles," p. 424; and Chapter 70, p. 349, note.

[2] See Toynbee, as cited, p. 67.
[3] Gaskell, as cited, p. 198.

2. AMERICA

a. *Slaves in the United States, 1790–1860*

(U. S. Census Reports)

NORTH

	1790	*1800*	*1810*	*1820*	*1830*	*1840*	*1850*	*1860*
California	....	....	....	....	....	....	....	....
Colorado	....	....	....	....	....	....	....	....
Connecticut	2,759	951	310	97	25	17	....	....
Dakota	....	....	....	....	....	....	....	....
Illinois	....	....	168	917	747	331	....	....
Indiana	....	135	237	190	3	3	....	....
Iowa	....	....	....	....	....	16	....	....
Kansas	....	....	....	....	....	....	....	2
Maine	....	....	....	....	2	....	....	....
Massachusetts	....	....	....	....	1	....	....	....
Michigan	....	....	24	....	32	....	....	....
Minnesota	....	....	....	....	....	....	....	....
Nebraska	....	....	....	....	....	....	....	15
Nevada	....	....	....	....	....	....	....	....
New Hampshire	158	8	....	....	3	1	....	....
New Jersey	11,423	12,422	10,851	7,557	2,254	674	236	18
New York	21,324	20,343	15,017	10,088	75	4	....	....
Ohio	....	....	....	....	6	3	....	....
Oregon	....	....	....	....	....	....	....	....
Pennsylvania	3,737	1,706	795	211	403	64	....	....
Rhode Island	952	381	108	48	17	5	....	....
Utah	....	....	....	....	....	....	26	29
Vermont	17	....	....	....	....	....	....	....
Washington	....	....	....	....	....	....	....	....
Wisconsin	....	....	....	....	....	11	....	....

SOUTH

	1790	1800	1810	1820	1830	1840	1850	1860
Alabama	...	...	...	41,879	117,549	253,532	342,844	435,080
Arkansas	...	...	...	1,617	4,576	19,935	47,100	111,115
Delaware	8,887	6,153	4,177	4,509	3,292	2,605	2,290	1,798
District of Columbia	...	3,244	5,395	6,377	6,119	4,694	3,687	3,185
Florida	...	...	...	...	15,501	25,717	39,310	61,745
Georgia	29,264	59,404	105,218	149,654	217,531	280,944	381,682	462,198
Kentucky	11,830	40,343	80,561	126,732	165,213	182,258	210,981	225,483
Louisiana	...	...	34,660	69,064	109,588	168,452	244,809	331,726
Maryland	103,036	105,635	111,502	107,397	102,994	89,737	90,368	87,189
Mississippi	...	3,489	17,088	32,814	65,659	195,211	309,878	436,631
Missouri	...	...	3,011	10,222	25,091	58,240	87,422	114,931
New Mexico	...	...	...	...	...	...	...	...
North Carolina	100,572	133,296	168,824	205,017	245,601	245,817	288,548	331,059
South Carolina	107,094	146,151	196,365	258,475	315,401	327,038	384,984	402,406
Tennessee	3,417	13,584	44,535	80,107	141,603	183,059	239,459	275,719
Texas	...	...	...	...	...	...	58,161	182,566
Virginia	293,427	345,796	392,518	425,153	469,757	449,087	472,528	490,865

For study of the above Table, see the Tables in Chapters 30 and 40.

b. *Exports of North and South Just Before the War*[4]

(See page 240)

Summary Statement of the Value of Exports of the Growth, Produce, and Manufacture of the United States, for the Year Ending June 30, 1859; the Productions of the North and of the South, Respectively, Being Placed in Opposite Columns; and the Articles of a Mixed Origin Being Stated Separately.—Report on Com. and Nav., 1859.

Exports of the North	
Product of the Forest	
Wood and its products	$7,829,666
Ashes, pot and pearl	643,861
Ginseng	54,204
Skins and furs	1,361,352
Product of Agriculture	
Animals and their products	15,262,769
Wheat and wheat flour	15,113,455
Indian corn and meal	2,206,396
Other grains, biscuit, and vegetables	2,226,585
Hemp, and Clover seed	546,060
Flax seed	8,177
Hops	53,016
	$45,305,541

Exports of the South	
Product of the Forest	
Wood and its products	$2,210,884
Tar and pitch	141,058
Rosin and turpentine	2,248,381
Spirits of turpentine	1,306,035
Product of Agriculture	
Animals and their products	287,048
Wheat and wheat flour	2,169,328
Indian corn and meal	110,976
Biscuit or ship bread	12,864
Rice	2,207,148
Cotton	161,434,923
Tobacco, in leaf	21,074,038
Brown sugar	196,935
	$193,399,618

Articles of Mixed Origin

Refined sugar, wax, chocolate, molasses	$ 550,937
Spirituous liquors, ale, porter, beer, cider, vinegar, linseed oil	1,370,787
Household furniture, carriages, rail-road cars, etc.	1,722,797
Hats, fur, silk, palm leaf, saddlery, trunks, valises	317,727
Tobacco, manufactured and snuff	3,402,491
Gunpowder, leather, boots, shoes, cables, cordage	2,011,931
Salt, lead, iron and its manufactures	5,744,952
Copper and brass, and manufactures of	1,048,246
Drugs and medicines, candles and soap	1,933,973
Cotton fabrics of all kinds	8,316,222
Other products of manufactures and mechanics	3,852,910
Coal and ice	818,117
Products not enumerated	4,132,857

[4] From Christy, p. 267.

Gold and silver, in coin and bullion 57,502,305
Products of the sea, being oil, fish, whalebone, etc. 4,462,974

$97,189,226
Add Northern exports 45,305,541
Add Southern exports 193,399,618

Total exports $335,894,385

EXPLANATORY NOTE.—The whole of the exports from the ports of Delaware, Baltimore, and New Orleans, are placed in the column of Northern exports, because there is no means of determining what proportion of them were from free or slave States, and it has been thought best to give this advantage to the North. Taking into the account only the heavier amounts, the exports from these ports foot up $11,287,898; of which near one-half consisted of provisions and lumber. The total imports for the year were $338,768,130. Of this $20,895,077 were re-exported, which, added to the domestic exports, makes the total exports $356,789,462, thus leaving a balance in our favor of $18,021,332.

For Table showing Cotton Manufacture since the Civil War, see Chapter 70.

c. *Production and Exports of Raw Cotton, 1790–1914* [5]

YEAR.	Production	Exports	YEAR.	Production	Exports
	Equivalent 500-pound bales, gross weight. Bales:			Equivalent 500-pound bales, gross weight. Bales:	
1914	16,134,930	8,931,253	1901	9,509,745	6,870,313
1913	14,156,486	9,256,028	1900	10,123,027	6,806,572
1912	13,703,421	9,199,093	1899	9,345,391	6,167,623
1911	15,692,701	10,681,332	1898	11,435,368	7,626,525
1910	11,608,616	8,025,991	1897	10,985,040	7,811,031
1909	10,004,949	6,491,843	1896	8,515,640	6,124,026
1908	13,241,799	8,889,724	1895	7,146,772	4,761,505
1907	11,107,179	7,779,508	1894	10,025,534	6,961,372
1906	13,273,809	8,825,236	1893	7,433,056	5,307,295
1905	10,575,017	6,975,494	1892	6,658,313	4,485,251
1904	13,438,012	9,057,397	1891	8,940,867	5,896,800
1903	9,851,129	6,233,682	1890	8,562,089	5,850,219
1902	10,630,945	6,913,506	1889	7,472,511	4,928,921

[5] Bulletin No. 131, Dept. of Commerce: Washington, 1915; p. 82.

Year.	Production (Equivalent 500-pound bales, gross weight) Bales:	Exports (Equivalent 500-pound bales, gross weight) Bales:	Year.	Production (Equivalent 500-pound bales, gross weight) Bales:	Exports (Equivalent 500-pound bales, gross weight) Bales:
1888	6,923,775	4,730,192	1844	2,078,910	1,745,812
1887	6,884,667	4,519,254	1843	1,750,060	1,327,267
1886	6,314,561	4,301,542	1842	2,035,481	1,584,594
1885	6,369,341	4,200,651	1841	1,398,282	1,169,434
1884	5,477,448	3,783,319	1840	1,347,640	1,060,408
1883	5,521,963	3,733,369	1839	1,653,722	1,487,882
1882	6,833,442	4,591,331	1838	1,092,980	827,248
1881	5,136,447	3,376,521	1837	1,428,384	1,191,905
1880	6,356,998	4,453,495	1836	1,129,016	888,423
1879	5,466,387	3,742,752	1835	1,061,821	847,263
1878	4,745,078	3,290,167	1834	962,343	774,718
1877	4,494,224	3,197,439	1833	930,962	769,436
1876	4,118,390	2,839,418	1832	815,900	649,397
1875	4,302,818	3,037,650	1831	805,439	644,430
1874	3,528,276	2,504,118	1830	732,218	553,960
1873	3,873,750	2,682,631	1829	763,598	596,918
1872	3,650,932	2,470,590	1828	679,916	529,674
1871	2,756,564	1,824,937	1827	564,854	421,181
1870	4,024,527	2,922,757	1826	732,218	588,620
1869	2,409,597	1,987,708	1825	533,473	409,071
1868	2,198,141	1,300,449	1824	449,791	352,900
1867	2,345,610	1,502,756	1823	387,029	286,739
1866	1,948,077	1,401,697	1822	439,331	347,447
1865	2,093,658	1,301,146	1821	376,569	289,350
1864	299,372	17,789	1820	334,728	249,787
1863	449,059	23,998	1819	349,372	255,720
1862	1,596,653	22,770	1818	261,506	175,994
1861	4,490,586	10,129	1817	271,967	184,942
1860	3,841,416	615,032	1816	259,414	171,299
1859	4,309,642	3,535,373	1815	209,205	163,894
1858	3,758,273	2,772,937	1814	146,444	165,997
1857	3,012,016	2,237,248	1813	156,904	35,458
1856	2,873,680	2,096,565	1812	156,904	38,220
1855	3,220,782	2,702,863	1811	167,364	57,775
1854	2,708,082	2,016,849	1810	177,824	124,116
1853	2,766,194	1,975,666	1809	171,548	186,523
1852	3,130,338	2,223,141	1808	156,904	101,981
1851	2,799,290	2,186,461	1807	167,364	21,261
1850	2,136,083	1,854,474	1806	167,364	127,889
1849	1,975,274	1,270,763	1805	146,444	71,315
1848	2,615,031	2,053,204	1804	135,983	76,780
1847	2,128,433	1,628,549	1803	125,523	70,068
1846	1,603,763	1,054,440	1802	115,063	75,424
1845	1,806.110	1,095,116	1801	100,418	47,768

Year.	Production	Exports	Year.	Production	Exports
	Equivalent 500-pound bales, gross weight — Bales:			Equivalent 500-pound bales, gross weight — Bales:	
1800	73,222	41,822	1794	16,736	9,414
1799	41,841	35,580	1793	10,460	3,565
1798	31,381	19,065	1792	6,276	1,097
1797	23,013	18,720	1791	4,184	277
1796	20,921	7,577	1790	3,138	379
1795	16,736	12,213			

d. *Value of Important Agricultural Exports, 1899–1914* [6]

(000 omitted)

	1899	*1904*	*1909*	*1912*	*1913*	*1914*
Vegetable Oils	$13,809	$12,618	$23,098	$26,908	$24,044	$16,251
[7] Oil Cake ...	14,548	17,069	25,836	28,228	29,444	21,668 [7]
Tobacco	25,467	29,640	30,902	43,251	49,354	53,964
Corn	68,977	30,071	25,194	28,957	28,801	7,008
Wheat Flour	73,093	68,894	51,157	50,999	53,172	54,454
Wheat	104,269	35,850	68,094	28,477	89,036	87,953
Total Grain Products ...	273,999	76,215	160,076	123,095	210,524	164,846
Cotton	210,080	372,049	417,390	565,849	547,357	610,475

For Table showing Cotton Manufacture since the Civil War, see Chapter 70.

[6] Year Book, U. S. Dept. of Agriculture.
[7] Should be credited to Cotton.

e. *Table Illustrating the Growth of Cotton Manufacture by Sections of the U. S., 1840–1914* [8]

[The quantities are given in running bales, except those for production in 1850, 1860, and 1870, which are in equivalent 400-pound bales, and those for consumption from 1840 to 1870, and for foreign cotton which are in equivalent 500-pound bales. Linters are included.]

Year.	Cotton produced (bales).[1]	Cotton Consumed (Bales).				Active Cotton Spindles.			
		United States.	Cotton-growing states.	New England states.	All other states.	United States.	Cotton-growing states.	New England states.	All other states.
1914 ..	14,613,964	5,884,733	3,023,415	2,251,041	610,277	32,107,572	12,711,303	17,408,372	1,987,897
1913 ..	14,090,863	5,786,330	2,960,518	2,210,813	614,999	31,519,766	12,227,226	17,311,451	1,981,089
1912 ..	16,109,349	5,367,583	2,712,223	2,108,360	547,000	30,578,528	11,582,869	17,139,945	1,855,714
1911 ..	11,965,962	4,704,978	2,328,487	1,911,092	465,399	29,522,597	11,084,623	16,510,981	1,926,993
1910 ..	10,386,209	4,798,953	2,292,333	2,016,386	490,234	28,266,862	10,494,112	15,735,086	2,037,664
1909 ..	13,432,131	5,240,719	2,553,797	2,144,448	542,474	28,018,305	10,429,200	15,591,851	1,997,254
1908 ..	11,325,882	4,539,090	2,187,096	1,894,835	457,159	27,505,422	10,200,903	15,329,333	1,975,186
1907 ..	13,305,265	4,984,936	2,410,993	2,073,355	500,588	26,375,191	9,527,964	14,912,517	1,934,710
1906 ..	10,725,602	4,909,279	2,373,577	2,059,900	475,802	25,250,096	8,994,868	14,407,580	1,847,648
1905 ..	13,697,310	[2]4,278,980	[2]2,140,151	[2]1,753,282	[2]385,547	23,687,495	7,631,331	14,202,971	1,853,193
1900 ..	9,507,786	3,873,165	1,523,168	1,909,498	440,499	19,472,232	4,367,688	13,171,377	1,933,167
1890 ..	7,472,511	2,518,409	538,895	1,502,177	477,337	14,384,180	1,570,288	10,934,297	1,879,595
1880 ..	5,755,359	[3]1,570,344	[3]188,748	[3]1,129,498	[3]252,098	[3]10,653,435	[3]561,360	[3]8,632,087	[3]1,459,988
1870 ..	3,011,996	796,616	68,702	551,250	176,664	7,132,415	327,871	5,498,308	1,306,236
1860 ..	5,387,052	845,410	93,553	567,403	184,454	5,235,727	324,052	3,858,962	1,052,713
1850 ..	2,469,093	575,506	78,140	430,603	66,763	3,998,022	264,571	2,958,536	774,915
1840 ..	2,063,915	236,525	71,000	158,708	6,817	2,284,631	180,927	1,597,394	506,310

1 Relates to crop of preceding year. 2 Does not include foreign cotton. 3 Cotton mills only.

8 Bulletin No. 128, U. S. Dept. of Commerce: Washington, 1914; p. 16.

3. The World

a. *The World's Cotton Crops, 1902–1914* [9]

(Bales of approximately 500 lbs.—000 omitted)

	1902–3	1903–4	1904–5	1905–6	1906–7	1907–8	1908–9	1909–10	1910–11	1911–12	1912–13	1913–14	1914–15 Estimate
America ..	10,758	10,124	13,557	11,320	13,551	11,582	13,829	10,651	12,132	16,043	14,129	14,610	16,500
India	3,367	3,161	3,791	3,416	4,934	3,122	3,692	4,718	3,853	3,288	4,395	5,201	5,000
Egypt ...	1,168	1,302	1,263	1,192	1,390	1,447	1,150	1,000	1,515	1,485	1,507	1,537	1,300
Russia ...	342	477	536	604	759	664	698	686	895	875	911	1,015	1,300
China	1,200	1,200	756	788	806	875	1,933	2,531	3,467	3,437	3,931	4,000	4,000
Others ...	801	751	803	936	1,027	950	969	950	967	1,058	1,171	1,340	1,300
Total ..	17,636	17,015	20,706	18,256	22,467	18,640	22,271	20,536	22,829	26,186	26,044	27,703	29,400

[9] From Todd, p. 395. Probably the most accurate cotton statistics published. But see note on page 339.

b. *The World's Cotton Spindles* [10]

Country	Spindles
Great Britain	55,576,108
United States	30,579,000
Germany	10,920,426
Russia	8,950,000
France	7,400,000
India	6,400,000
Austria	4,864,453
Italy	4,580,000
Mexico, Brazil, etc.	3,100,000
Japan	2,250,000
Spain	2,200,000
Belgium	1,468,838
Switzerland	1,398,062
Canada	855,293
Sweden	529,772
Portugal	482,000
Holland	470,956
Denmark	86,836
Norway	74,564

In 1909 Sir Charles Macara, who compiled the above table, addressed the President of the British Board of Trade as follows:

"Lancashire, the center of the cotton industry of England, has during the last 50 years doubled her population; she has also doubled her cotton machinery, considerably improved its efficiency, and increased the speed at which it is run, with the result that not only is there a proportionately greater output, but the output is of immensely increased value. The importance of the cotton industry of England may be judged from the fact that its products, in addition to providing for our home requirements, represent about a third of our total exports of manufactures.—These exports go to the great neutral markets, as well as largely to the countries which have a cotton industry of their own, forming part of their exports.—In round figures, the cotton crop of the world now averages about 20,000,000 bales, and a common fallacy is to gauge the value of the cotton industry by the weight of raw cotton consumed. England, with considerably over one-third of the spindles of the world, consumes annually 4,000,000 bales of cotton, whereas

10 As of March 1, 1913. Sir Chas. Macara, as cited, p. 9.

the United States of America, with about half the number of spindles there are in England, consumes 5,000,000 bales, and Germany, with considerably less than a fifth of the spindles in England, consumes 1¾ million bales. The value of the cotton trade of the respective countries can really only be gauged by the extent of the machinery, the labor employed, the fineness, variety, excellence, and value of the fabrics produced."[11]

See also figures in Chapters 70, 71, 72.

[11] Cited by Porter, p. 312.

APPENDIX G

AUTHORITIES

Book I

FROM INDIA TO ENGLAND

BAINES, EDWARD, JR.—History of the Cotton Manufacture: London, 1835.

BALLS, W. L.—The Cotton Plant in Egypt: London, 1912.

CHISHOLM, G. G.—Handbook of Commercial Geography: London, 1904.

DANA, W. B.—Cotton from Seed to Loom: New York, 1878.

DARWIN, ERASMUS.—The Botanic Garden, Part I: The Economy of Vegetation: London, 1791; Part II: The Loves of the Plants: London, 1790.

DRAPER, J. W.—A History of the Intellectual Development of Europe: New York, 1863.

DYER, JOHN.—The Fleece: London, 1757.

FERRERO, G.—Characters and Events of Roman History; Translation: New York, 1909.

HALLAM, H.—View of the State of Europe during the Middle Ages: New York, 1896.

HALLIWELL, J. O. (editor)—The Voiage & Travaile of Sir John Maundevile, Kt. Reprinted from the edition of 1725: London, 1883.

HERODOTUS.—Historia; Edited by Dietsch: Leipzig, 1899.

KING, HENRY (translator)—The Metamorphoses of Publius Ovidius Naso: Edinburgh, 1871.

LARNED, J. N. (compiler)—History for Ready Reference and Topical Reading: Springfield, Mass., 1895, 1901, 1910.

LEE, HENRY.—The Vegetable Lamb of Tartary: London, 1887.

REYBAUD, L.—Le Coton: Paris, 1863.

ROGERS, J. E. T.—The Economic Interpretation of History: New York, 1909.

ROYLE, J. F.—The Culture and Commerce of Cotton in India: London, 1851.

SCHULZE-GAEVERNITZ, G. VON—Der Grossbetrieb: Leipzig, 1892. (See also Bk. II.)

SONNERAT, M.—Collection des Planches pour servir Au Voyage aux Indes Orientales et à La Chine: Paris, 1806.

WHEELER, B. I.—Alexander the Great: New York, 1900.

YULE, HENRY (editor)—Cathay and the Way Thither: London, 1866.

The Cotton Plant: Washington, 1896.

Encyclopedia Britannica, 9th and 10th editions.

The Naked Truth, in an Essay upon Trade: 1696.

The Charleston *News and Courier*.

BOOK II

THE TRANSFORMATION OF ENGLAND

BAINES, E., JR.—See Bk. II.

BLACKSTONE, W.—Commentaries on the Laws of England (1765): London, 1809.

BROUGHAM, H.—Lives of Men of Letters and Science: London, 1846.

CARLYLE, T.—Past and Present (1843); London, 1889; Critical and Miscellaneous Essays (1839): New York, n. d., vol. iv.

CARNEGIE, A.—James Watt: New York, 1905.

CHEYNEY, E. P.—An Introduction to the Industrial and Social History of England: New York, 1905.

DARWIN, E.—See Bk. I.

DEFOE, D.—Tour Through the Whole Island of Great Britain: London, 1727.

ELLISON, T.—The Cotton Trade of Great Britain: London, 1886.

GASKELL, E. C.—Mary Barton (1848): London, 1906.

GASKELL, P.—Artisans and Machinery: London, 1836.

GIBBINS, H. DE B.—The Industrial History of England: London, 1904.

GREEN, J. R.—A Short History of the English People: New York, 1895.

HOBSON, J. A.—The Evolution of Modern Capitalism: London and Felling-on-Tyne, 1906.

HOWE, H.—Memoirs: New York, 1857.

INNES, A. D.—England's Industrial Development: New York, 1912.

MACGREGOR, D. H.—The Evolution of Industry: London, 1914.

MALTHUS, T. R.—An Essay on the Principle of Population: London (1803), n. d.

MOORE, T.—Poetical Works: Philadelphia, 1856.

NORTH, S. N. D.—The Development of American Industries since Columbus, *Popular Science Monthly*, vol. xxxix: New York, 1891.

PERRIS, G. H.—The Industrial History of Modern England: New York, 1914.

POLLARD, A. F.—The History of England: London, n. d.

PORTER, G. R.—The Progress of the Nation (1838): London, 1912.

RAND, B. (compiler).—Selections illustrating Economic History: New York, 1903.

SCHULZE-GAEVERNITZ, G. VON.—Social Peace (Zum Socialen Frieden): London, 1900. (See also Bk. I.)

SELIGMAN, E. R. A.—The Economic Interpretation of History: New York, 1912.

SEWARD, A. C. (editor).—Darwin and Modern Science: Cambridge, 1909.

SUTCLIFFE, T.—An Exposition of Facts relating to the Rise and Progress of the Woolen, Linen, and Cotton Manufactures of Great Britain: Manchester, 1843.

THOMSON, J. A. (with P. GEDDES).—Evolution: London, n. d. (See also Seward, above.)

TOYNBEE, A.—Lectures on the Industrial Revolution: London, 1908.

TRAILL, H. D. (editor).—Social England: London, 1905.
WALPOLE, S.—History of England since 1815: London, 1878.
WARNER, T.—Landmarks in English Industrial History: London, n. d. (Also in Traill's Social England.)
WILKINSON, F.—The Story of the Cotton Plant: New York, 1906.
WOOD, H. T.—Industrial England in the Middle of the Eighteenth Century: London, 1910.
WOODCROFT, B.—Brief Biographies of the Inventors of Machines for the Manufacture of Textile Fabrics: London, 1863.

The London *Times*, Textile Number, June 27, 1913.

BOOK III

AMERICA: SECTIONAL EVOLUTION

BALLAGH, J. C. (editor)—The South in the Building of the Nation: Richmond, 1910.
BISHOP, J. L.—A History of American Manufactures from 1608 to 1860: Philadelphia, 1866.
BOGART, E. L.—The Economic History of the United States: New York, 1907.
BRUCE, P. A.—Economic History of Virginia in the Seventeenth Century: New York, 1907.
CALLENDER, G. S. (editor)—Selections from the Economic History of the United States, 1765–1860: Boston, 1909.
CURTIS, W. E.—The True Thomas Jefferson: Philadelphia, 1901.
DAY, C.—A History of Commerce: New York, 1907.
DIAZ, B. (DEL CASTILLO)—The True History of the Conquest of Mexico, Written in the year 1568; Maurice Keating, Translator: London, 1800.
ELLIOTT, O. L.—The Tariff Controversy: Palo Alto, 1892.
FISKE, J.—The Discovery of America: Boston, 1892. The Critical Period of American History: Boston, 1892.

GOODRICH, M.—Pawtucket and the Slater Centennial: *New England Magazine*, vol. iii, Boston, 1891.

HALE, E. E.—Memories of a Hundred Years: New York, 1902. Cotton from First to Last, *New England Magazine*, vol. iii, Boston, 1891.

HALLE, E. VON.—Baumwollproduktion und Pflanzungswirtschaft in den Nordamerikanischen Südstaaten, I: Die Sklavenzeit: Leipzig, 1897. (See also Bk. IV.)

HAMILTON, A.—Works: New York, 1850.

HAMMOND, M. B.—The Cotton Industry: New York, 1897. (See also Eli Whitney, below.)

HART, A. B.—Slavery and Abolition: New York, 1906. Formation of the Union: New York, 1909. American History Told by Contemporaries: New York, 1909.

JEFFERSON, T.—Writings: Washington, 1904.

JOHNSON, A.—Union and Democracy: Boston, 1915.

JOHNSTON, A.—American Political History: New York, 1905. (See also Bk. IV.)

LARNED, J. N.—See Bk. I.

LINCOLN, A.—Complete Works: New York, 1894.

MADISON, J.—Journal of the Federal Convention: Chicago, 1898.

MCHENRY, G.—The Cotton Trade: 1863.

MCLAUGHLIN, A. C.—The Confederation and the Constitution: New York, 1906.

MCMASTER, J. B.—A History of the People of the United States: New York, 1892. Cambridge Modern History, vol. vii: New York, 1906.

NORTH, S. N. D.—See Bk. II.

OLMSTED, D.—Memoir of Eli Whitney: *American Journal of Science*, vol. xxi: 1832.

PRESCOTT, W. H.—History of the Conquest of Mexico: New York, 1844.

PHILLIPS, U. B. (editor)—A Documentary History of American Industrial Society; vol. i: Cleveland, 1910.

RAMSAY, D.—History of South Carolina: Charleston, 1809.

RICH, G.—The Cotton Industry in New England: *New England Magazine*, vol. iii, Boston, 1891.

ROGERS, J. E. T. (compiler)—Copy of Tracts relating to America (17th and 18th centuries) found in the Bodleian Library at Oxford: n. d.

SMITH, G.—The United States; an Outline of Political History: New York, 1889.

TURNER, F. J.—The Rise of the New West: New York, 1906.

TOMPKINS, D. A.—American Commerce: Charlotte, N. C., 1900. Cotton and Cotton Oil: Charlotte, N. C., 1901. The Cotton Gin: the History of its Invention; exhibiting copies of Original Patent Specifications and Drawings, with synopsis of testimony in the 27 law-suits relating to infringements in Ga., 1796–1805: Charlotte, N. C., 1901.

WALKER, F. A.—The Making of the Nation: New York, 1909.

WEEDEN, W. B.—Economic and Social History of New England: Boston, 1894.

WHITE, G. S.—Memoir of Samuel Slater: Philadelphia, 1836.

WHITNEY, ELI.—Correspondence, Edited by M. B. Hammond: *American Historical Review,* October, 1897.

WINSOR, J.—Narrative and Critical History of America: Boston, 1889.

WRIGHT, C. D.—The Industrial Evolution of the United States: New York, 1902.

The *American Historical Review.*

BOOK IV

AMERICA: THE GREAT CONTROVERSIES

ADAMS, C. F.—Studies Military and Diplomatic: New York, 1911. (See also Bk. V.)

ALDERMAN, E. A. (editor)—The Library of Southern Literature: Atlanta, 1908.

BANKS, E. M.—The Economics of Land Tenure in Georgia: New York, 1905.

BINGHAM, R.—Sectional Misunderstandings: Reprinted, with additional matter, from *North American Review*, for Sept., 1904.

BRADFORD, G., JR.—Lee the American: Boston, 1912.

BROWN, W. G.—The Lower South in American History: New York, 1902.

CALHOUN, J. C.—A Disquisition on Government, etc.: Columbia, S. C., 1851.

CALLENDER, G. S.—See Bk. III.

CHADWICK, F. E.—Causes of the Civil War: New York, 1906.

CHRISTY, D.—See Elliott, E. N.

ELLIOTT, E. N., and others.—Cotton is King: Augusta, 1860.

ELLIOTT, O. L.—See Bk. III.

GORDY, J. P.—A History of Political Parties in the United States: Athens, O., 1895. Political History of the United States: New York, 1902.

HALLE, E. VON.—Baumwollproduktion und Pflanzungswirtschaft in den Nordamerikanischen Südstaaten, II: Sezessionskrieg und Rekonstruktion: Leipzig, 1906. (See also Bk. III.)

HAMMOND, H.—Sketch of James Henry Hammond. Printer's proof.

HAMMOND, J. H.—Speech on the Admission of Kansas; Speech on the Relation of States: Washington, 1858, 1860.

HAMMOND, M. B.—See Bk. III.

HART, A. B.—See Bk. III.

HELPER, H. R.—The Impending Crisis: New York, 1857.

JOHNSON, O.—William Lloyd Garrison and His Times: Boston, 1880.

JOHNSTON, A.—American Orations: New York, 1906. (See also Bk. III.)

LARNED, J. N.—See Bk. I.

LINCOLN, A.—See Bk. III.

LODGE, H. C.—Daniel Webster: Boston, 1895.

MCMASTER, J. B.—See Bk. III.

MORSE, J. T., JR.—John Quincy Adams: Boston, 1895.

RHODES, J. F.—History of the United States from the Compromise of 1850: New York, 1906.
SMITH, G.—See Bk. III.
TAUSSIG, F. W.—The Tariff History of the United States: New York, 1905. (See also Bk. VII.)
TOMPKINS, D. A.—See Bk. III.
WEBSTER, D.—Writings and Speeches: Boston, 1903.
WILSON, W.—Division and Reunion: New York, 1909. Cambridge Modern History, vol. vii: New York, 1906.

BOOK V

AMERICA: THE CIVIL WAR

ADAMS, C. F.—Charles Francis Adams: Boston, 1900. Transatlantic Historical Solidarity: Oxford, 1913. A Crisis in Downing Street: Boston, 1914. (See also Bk. IV.)
ALDERMAN, E. A.—See Bk. IV.
DAVIS, J.—The Rise and Fall of the Confederate Government: New York, 1881.
FITE, E. D.—Social and Industrial Conditions in the North during the Civil War: New York, 1910.
GRANT, U. S.—Personal Memoirs: New York, 1885.
HALLE, E. VON.—See Bks. III and IV.
HAMMOND, M. B.—See Bk. III.
LARNED, J. N.—See Bk. I.
MORLEY, J.—The Life of Richard Cobden: Boston, 1890.
"NAUTICUS."—Beiträge zur Flotten-Novelle: Berlin, 1900.
REED, J. C.—The Brothers' War: Boston, 1906.
RHODES, J. F.—See Bk. IV.
SCHWAB, J. C.—The Confederate States of America: New York, 1901. Cambridge Modern History, vol. vii: New York, 1906.
TREVELYAN, G. M.—The Life of John Bright: Boston, 1913.

The Charleston *Courier*.
The London *Times*.
Proceedings of the Massachusetts Historical Society.

Book VI

THE OLD SOUTH AND THE NEW

Alderman, E. A.—See Bk. IV.
Burkett, C. W. (with C. H. Poe)—Cotton: New York, 1906.
Copeland, M. T.—The Cotton Manufacturing Industry of the United States: Cambridge, 1912..
Curtis, W. E.—See Bk. III.
Derrick, S. J.—The Cotton Mills of the South: Newberry, S. C., 1915.
Emery, H. C.—Economic Development of the United States, in Cambridge Modern History, vol. vii: New York, 1906.
Goldsmith, P. H.—The Cotton Mill South: Boston, 1908.
Grady, H. W.—Writings and Speeches: New York, 1890.
Hand, W. H.—Report of State High School Inspector: Columbia, S. C., 1915.
Kohn, A.—The Cotton Mills of South Carolina: Charleston, 1907.
McCulloch, J. E. (editor)—The Human Way: Nashville, 1913.
Page, W. H.—The Rebuilding of Old Commonwealths: New York, 1905.
Payne, E. J.—Colonies and Colonial Federations: London, 1904.
Reed, J. C.—See Bk. V.
Thompson, H.—From the Cotton Field to the Cotton Mill: New York, 1906.

The *American Historical Review.*
Annals of the American Academy of Political and Social Science.
Reports of the American Historical Association, and of the Thirteenth Census.

Book VII

COTTON AND WORLD TRADE

Alderman, E. A.—See Bk. IV.

Ashley, W. J.—Germany and Cotton: The *Atlantic Monthly,* Jan., 1916.

Atkinson, E.—The Industrial Progress of the Nation: New York, 1889.

Balls, W. L.—See Bk. I.

Burkett, C. W.—See Bk. VI.

Grady, H. W.—See Bk. VI.

Law, W. A.—Cotton as a Factor in American Trade: Philadelphia, 1907.

Macara, C.—Leading the World: London, 1913.

Mather, W.—Egypt and the Anglo-Egyptian Sudan: Southampton, 1910.

Porter, G. R.—See Bk. II.

Price, T. H.—*Cotton and Finance:* New York, 1912.

Ramsay, W.—Article in the *English Review,* May, 1915.

Ritter, W. E.—War, Science and Civilization: Boston, 1915.

Rogers, H. J. (editor)—Congress of Arts and Sciences, vol. vi: Boston, 1906.

Schmidt, A.—Cotton Growing in India: Manchester, 1912.

Sully, D. J.—Articles in the *Cosmopolitan Magazine:* New York, Feb., Mar., and Apr., 1909.

Taussig, F. W.—Some Aspects of the Tariff Question: Cambridge, 1915. (See also Bk. IV.)

Thomson, J. A.—See Bk. II.

Todd, J. A.—The World's Cotton Crops: London, 1915.

Tompkins, D. A.—Cotton Values in Textile Fabrics: Charlotte, N. C., 1902. (See also Bk. III.)

Whelpley, J. D.—The Trade of the World: New York, 1913.

Wickware, F. G. (editor)—American Year Book: New York, 1915, 1916.

The Charlotte *Observer*.
The London *Times*.
The Manchester *Guardian*.
Reports of the Thirteenth Census, the United States Departments of Commerce and of Agriculture, the International Congress of Tropical Agriculture, the British Cotton Growing Association, and the Master Cotton Spinners' and Manufacturers' Associations.

THE END

INDEX

For use in topical reading, consult titles such as Blockade, Constitution, Great War of 1914, England, Slavery, Southern Characteristics, and Statistics.